A NEW WAY OF BELONGING

THE HISTORICAL SERIES OF THE REFORMED CHURCH IN AMERICA
IN COOPERATION WITH ORIGINS STUDIES IN
DUTCH-AMERICAN HISTORY
NO. 70

A NEW WAY OF BELONGING

Covenant Theology, China, and the
Christian Reformed Church, 1921–1951

Kurt D. Selles

WILLIAM B. EERDMANS PUBLISHING COMPANY
Grand Rapids, Michigan / Cambridge, U.K.

Wm. B. Eerdmans Publishing Co.
2140 Oak Industrial Drive S.E., Grand Rapids, Michigan 49503 /
P.O. Box 163, Cambridge CB3 9PU U.K.
www.eerdmans.com

Printed in the United States of America

ISBN 978-0-8028-6662-2

Library of Congress Cataloging-in-Publication Data

Selles, Kurt D.
  A new way of belonging : covenant theology, China, and the Christian
Reformed Church, 1921-1951 / Kurt D. Selles.
      p. cm. -- (The historical series of the Reformed Church in America
; no. 70)
  Includes bibliographical references and index.
  ISBN 978-0-8028-6662-2 (pbk. : alk. paper) 1. Christian Reformed
Church--Missions--China--Rugao   Shi--History--20th   century.   2.
Missions, American--China--Rugao   Shi--History--20th   century.   3.
Rugao Shi (China)--Church history--20th century. I. Title.
  BV3425.R84S45 2011
  266'.5731510904--dc22
                          2010048389

To Wang Aitang

who faithfully served the church in Rugao

from 1925-1966

The Historical Series of the Reformed Church in America

The series was inaugurated in 1968 by the General Synod of the Reformed Church in America acting through the Commission on History to communicate the church's heritage and collective memory and to reflect on our identity and mission, encouraging historical scholarship which informs both church and academy.

www.rca.org/series

General Editor
　　Rev. Donald J. Bruggink, Ph.D., D.D.
　　Western Theological Seminary
　　Van Raalte Institute, Hope College

Associate Editor
　　George Brown, Jr., Ph.D.
　　Western Theological Seminary

Copy Editor
　　Laurie Baron

Production Editor
　　Russell L. Gasero

Commission on History
　　Douglas Carlson, Ph.D., Northwestern College, Orange City, Iowa
　　Mary L. Kansfield, M.A., East Stroudsburg, Pennsylvania
　　Hartmut Kramer-Mills, M.Div., Dr.Theol., New Brunswick, New Jersey
　　Jeffery Tyler, Ph.D., Hope College, Holland, Michigan
　　Audrey Vermilyea, Bloomington, Minnesota
　　Lori Witt, Ph.D., Central College, Pella, Iowa

Contents

Illustrations

Abbreviations

ABCFM	American Board of Commissioners for Foreign Missions
CCC	Church of Christ in China
CRC	Christian Reformed Church
CRWM	Christian Reformed World Missions
CSSU	China Sunday School Union
DRCM	Dutch Reformed Church Mission
FCMS	Foreign Christian Missionary Society
NCH	*North China Herald*
NCTS	North China Theological Seminary
NKM	North Kiangsu (Jiangsu) Mission
NLM	New Life Movement
PCUS	Presbyterian Church in the U.S. (South)
PCUSA	Presbyterian Church in the U.S.A. (North)
RAB	Religious Affairs Bureau
RCA	Reformed Church in America (formerly part of the Dutch Reformed Church and known as the Reformed Protestant Dutch Church)
SVM	Student Volunteer Movement (for Foreign Missions)
UPC	United Presbyterian Church

Aknowledgments

On my first trip to China in April of 1989, I had the opportunity to visit Rugao, the city and county where a Christian Reformed Church mission was located from 1921-1950. I was traveling with Ed Van Baak, who had served with the mission in its closing days, from 1948 until 1949. From Shanghai we took a ferry up the Yangzi River (as the missionaries did so many times) to Nantong, the river port just south of Rugao, and then went by taxi into the city. This was Ed's first trip back to Rugao forty years after he was evacuated from the country in the fall of 1949, and we were looking for Christians and for clues about what had happened to the church after the missionaries had left.

Unable to find any Christians or anything about the fate of the church on our own, we went to the city's Religious Affairs Bureau office, where we were told that the church in Rugao had died out at the beginning of the Cultural Revolution (1966-1976), and that there were no Christians left in the city. But the house of "the doctor," the officials told us, still stood in the city, and they asked if we would like to see it. So the officials took us to the residence that Lee Huizenga had built in Rugao City in the 1920s. They left us at the house while they went off to what they described as a "meeting." When they did not return for more than two hours, we decided to leave the city quietly (it felt a little like *flight*—something else the missionaries experienced more than once). As we returned to Shanghai, we still wondered what had happened to the Christians and church in Rugao.

Over the years I continued to wonder about Rugao. Almost ten years after my first visit to the city, while I was doing graduate work at Vanderbilt University, Ed Van Baak encouraged me to write about the history of the mission in Rugao as a contribution to the history of the Christian Reformed Church. The subject appealed to me as an academic topic and for personal reasons. Because my grandparents, Albert and Trena Selles, had worked in China with the Christian Reformed China mission for more than twenty years, and my father, Donald Selles, had spent part of his boyhood in China, I had heard many stories about the mission in China. Consequently, this project grew from my family's connection to China, from a desire to make a contribution to the Christian Reformed Church's mission history, and from a scholarly interest in the history of Christianity through the lens of one small piece of its mosaic.

In completing this book, I have incurred debts of gratitude on both sides of the Pacific. The late Ed Van Baak—missionary, field director, traveling companion, historian, raconteur, good friend, and brother—encouraged me to begin the project and answered countless questions, many from firsthand experience. Professors Dale Johnson (Vanderbilt University) and Daniel Bays (Calvin College) provided scholarly advice and personal support with great patience. Richard Harms, Wendy Blankespoor, and Hendrina Van Spronsen at the Heritage Hall archives of the Christian Reformed Church answered many questions and hauled folders back and forth from the storage room with consistent cheerfulness. Professor Henry Zwaanstra (Calvin Theological Seminary) provided invaluable assistance with translating several articles from Dutch. Fran Van Baak, former Christian Reformed missionary to China and Japan, helped identify faces in some of the group photographs. Felicia Cooper, my teaching assistant at Beeson Divinity School, helped with proofreading.

On the other side of the Pacific, Sheng Songru in Jingjiang offered insight into the church and mission work in that city. From Nanjing, Lin De'en opened doors for me to contact church and city officials in Rugao. Lu Youcai and Yan Shiji in Rugao not only answered many questions but also allowed me to scribble notes for several hours from a number of tattered notebooks squirreled away in a cabinet in the local

Religious Affairs Bureau office. These notebooks contained church records kept by the Christian Reformed missionaries in the 1930s and 1940s and included one notebook kept by Rugao evangelist Wang Aitang from 1950 to 1962. Though it took several years to find her, Wang Shuangen, Wang Aitang's youngest daughter, gave me a glimpse of her father's life and church work in Rugao after the missionaries left in 1950. I am thankful for the help of all these friends, teachers, and colleagues. Most of all, however, I am grateful to my wife, Vicki, for her support, help, and unfailing good humor in seeing this project through to the end. I think it's done now, finally.

INTRODUCTION

In 1920, after several years of study, the Synod of the Christian Reformed Church (CRC) decided to send its first overseas missionaries to China. When it came down to a choice between establishing a mission in Africa or China, the synod chose China, in part, it said, because "the conservative, intellectual spirit of the Chinese is more in harmony with our people." The synod's delegates believed that through their "many points of contact" with the Chinese people they would have the best opportunity to transplant their distinctively Reformed faith on foreign soil. A few months later, three Christian Reformed missionaries and their families departed for Shanghai. The next year they took over a section of the mission field of the Presbyterian Church in the U.S. (Southern) in Rugao County of northern Jiangsu Province.[1]

---

[1] When the CRC missionaries were in China during the first half of the twentieth century, English-speaking foreigners used the Wades-Giles system of Romanization for transcribing Chinese characters into English writing. Thus, the capital of China was "Peking," and the province and city where the missionaries worked was "Jukao, Kiangsu Province." Today the Chinese-devised *pinyin* system for transcribing Chinese characters into

For the next thirty years, the Christian Reformed Mission worked to plant a church in Rugao, until the last missionary was forced out of the country in early 1950. This book is the story of that attempt to plant a church in Rugao with Reformed characteristics.

I will argue that the Christian Reformed missionaries went to China because they believed they had "many points of contact" with the Chinese; yet their own cultural and theological perspective, combined with their inexperience and unrealistic expectations, clashed radically with the reality of Rugao. Ironically, what they originally thought of as "many points of contact" turned out to be *one* fundamental point of contact in *covenant theology*, which connected with the culture, worldview, and social needs of Rugao. Indeed, in the upheaval of China's Republican Era (1911–1949), when almost every aspect of traditional society was under siege, covenant theology, as a way to preserve family and form new communities, proved remarkably resonant with the times. Moreover, though conflict and negotiation were parts of the process, the cultural translation that took place in Rugao actually seems more like discovery, both by the missionaries and by the Chinese.

This narrative tells the story of the Christian Reformed Church's China mission, beginning with the choice of China as the first overseas mission of the denomination and ending with the closing of Rugao church after the missionaries had left at the outset of China's Great Proletariat Cultural Revolution in 1966. This account does not, however, chart every event during the period under discussion or include every person (American or Chinese) who served in Rugao.[2] Instead, the story focuses on the effort of the Christian Reformed Mission to translate its version of the Christian faith in one county during one of the most tumultuous periods in Chinese history.

Any portrayal of mission work in China in the first half of the twentieth century must be placed in the context of the massive upheavals taking place there during the 150 years between the beginning of the nineteenth century and the middle of the twentieth

---

Roman letters is used in China and in most other parts of the world. Thus, I use "Beijing" and "Rugao, Jiangsu Province," and for writing most other Chinese words, only using Wade-Giles for commonly accepted names of historical figures and places such as Chiang Kai-Shek, Sun Yatsen, and Canton.

2   For a list of Americans and Chinese who served in the Rugao mission between 1920 and 1952, see Appendix.

century.[3] At the end of the eighteenth century, the Qing dynasty (1644–1911) stood at the apex of its power. Under the sage guidance of the early Qing emperors, China had expanded its territory to historic proportions, created a vast infrastructure that contributed to peace and a state treasury overflowing with silver, and obtained new heights in the arts and the traditional crafts of China. Westerners coming to China were impressed with the greatness of the country and, lured by the possibility of selling to millions of Chinese, wanted to tap into its markets. The Middle Kingdom, however, had no need of contact with or goods from "barbarians," and the Westerners were turned away at the door.

If Qing China had reached a pinnacle of power and wealth in the eighteenth century, it experienced precipitous decline during the nineteenth century, largely due to the inability of a series of weak emperors to handle surging foreign and domestic pressures. From the outside, foreigners began knocking with increasing regularity and intensity at China's doors. Although British attempts to open the China market had failed earlier to balance trade, by the early decades of the nineteenth century the British had swung the balance of trade in their favor by importing opium from their Indian colony. Using opium to balance trade unfortunately created millions of Chinese addicts and resulted in deep social problems and political crisis. The Chinese and British went to war over opium in 1838, and following China's defeat in the First Opium War in 1842, foreigners claimed the right to occupy five treaty port cities along China's east coast. Less than twenty years later, China suffered a second defeat in another war fought over opium, and this time the country was flung open to the outside world. These outside pressures from foreigners intensified various internal pressures that resulted in several ethnic and religious rebellions, the most disastrous being the Taiping Rebellion (1850–1864), in which as many as thirty million Chinese may have died and which almost succeeded in toppling the Qing dynasty. By the end of the nineteenth century, China was exhausted and on the verge of collapse.

Though the Qing dynasty frantically tried to save itself and the country through a series of modernizing reforms at the end of the nineteenth century, its attempts were too little too late: In 1911, after two thousand years of holding the country together, China's imperial

---

3   For an excellent and highly readable overview of China between the end of the eighteenth century and the middle of the twentieth century, see Jonathan Spence, *The Search for Modern China*, 2nd ed. (New York: Norton,

system of government collapsed. The crumbling of this ancient pillar of China's stability produced a chaotic heap of social, political, and cultural rubble. Following this collapse, while the Chinese struggled to find a new way of rebuilding their country and their culture, foreigners carved China up like a watermelon, creating spheres of influence in large swaths of the country and in important cities, such as Shanghai and Beijing, where they took control of important sectors of China's legal and economic systems. China was being dragged willy-nilly into the modern world. Out of the chaos, the ever-resilient Chinese began to reinvent themselves and to reorganize their country; from the New Culture Movement and May Fourth Movement of the 1910s came important political, linguistic, social, educational, and cultural changes and resources for rebuilding the nation. As the country's confidence grew, the Chinese began to stand up to the foreign powers.

By the end of the 1920s, Chiang Kai-shek and his Nationalist government had taken back much of the country from warlords, established a new capital in the ancient city of Nanjing, and set the country on a path to becoming a modern nation state. But the so-called "Nanjing Decade" (1928–1937) came to a sudden halt with the Japanese invasion in 1937 and the onset of World War II. For the next twelve years China was plunged into war, first with the Japanese, and then in a brutal civil war between Nationalist and Communist forces fighting for control of the country. When the Communists defeated the Nationalist armies in 1949, Chiang and his government fled to Taiwan, and Mao Zedong stood on the rostrum at Tiananmen Square in Beijing and proclaimed that with the founding of the People's Republic, an old world had passed away and a "new" China had been born.

The Christian Reformed missionaries came to China in 1920, when the country was in the throes of trying to stabilize and reorganize itself. Protestant missionaries had already been in the country for about eighty years. First they had set up mission stations in the five treaty ports opened after the First Opium War (1838–1842), where they built missionary compounds, churches, schools, and hospitals. Not until after the Second Opium War (1856–1860) was the country opened for missionaries to bring Christianity to the interior regions. The advance of the Christian faith in China was often hindered by the opposition of China's intellectual elite, because Christianity was perceived to have played a role in tearing down the ancient structures of Chinese society and competed with China's traditional values. The faith grew slowly and sometimes was used by Chinese converts as a way to advance, enhance, or protect themselves through association with foreign privilege. At the end of the nineteenth century, Chinese anger at foreign intrusion was unleashed in the Boxer Uprising of 1900, when almost twenty thousand Chinese Christians were killed along with several hundred foreigners. When the Qing dynasty fell in 1911, however, many educated Chinese saw Christianity as a potential resource for rebuilding the country, and during the second decade of the twentieth century missionaries and Chinese Christians played an important role in helping sort out the chaos. But the Chinese felt betrayed following World War I, when the allied forces handed most of Shandong Province to the Japanese. Christianity became once again embattled in the country. After eight decades of missionary presence, there were perhaps 300,000 Protestants in the country.[4]

It was into this setting that the Christian Reformed missionaries came to plant a Reformed church.

---

[4]   For information about the state of Protestant Christianity in China in 1920, see Milton Stauffer, ed., *The Christian Occupation of China: A General Survey of the Numerical Strength and Geographical Distribution of the Christian Forces in China Made by the Special Committee on Survey and Occupation, China Construction Committee, 1918-1921* (Shanghai: China Continuation Committee, 1922), 38.

CHAPTER 1

The Greatest Strategic Significance: Choosing China, 1920

Beginning at Jerusalem

Though it took more than sixty years to send its first foreign missionaries, the Christian Reformed Church's interest and concern for missions showed itself from church's earliest days. In 1857, at the second classis meeting of the newly formed denomination, one elder called on the four charter churches to set aside time each month to pray for the extension of God's kingdom and to collect funds for Bible distribution in the Dutch churches of Indonesia.[1] The churches agreed to do so, but following through proved more difficult, and the same elder who had raised the question of missions complained several years later that the church was not fulfilling its pledge to further the extension of God's kingdom.[2]

---

[1] "Klassiekale Vergadering Gehouden den 7 October 1857, te Vriesland, Staat Michigan," p. 1, Art. 1.
[2] "Klassiekale Vergadering Gehouden den 5 Februari 1862, te Graafschaap," p. 19, Art. 5 and 6.

The early mission efforts of the Christian Reformed Church were carried out under the catchphrase, "Beginning at Jerusalem."[3] Initially this meant reaching out to fellow Dutch immigrants, or, as Henry Beets, one of the most vocal missions advocates in the church and editor of a denominational weekly, put it, "All ecclesiastical efforts to extend the Kingdom of God among people in America who are somewhat akin in religious beliefs and language to the members of our church."[4] The Dutch immigrants who came to the United States during the second half of the nineteenth century were looking for a home and a church. Finding a church was not so difficult after the 1850s, since the church was at the center of the Dutch enclaves that began sprouting up, first in western Michigan and then in scattered locations across the northern part of the United States. While most Dutch immigrants were already committed church members, Christian Reformed efforts to establish churches in immigrant communities included those neglecting their church heritage.[5]

Later, "beginning at Jerusalem" took on a new and more literal meaning when some members of the Christian Reformed Church began evangelistic mission work with Jewish Americans. In the last decades of the nineteenth century, Christian Reformed members in Chicago and in Paterson, New Jersey, began working with other Protestants in Jewish neighborhoods adjacent to Dutch ghettos. The Reverend Isaac Fles, a Jewish-Dutch convert to the Christian Reformed Church, played an important role in stimulating interest in mission work to Jews, persuading the denomination to open a mission in Chicago just before the turn of the century.[6] According to Beets, Christian Reformed work among Jews was a debt of obligation to the Jewish race for its contribution to the development of Christianity.[7]

---

[3]   The phrase comes from Luke 24:47 and is part of Jesus' command to his followers that "repentance and remission of sins should be preached in his name unto all the nations, beginning from Jerusalem." [All Bible quotes come from the American Standard Version, the version used in the CRC during the period under study.]

[4]   Henry Beets, "Home Missions of the Christian Reformed Church," *Banner* (until 1907 the *Banner of Truth*) 40 (March 31, 1905): 135.

[5]   For CRC mission work among Dutch immigrants, see John Knight, "1887-1908, Reaching the Dispersed Dutch," in *Echoes of Mercy, Whispers of Love* (Grand Rapids.: Grand Rapids Area Ministries, 1989), 15ff.; John H. Bratt, "The Missionary Enterprise of the Christian Reformed Church of America," Ph.D. diss. (New York: Union Theological Seminary, 1955), 53ff.; and John Kromminga, *The Christian Reformed Church: A Study in Orthodoxy* (Grand Rapids: Baker, 1949), 153.

[6]   For Jewish missions, see John Bratt, "Missionary Enterprise," 133ff.

[7]   Beets, "Our Indebtedness to Israel," *Banner* 50 (Nov. 25, 1915): 733.

Before the end of the nineteenth century, "beginning at Jerusalem" also came to mean mission work among Native Americans. In 1889 the denomination's newly established "Board of Heathen Mission" sent the Reverend Tamme Vanden Bosch to work among the Sioux on the Rosebud Indian reservation in South Dakota.[8] But Vanden Bosch left after less than a year of work, and the board could not find a replacement for almost six years. Finally, in 1896, the board sent two families to Fort Defiance, Arizona, to begin work on the Navajo reservation.[9] Strong opposition from Catholic missionaries there, however, forced the families to move to Gallup, New Mexico.

By the turn of the century, then, Christian Reformed mission work had begun, but it was a small beginning. One minister in a sister denomination, the Reformed Church in America (RCA), openly chided the Christian Reformed Church for its paltry missionary efforts.

> It seems hardly possible that a denomination which holds to the Calvinistic principle, and rightly so, that the Bible is our only rule of faith and practice, should be so sadly negligent or indifferent to the great command of the Savior, when he said: "Go ye therefore, and make disciples of all nations." We refer to our sister denomination, the Christian Reformed Church, which has no missions abroad. A little mission among the American Indians, and that of recent origin, and to which they contribute less than ten-thousand dollars a year, is all that they are doing,

---

[8]   The original name of the Board of Heathen Mission was "Board of Foreign Missions" because when the board was founded the church was interested in work outside of the United States. When the synod of 1886 decided to begin work among the Indians of North America, however, the name of the mission organization was changed from "foreign" to "heathen" to reflect the fact that this work would be carried on in the United States among people whose culture had no affinity with "Christian culture." In 1918, when the CRC began considering seriously where to send its first overseas missionaries, discussion about the name of the mission board came up again. Henry Beets, who was at the time lobbying for the position of full-time secretary of missions, argued that "foreign" was less offensive, was currently used by other American mission agencies, and was a more accurate term. Though he was successful in securing the position (for the denomination and for himself), the name remained unchanged until 1924, when it was changed back to the "Board of Foreign Missions."

[9]   Dick L. Van Halsema, "The Rise of Home Missions in the Christian Reformed Church," S.T.M. diss. (New York: Union Theol. Seminary, 1953), 20-24.

as a Church, to bring the light of the Gospel to those who are in utter darkness.[10]

While accurately describing the denomination's meager efforts, the critic failed to mention reasons why the CRC was slow to engage in mission activity. One important reason was that many of its members were recent immigrants.

The Christian Reformed Church traced its origins to a band of Dutch immigrants who had arrived in west Michigan in the late 1840s looking for a better life and hoping "to enjoy freedom of worship, train their children in accordance with Scriptures, and be a blessing for the Kingdom of God."[11] Alone in the new world, these "new" Dutch at first accepted the care and hospitality extended to them by the "old" Dutch of the Reformed Church in America, many of whom had been living on the East Coast for more than two hundred years.[12] Theological and cultural differences came to a head in 1857, when four churches broke away from the Reformed Church to form a new denomination.[13] One of the breakaway churches immediately returned to the RCA fold and, for the first decade or so, the fledgling denomination barely survived. Starting in the late 1860s, however, the Christian Reformed churches

---

[10]   Evert J. Blekkink, "A Better Day in a Sister Church," *Leader* 1 (July 1906): 137. Quoted in Beets, "Our Lack of Mission Zeal," *Banner* 42 (Jan. 3, 1907): 2.

[11]   Henry Beets, *De Christelijke Gereformeerde Kerk in Noord Amerika* (Grand Rapids: Grand Rapids Publishing, 1918), 56. For origins of the CRC, see James Bratt, *Dutch Calvinism in Modern America: A History of a Conservative Subculture* (Grand Rapids: Eerdmans, 1984); Henry Zwaanstra, *Reformed Thought and Experience in a New World* (Kampen: J.H. Kok, B.V., 1973); and Robert P. Swierenga, "True Brothers: The Netherlandic Origins of the Christian Reformed Church in North America, 1857-1880," in *Breaches and Bridges: Reformed Subcultures in the Netherlands, Germany, and the United States*, George Harinck and Hans Krabbendam, eds. (Amsterdam: VU Uitgeverij, 2000), 61-84.

[12]   The RCA (in the nineteenth century the "Dutch Reformed Church") claims the distinction of being the oldest Protestant denomination in North America, having been established at the beginning of the seventeenth century by Dutch colonists in New Amsterdam (New York City). See Gerald F. De Jong, *The Dutch Reformed Church in the American Colonies* (Grand Rapids: Eerdmans, 1978).

[13]   Until it settled on its current name in 1904, the Christian Reformed Church was called successively the "Holland Reformed Church" (1859-1861), "True Dutch Reformed Church" (*Ware Hollandsche Gereformeerde Kerk*) (1865-1879), the Holland Christian Reformed Church (1880), and the (Holland) Christian Reformed Church (1894-1904). See Kromminga, *Christian Reformed Church*, Appendix IV, 234.

began receiving new immigrant members, so that by the 1880s the denomination was on solid ground. These years of assimilating newcomers were also years of building: homes, farms, businesses and—most important for the members of this strongly religious subculture—churches, parsonages, and a theological school to train clergy.

While accepting the Reformed "brother's words" of criticism in 1906 as "a merited, loving rebuke," Henry Beets, in a January 1907 editorial, offered "two or three reasons in extenuation of our negligence." Since, as Beets pointed out in answer to the charge of "indifference to missions," the members of the Christian Reformed Church were "not of noble birth or rich," this building took time and money. Beets added, rather defensively, that unlike the "new" Dutch members of the RCA, the members of his denomination had to build "from the bottom up and single handedly, without any aid from the outside such as our Reformed brethren in the West enjoyed for over a half century and are enjoying today, more or less." Further, said Beets, CRC members provided for the poor in their midst and supported "free Christian primary schools," while "other denominations like the Reformed Church expend comparatively little for these."[14]

Stretched to its limits financially during this period, the Christian Reformed Church naturally gave little to missions. The denominational total for giving in 1906 came to ten thousand dollars for missionary work with Native Americans. According to Beets, this meant that out of 160 churches, less than a hundred gave more than one dollar per family for either "home" or "heathen" missions, which, calculated on a weekly basis, came to less than two cents per week.[15] To raise even this much, Henry Beets had to coax, cajole, and at times even shame the reluctant members of the CRC to support the cause of missions.

Lack of money was not the only problem facing Christian Reformed missions. Recruiting missionary workers also proved extraordinarily difficult. The Reverend Tamme Vanden Bosch provides an apt example. He was the first to volunteer to serve as a "home" missionary in the denomination in 1879, but, like the few others who took up work among the "scattered Hollanders" in North America, he lasted only a short time at the task. So desperate was the church to recruit missionary candidates that the synod of 1886 suggested that anyone receiving financial aid for ministerial training should serve for a time as a missionary.[16] That same year, Vanden Bosch, by then a member

---

14 Beets, "Our Lack of Mission Zeal," 2.
15 Beets, "Our Giving for Missions," *Banner* 41 (Aug. 3, 1906): 202.
16 The church never acted on this proposal. See *Acta Synode CRC*, 1886, Art. 7, 29.

of the Board of Heathen Missions, volunteered to begin mission work with the Sioux when a denomination-wide appeal failed to turn up any willing workers.[17] Because of the turmoil roiling the reservation and what was later described as Vanden Bosch's own "erratic behavior," he left after less than a year of service.

Beets ended his 1907 reflection on the lack of mission zeal in the denomination acknowledging that more could be done "if pastors and consistories would take the matter up with more enthusiasm and regularity, and if every member would make it a matter of conscience. Brethren, let us try," he urged.

Just three years later, in a 1910 *Banner* editorial, Beets noted with enthusiasm some hopeful signs of increased mission zeal in the church. After heralding the work of the nationwide, ecumenical Laymen's Missionary Movement, he noted several proposals adopted by the synod of 1910 for bolstering missionary support. That year the synod recommended that missionary sermons be preached in all churches several times a year, and it called on the church to include "missionary subjects" in its catechism and Sunday school curriculum.[18] The synod also urged young people and men's societies to study missionary subjects. Last, but certainly not least, the synod recommended "weekly, systematic offerings for the cause of missions."[19]

The recommendations paid off, and two years later the synod of 1912 could report that "more love" for missions was apparent in the denomination. Signs of this increased love for missions included the fact that several urban churches had established city missions. In Grand Rapids, Michigan, the center of the denomination, one church had opened a "missionary Sunday school, another church had opened the "Way of Life Mission," a street ministry in the southeast section of the city, and a third church was doing mission work with German and Polish immigrants in the northeast section of the city.[20] Churches in Paterson, New Jersey, and Chicago had also established city missions. Commenting on the interest in city missions, John Dolfin, secretary

[17] Henry Beets, *Toiling and Trusting: Fifty Years of Mission Work of the Christian Reformed Church among Indians and Chinese* (Grand Rapids: Grand Rapids Company, 1940), 26.
[18] The synod suggested this could be done without harming the integrity of the rigorously biblical curriculum by substituting relevant mission materials for review lessons or temperance lessons. Beets, "Missionary Plans," *Banner* 45 (Sept. 8, 1910): 560.
[19] Ibid.
[20] Knight, *Echoes of Mercy*, 21.

of the Board of Heathen Missions, saw the movement as a sign of "a marvelous awakening in mission interest that is felt throughout our whole church but especially strong in some localities."[21]

Mission societies and mission fests also revealed growing mission enthusiasm. The first Christian Reformed mission society had been organized in Grand Haven, Michigan, in 1885. By 1910 there were seventeen such societies in the denomination, and five years later the number had grown to twenty-six. These societies organized activities to spark mission enthusiasm. One important activity was the mission "fest." Usually held outdoors during September and October as a harvest festival, mission fests featured special worship services led by missionary speakers. The annual events were highlights for many churches and stimulated not only interest in missions but also romantic interests, playing a sociological function in many Christian Reformed enclaves.[22] As the number of societies and festivals grew, perhaps fearing that mission enthusiasm could get out of hand or dilute theological purity, some church leaders suggested ways to insure that materials were in keeping with denominational standards.[23]

A rise in mission giving provides another strong (perhaps the strongest) indication of increased missionary zeal in the Christian Reformed Church after 1910. While at times still having occasionally to urge members to increase their mission giving, Henry Beets could report in 1916 that in some churches giving had increased to ten cents per week per family, which, he estimated, if realized throughout the denomination, would mean a $200,000 annual budget for missions.[24]

Mission societies, street missions, mission fests, and increased giving all clearly indicate an increased interest in missions in the Christian Reformed Church in a relatively short period of time after 1910. What accounts for this rise of enthusiasm for missions? Certainly, synodical suggestions and prodding by denominational leaders, most notably Henry Beets, played a role in fanning mission enthusiasm in the church. But the real source of increased missionary enthusiasm came from another direction: the young people of the denomination. After 1910, the rise of interest among Christian Reformed young people forced the issue of missions to the forefront of the church's agenda.

[21]   John Dolfin, "Something to Think About," *Banner* 47 (Oct. 10, 1912): 640-41. See also Knight, *Echoes of Mercy*, 20-23.
[22]   Malcolm McBride, "Mission Fests: Fun, Faith-filled While They Lasted," *Banner* 121 (Sept. 15, 1986): 25-26.
[23]   John Bratt, "Missionary Enterprise," 151.
[24]   Beets, "Mission Giving," *Banner* 51 (Dec. 21, 1916): 806-07.

Rallying the Volunteers

Calls for the Christian Reformed Church to open a foreign mission reached a crescendo between 1916 and 1918. In 1916, the synod called on the church to make a decision about the feasibility of establishing a foreign mission by 1918, and it appointed a committee to investigate the venture. The committee was made up of the Reverend K.W. (Karel) Fortuin, the Reverend M. (Marinus) Van Vessem, and the Reverend Harold Bode, and it was divided in its opinion, with Fortuin and Van Vessem favoring South America as a mission field and Bode recommending China in a minority report. The committee published its recommendation just months before the synod met in June of 1918. While agreeing that a foreign field should be established, the majority report cautioned the church to examine its motives for doing so, warning, "The guiding motive for our churches must not be to imitate others, but for the Church of God the thought must prevail: to what does the Lord through His Spirit call the Church to do, thereby taking in consideration the special leadings of His Providence."[25]

These stern words were aimed directly at Calvin College and Calvin Theological Seminary students who in 1918 were forcefully lobbying the church to initiate foreign mission work. Specifically, the majority report's words were a response to a discussion that had taken place in the *Calvin College Chimes* during the school year of 1917–1918, a discussion that had already started eight years earlier when Fortuin had been a student at Calvin Seminary.

The discussion of motivation for missions had begun already in 1910 when John Luidens, the organization editor of the *Chimes*, had written an article lamenting the poor turnout for a missions lecture given by a Reformed Church missionary serving in Japan.[26] According to Luidens, the low attendance demonstrated a lack of missionary zeal. Another symptom Luidens pointed to was the decline of mission societies on campus from three groups with sixty members in 1907 to only one group with twelve members in 1910. In the next issue of *Chimes*, Lee Huizenga, a tireless missions advocate during his seminary days who was serving a pastorate in New Jersey while preparing for overseas mission work, supported Luidens's assessment of the tepid enthusiasm

25 M. Van Vessem and K.W. Fortuin, "Report, Extension of Mission Work," *Banner* 53 (April 4, 1918): 242.
26 Harvey Smit, "Mission Zeal in the Christian Reformed Church," in *Perspectives on the Christian Reformed Church*, Peter DeKlerk and Richard DeRidder, eds. (Grand Rapids: Baker, 1983), 235-39.

for missions in the church and offered a stark explanation. The church, he said, was simply disobedient to the Lord's final command: "GO." Huizenga then called on the churches to "pray for a true revival of mission spirit, for we are *all* guilty."[27]

Responding to these calls for mission enthusiasm, the next fall Fortuin offered in the *Chimes* a word of caution about the motivation or "spirit" for missions. While supporting stronger mission interest, he urged the church to distinguish clearly between the "American mission spirit...with its dollar standard and methodistic ideas of why and how we should do evangelism," and "the biblical approach...best expressed in Reformed principles."[28] According to Fortuin, the American missionary spirit was most clearly expressed in the watchword of the Student Volunteer Movement: "The Evangelization of the Whole World in This Generation." He went on to add, "Many students could not accept this motto because it was a purely human construct, based not on scripture but on 'methodistic,' emotional urging of us to win souls for Jesus. It stresses not the Lord's command but the need of poor, blind heathen."[29]

The back-and-forth discussion between Luidens and Fortuin and several others about motivation for missions continued into 1911. At the discussion's vortex was the Student Volunteer Movement for Foreign Missions. How did that broadly evangelical parachurch movement come to be so involved in the internal discussions of the Christian Reformed Church?

The Student Volunteer Movement for Foreign Missions was both a cause and a result of the flowering of the late nineteenth-century Protestant enthusiasm for foreign missions.[30] At a student conference organized by revivalist Dwight L. Moody in 1876 at Mount Hermon, Massachusetts, one hundred students pledged to become missionaries. Over the next several decades the number of volunteers grew

27 Lee Huizenga, "Mission-Symposium," *Chimes* 4 (1910): 205.
28 K.W. Fortuin, "Zendinggeest," *Chimes* 4 (1910): 257. Quoted in Smit (from Dutch trans.), "Mission Zeal," 236.
29 Ibid., 236.
30 For the history of the SVM, see Michael Parker, *The Kingdom of Character: The Student Volunteer Movement for Foreign Missions (1886-1926)* (Lanham, Md.: Univ. Press of America, 1998); Nathan Showalter, *The End of the Crusade: The Student Volunteer Movement for Foreign Missions and the Great War* (Lanham, Md.: Scarecrow, 1998); and Clifton Philips, "The Student Volunteer Movement and Its Role in China Missions, 1886-1935," in John K. Fairbank, ed., *The Missionary Enterprise in China and America*, (Cambridge: Harvard Univ. Press, 1974), 91-109.

exponentially, reaching 33,726 by 1920.[31] Only about 26 percent of the volunteers went overseas; the rest dedicated themselves to promoting the missionary enterprise at home "by their intelligent advocacy, by their gifts, and by their prayers."[32] Some of those who stayed at home served as traveling secretaries, visiting campuses across North America and around the world. The student movement also promoted missions through its quadrennial conventions, which by 1920 were drawing more than eight thousand participants to listen to missionaries from around the world.

By the middle of the second decade of the twentieth century, the Student Volunteer Movement was also playing an important role in the politics of the Christian Reformed Church. Though Calvin was not officially a part of the movement, students at the college and seminary had organized a "Student Volunteer Band" in 1907. Shortly after its first meeting, Calvin student Edward Tanis wrote that the Student Volunteer Movement "...has sprayed our school. Just enough moisture has been received to assure, under God's nourishment, a steady, vigorous growth of mission zeal."[33] Tanis's optimism proved premature, but a decade later, by 1917, "The Band," as it came to be known in Christian Reformed student circles, was *the* missionary force to be reckoned with in the denomination.

Changes in the church also help explain the growth and strength of student mission forces in the church. By the end of the first decade of the twentieth century, the waves of Dutch immigrants had slowed and, with the onset of the Great War, virtually came to a halt. While more recent arrivals clung tenaciously to their Old World identity and roots, some in the church wanted to make peace with the larger American world and with American Protestantism. Young people were especially keen to become American Christians.[34] The Student Volunteer Movement provided the young people of the church a direct line to the American Protestant world.

---

[31]   Parker, *Kingdom of Character*, 18.
[32]   Albert H. Smit, "The Significance of the Student Volunteer Movement," *Chimes* 14 (Jan. 1920): 16-17.
[33]   Edward J. Tanis, "Students and Missions," *Chimes* 1 (April, 1907): 13.
[34]   For Americanization in the CRC, see James Bratt, *Dutch Calvinism in Modern America: A History of a Conservative Subculture* (Grand Rapids: Eerdmans, 1984), 41ff., and Henry Zwaanstra, *Reformed Thought and Experience in a New World: A Study of the Christian Reformed Church and its American Environment 1890-1918* (Kampen: J.H. Kok, 1973), 297ff.

Though The Band at Calvin was an exclusively male bastion, women students organized their own "Girls Mission Society" around the slogan "more love for missions."[35] Together the two groups organized activities to foster missionary zeal in the schools and the church. Perhaps their most important activity (certainly the most exciting) was hosting missionary speakers. On these intense, activity-filled days, a guest missionary would lead the morning "chapel exercises" at the college and speak to a denominational audience in the evening. Between these two main events, the guest missionary would meet privately with students considering mission work or lead sessions on spiritual preparation, meetings from which students at times were turned away "because the room could not contain them."[36] Many of these missionaries worked with the Reformed Church, but missions opened other ecumenical doors as well, including Methodist missionaries. One of these, Dr. Charles S. Buchanan, who was superintendent of the Methodist Missions in the East Indies, an Englishman who spoke Dutch and who was fond of Calvinism, packed the school's auditorium in January 1918 despite "a blizzard raging outside."[37]

Contact with the Student Volunteer Movement also drew Christian Reformed students out of the shelter of their religious subculture. At first the students were timid about being in the larger Protestant world, something one member of the Student Volunteer Movement noticed about Calvin students attending a conference in 1917, commenting that "some of your delegates seemed shy, they didn't mix."[38] By 1920, when The Band's influence in the denomination had increased, Christian Reformed students were attending Student Volunteer Movement conferences in large numbers, both women and men, mixing better with the speakers and other delegates, and "finding little time to be together during the day but huddling together at night to smoke cigars and compare notes."[39] The students' exposure to American Protestantism extended beyond the conference itself. Carolyn Van der Meer, a member of the Girls Mission Society, reported that one night, "out of curiosity," she attended a "Holy Rollers' Meeting" with a group of Christian Reformed students, who found that though the

---

[35] "The Girl's Mission Society," *Chimes* 11 (Nov. 1917): 283-84.

[36] Richard H. Pousma, "Dr. Zwemer's Lecture," *Chimes* 13 (May 1919): 228-29.

[37] "Mission Enthusiasm," *Chimes* 12 (Feb. 1918): 79.

[38] "Student Volunteer Band at Calvin College," *Chimes* 11 (May-June 1917): 155-56.

[39] Nicholas De Vries, "Our Delegation at Des Moines," *Chimes* 14 (Feb. 1920): 66-68.

meeting was strange, the testimonies were "sincere." About this meeting, Van der Meer noted, "The same blessedness of the life in Jesus Christ, which we, who are His, experience, was related in this evening."[40]

Christian Reformed students brought the enthusiasm of the conferences back to Calvin. Van der Meer wrote, "Coming home, I was filled with an eagerness to bring back some of the spirit of the Convention to my own beloved Calvin."[41] As a result of connections with the student movement, mission enthusiasm grew at Calvin, especially between 1915 and 1920. In 1915, The Band had nine members, but in the next five years the numbers had grown to twenty-seven. By 1917, Christian Reformed students studying at other schools—schools specifically for training missionary candidates—had organized their own "Bands" along the lines of the Calvin Band. At the Union Missionary Training Institute in Brooklyn, thirteen Christian Reformed students, men and women, were studying and working in city missions, in order to prepare for the mission field. Another eleven were studying at the Moody Bible Institute in Chicago. In the effort to push the CRC to establish a foreign field, these Bands together proved a formidable lobbying force.

The Bands were determined to push the cause of missions to victory, as one article in the *Chimes* declared in its title in the spring of 1917: "A Christian Reformed Foreign Mission Field by 1918."[42] To do so, however, they had to overcome suspicions about the nature of their connection to the wider Student Volunteer Movement. While not all denominational leaders were opposed to the movement and its incarnation as "Bands," many were suspicious of this movement, originating as it did from outside the denomination.[43] After The Band declared its determination to have a foreign field by 1918, one member

---

[40]   Carolyn M. Van der Meer, "My Trip to Des Moines," *Chimes* 14 (Feb. 1920): 64.
[41]   Ibid.
[42]   John De Korne, *Chimes* 11 (May-June 1917): 154.
[43]   Henry Beets, for one, supported the CRC Bands. In an address to The Band at Calvin College in October 1915, he encouraged students to support missions because of the world's tremendous needs and because mission led to the "best kind of consecration." Another denominational leader to promote mission and support the Volunteer Bands was Gelmer Kuiper, a CRC businessman from New Jersey. Kuiper spoke at Calvin in 1910 pleading for support of the SVM's "watchword." For Kuiper's views of the CRC and missions, see Gelmer Kuiper, "The Mission of our Church from a Member's point of view," in *Gedenkboek van het Vijftigjarig Jubileum der Christelijke Gereformeerde Kerk, 1857-1907* (Grand Rapids: J.B. Hulst, 1907), 239-43.

responded in the *Chimes* to what he took as severe criticism by some individuals in the church. "Two things ought to be clear about this organization [The Band]," he wrote. "The first is that this organization is not affiliated with The Student Volunteer Movement."[44] Second, this anonymous student wrote, "If students knew The Band was open to students interested in both foreign *and* home missions, the numbers would be even higher."

The most serious criticism of The Band, however, was its attempt to usurp the church's prerogative to lead its members; in other words, instead of being led by the legitimate leaders of the church, Band members were attempting to lead the church and thus were "disregarding the guiding hand of God." During the 1917–1918 school year, another debate broke out in the *Chimes* over the issue of who should lead whom. In the fall, John W. Brink, a missionary to the Indians in New Mexico, addressed an alumni letter to the *Chimes* about the rising interest among students for a foreign mission field. On the one hand, Brink expressed approval of the students' interest in missions and his belief that their "calls" came "as a part of whole-hearted consecration."[45] But Brink wondered why students were agitating for a foreign field when there was plenty of work to do on the Indian field. He questioned their approach of pushing for a foreign field and rejected the idea that individuals should lead the church. The rule according to Holy Scripture, Brink stated, is that the "Spirit leads the Church into all truth and the individual believer in and through that Church." He put the matter bluntly:

> *First the Church and then the men.* Nobody should strive to induce the Church to go abroad because some of her sons are called to do so. But rather *the sons should be urged to go when and because the Church, their spiritual Mother, is Spirit-led to a foreign field.*[46]

Careful to show this missionary statesman all due respect, students nonetheless challenged Brink in the next several issues of the *Chimes*. In an article entitled, "'First the Church and then the Men': What does history say about it?" student editor William Goudberg disagreed with Brink about the principle at stake. Citing a long list of examples, Goudberg argued that throughout its history the church

---

[44] "The Student Volunteer Band of the Theological School and Calvin College," *Chimes* 11 (May-June, 1917): 154-55.
[45] John W. Brink, "A Foreign Mission Field," *Chimes* 11 (Nov. 1917): 349.
[46] Ibid., 351.

had not been interested in missions but had been prodded to missions by visionary prophets, such as William Carey, calling the church to faithfulness.[47] Usually, he concluded, the Holy Spirit called the church by means of the very men whom the Spirit had set aside for the work, and that sometimes these men were 'voices crying in the wilderness.'" Simon Dykstra, another student respondent, suggested that Brink's "polemical attitude" was, perhaps, an indirect response to the "many shafts of criticism" directed at the Indian field.[48] Dykstra went on to reject Brink's principle of "first the church, then the men," as a "misleading antithesis." "The antithesis is wanting," he wrote:

> We have imbibed our mission enthusiasm in our own Church. We have labored in her mission societies, we have listened to her missionaries, we have been inspired by the sacrifice of her own sons. No Methodistic revival has stirred our emotions. Our own Reformed principles impel us to action. They err who question our Calvinism. Is there no mission spirit possible in our own circles except it be imported? [49]

In his conclusion, Dykstra reiterated his rejection of the antithesis and stated that the operative principle should be *first the Church through the men."*

A month after Dykstra's March 1918 article appeared, the majority report of the synodical committee on recommending foreign missions reported in the *Banner*. Although the committee's report did not refer directly to the argument taking place in the *Chimes*, it clearly had that discussion in mind when it reminded students sternly that the desire to imitate others was not a legitimate reason for extending the mission work of the church. "The extension of heathen mission is possible," the committee wrote, "but it should be done primarily out of obedience to the Lord's command in the Great Commission and in

[47] *Chimes* 12 (Feb. 1918): 59-63.
[48] Sam A. Dykstra, "A Foreign Mission Field," *Chimes* 12 (March 1918): 107.
[49] Ibid., 108. See also Dykstra's letter to John De Korne on the controversy. His letters not only reveal the deep sense of camaraderie the CRC students felt in their cause to push for a foreign mission field, but also Dykstra's conviction that one of the professors at the seminary, Samuel Volbeda, would oppose the students because he always "fought the tendency to seek norms in mission history, and our sturdy Calvinists perhaps would never consent to copy history even if it prove the usual method of the Holy Spirit which Goudberg has presented." Sam Dykstra to De Korne, Feb. 21, 1918, and April 27, 1918, De Korne, personal folder.

order to glorify God."[50] As to where the church should begin its first overseas venture, in another shot clearly aimed at the student Bands, the committee suggested it should be a decision of the church and not according to the whims of students.

Two months later, the synod of 1918, remembered as a "visionary synod," decided to extend the denomination's mission program overseas.[51] From being a nagging obligation less than a decade earlier, the cause of foreign missions had moved to an important place at the forefront of the church's agenda. The role of Student Volunteer Bands in this shift cannot be overestimated. At a pivotal time in the denomination's history, as immigration slowed down and the process of Americanization had reached a critical phase, students, with their ties to the larger American Protestant world, aggressively campaigned to force their largely reluctant elders to participate in missions.

About their victory, John De Korne, formerly head of the Calvin Band and in 1918 serving as a pastor in New Jersey, wrote to fellow Band members: "Nothing but a solid stone wall of indifference will keep us from reaping for our church the fruits of the victory for which our CRC mission enthusiasts have been fighting so long."[52] A significant number of these "mission enthusiasts" (including John De Korne, Lee Huizenga, the brothers Simon and Harry Dykstra, and Nicholas De Vries) went on to become the pioneer missionaries of the denomination, carrying their ideas, passions, and conflicts with them to the field. Though they had won this fight to establish a foreign mission, the next battle lay in choosing where that work would be established.

A "Neglected Continent"

At various times, voices in the church had called for opening mission work in Cuba, Latin America, South America, Indonesia, Arabia, Abyssinia, Africa, and China.[53] Even the committee appointed by the synod to recommend the feasibility of a foreign field could not agree on where that field should be.

The committee's majority report recommended extending the denomination's Indian work in the southwest United States down

---

[50]   M. Van Vessem and K. W. Fortuin, "Report: Extension of Mission Work," *Banner* 53 (April 4, 1918): 242-43.
[51]   See Henry Zwaanstra, *Catholicity and Secession: A Study of Ecumenicity in the Christian Reformed Church* (Grand Rapids: Eerdmans, 1991), 30.
[52]   De Korne to fellow members, Nov. 27, 1918, De Korne, personal folder.
[53]   John Bratt, "Missionary Enterprise," 183.

through Mexico and Central America to South America, in order to form a chain of connected mission stations. Such a plan, the report argued, would employ the church's valuable experience gained in Indian work and make a contribution to what it termed a field "ripe for the harvest."[54] Work in South America, the report continued, would also be commensurate with the "relatively small strength of our Church." Most importantly, the majority report concluded, extending from the church's existing work would allow the denomination to work independently of other churches, because, it warned, "Co-operation with others endangers our confessional character and authority, both of which are necessary for the teaching of the Word and for discipline."[55]

Though Fortuin and Van Vessem's majority report claimed that "this extension [to South America] is favored by a majority of our people," one of those advocates stood out: Lee Huizenga.[56] By 1918 Huizenga had been agitating for a foreign mission in South America for almost a decade. At his graduation from Calvin Seminary in 1909, he had given a commencement address entitled "South America, an Open yet Neglected Mission Field," in which he had outlined the dimensions of the continent and then had pleaded for the church to send missionaries to meet the dire spiritual needs of the South American people who, he said, lived under the "pall of Roman Catholicism."[57]

A year after graduation, while serving a church in New Jersey and studying medicine in preparation for work as a missionary doctor, Huizenga wrote a five-part series of articles lobbying for Christian Reformed mission work in South America, expanding on the themes of his commencement address and drawing particular attention to the plight of South American Indians.[58] Huizenga's campaign for South America reached a climax in 1913: Avoiding the difficulty of a synodical appointment, he convinced Classis Hudson to send him there as its missionary. When the synod rejected this power play to force the issue,

[54] Van Vessem and Fortuin, "Report, Extension of Mission Work," 242.
[55] Ibid.
[56] Ibid.
[57] Huizenga, "South America, an Open yet Neglected Mission Field," *Chimes* 3-4 (1909-1910): 157-60.
[58] Huizenga, "The Indians of South America" (five parts), *Banner* 45 (May 19, 26, June 2, 9, and 16, 1910): 319, 337, 348, 366, and 384. The phrase "neglected continent" as well as Huizenga's information about South America comes—much of it verbatim—from James Dennis's landmark work on missions at the end of the nineteenth century. See Dennis, *Foreign Missions after a Century* (New York: Revell, 1893), 132ff.

Huizenga moved to New Mexico to work on the Indian field, where he continued to agitate for South America.[59]

Not everyone agreed with Huizenga and the recommendation for South America; in fact, the subject touched a raw nerve in the church. Soon after the recommendation was made, Henry Beets, in a three-part article, took strong issue with South America as a Christian Reformed mission field. Though he cautiously agreed with the idea of opening a foreign field, suggesting that the church wait until the end of the war in Europe, he rejected the recommendation that mission work be done among the Indians: "Without desiring to in the least belittle the majority report,...we do not agree with its findings and are not in accord with its advice and recommendation."[60]

Beets argued, "Native Americans are uncivilized and ingrainedly prejudiced against whites...making them extremely difficult subjects for the missionary venture." Taking a not-so-subtle jab at the chief proponent of South American work, Beets continued: "In last week's '*Wachter*' Dr. Huizenga informed us that he 'often' meets cases of our 'converts' reverting to heathenism, while but a 'few' 'remain faithful to the Lord.'" Only through their children can they be reached with the gospel, a method, Beets added, which "is not always crowned with success." Anticipating the question of why the Christian Reformed Church had started a mission among Indians in the first place, Beets wrote: "The main argument set forth was that we robbed the Indian of so many things of a material kind that we should try to bring him a substitute of a spiritual nature, in fact, the best substitute in the world: the Gospel."[61]

"Humanitarian, patriotic, and altruistic" motives were fine for selecting Indians as a domestic focus for missionary work, but in selecting a foreign field, Beets continued, biblical principles—specifically Pauline principles—should govern the choice of extension. When the Apostle Paul chose new areas for mission work, according to Beets, he chose locations that would be relatively easy and in highly populated urban centers. Moreover, Paul chose people of promise, who would in turn make a contribution to the development of the Christian faith. In Beets's mind, the Pauline principles for choosing a mission location could be summarized in the term "strategicity."

Beets expanded on the idea of "strategicity" in a series appearing just before the synod met in 1918. While he may have coined the term,

[59] John Bratt, "Missionary Enterprise," 127.
[60] Beets, "New Mission Work—Where?" *Banner* 53 (May 9, 1918): 336-38.
[61] Ibid.

the ideas were those of John R. Mott, leader of the Student Volunteer Movement and a leading missionary spokesperson.[62] According to Mott, stated Beets, "While all men everywhere are in need of the gospel, there are what are called **strategic races and places** the reaching of which means **much more** for the whole cause of missions than the reaching of others, in less significant positions."[63] As an example of a strategic race, Mott pointed out the importance of the Chinese, and Beets, supporting this conclusion, added: "Comparatively speaking, the Amarinds [sic] are far inferior to the Chinese....Indeed, the Chinamen have been called the Anglo-Saxons of the Orient."

As far as strategic places were concerned, Beets argued that it was not good stewardship to send "a consecrated and highly educated worker" to minister to a handful of Indians when he could minister to "hundreds more if located in a more thickly populated" area, such as Tokyo, Shanghai, or Bombay. At the end of the article, although Beets refused to be pinned down on where he thought the church should establish a foreign mission, he did suggest China as a good possibility and, perhaps, the Dutch Indies. The church's choice, he concluded, should also be based on what Mott had called at the World Missionary Conference in Edinburgh in 1910, the "**principle of urgency**," which was evident in the Christian movements taking place in India and China.[64]

Beets's articles rejecting South America as a mission field show that missions was a portal through which some Christian Reformed leaders could sympathetically view the larger Protestant world. They also reveal the frustration many in the church felt about Indian missions. After more than a decade of work in the southwest, the Christian Reformed Church could claim only one convert—a girl of thirteen who died shortly after her baptism.[65] Denominational critics continually questioned the wisdom of mission work among the Indians. Some wondered if Indians, given their nomadic lifestyle, could be gathered into one place to hear the message of the gospel. Others were harsh in their estimation of Indians' ability to receive Christianity

---

[62] It is unclear where Beets found the term "strategicity."

[63] Beets, "Why Not among the Indians," *Banner* 53 (May 16, 1918): 352-54. The quote from Mott comes from *The Decisive Hour of Missions* (New York: Missionary Education Movement of the United States and Canada, 1911), 108. The bold text is Beets's.

[64] Ibid.

[65] Scott Hoezee and Christopher H. Meehan, *Flourishing in the Land: A Hundred-Year History of Christian Reformed Missions in North America* (Grand Rapids: Eerdmans, 1996), 12.

at all. One critic stated that "preaching would have little effect on Indians because they were stupid and hardhearted, and should they be converted, their lazy and roaming nature would prevent them from forming well-organized, self-supporting churches."[66] On the floor of the synod, another opponent even went so far as to suggest that "any race which ate the entrails of animals was simply 'beyond redemption.'"[67]

Less than a month later, the synod of 1918 took Beets's advice and rejected the majority report's call for expanding missionary work from the southwest into South America, noting that work with Indians was expensive and that "there is in our church a strong antipathy against further expansion of mission to the Indians."[68] After rejecting South America, the synod narrowed the choice of foreign fields down to two possible locations: Central Africa or China.

"Ethiopia Shall Haste To Stretch out her Hands"

To investigate whether the church should establish a mission in Africa or China, the synod appointed two ordained men to provide the next synod of 1920 with a recommendation. The men selected for the task, Lee Huizenga and John De Korne, were both obvious choices.

Huizenga, as noted above, had been an early and strong proponent of work with the Indians of South America. After suffering a nervous breakdown during his seminary years, Huizenga had gone to New Mexico to rest and to do maintenance work for the Christian Reformed Church's Indian mission. After graduating from Calvin Seminary in 1909, Huizenga had alternated between serving as pastor of the Christian Reformed Church in Englewood, New Jersey, and doing mission work in the Southwest, all while studying for a medical degree and teaching at the Union Missionary Training Institute in Brooklyn. He also continued to agitate for missions in the denominational papers.[69]

John De Korne, though less well known in the church, was also an important missions advocate. First as president of the student missions Band and then later as pastor, De Korne more than any other person

---

[66]   Robert J. Groelsema, "Christian Assimilation: The Pioneer Christian Reformed Indian Mission," *Origins* 5:1 (1987): 43. See also, Beets, *Toiling and Trusting*, 32.

[67]   From Herman Fryling, personal memoir. Quoted in Hoezee and Meehan, *Flourishing*, 3.

[68]   *Acta Synode CRC*, 1918, Art. 65, 86 (trans.).

[69]   Huizenga frequently contributed mission articles to the *Banner*, *De Wachter*, *De Heidenwerld*, and the *Sabbath Day Instructor*.

rallied the student mission enthusiasts during the crucial years leading up to the 1918 decision to open a foreign field. After graduating from seminary in 1917, De Korne had taken over as Huizenga's replacement at the Englewood church, while at the same time serving as an army chaplain at Fort Merit, New Jersey.[70]

From their base in New Jersey, De Korne and Huizenga began investigating the two possible locations selected by the synod. They gathered the bulk of their information at the Missionary Research Library in New York, which touted itself at the time as the best missionary library in North America.[71] In addition to reading, the two attended meetings sponsored by the Foreign Missions Conference of North America and interviewed some of the leading mission experts of the day. About this last activity, in a letter to a friend De Korne boasted that they had "been able to have conferences with the biggest missionary men our country can boast. How is this for a partial list: Zwemer, Kumm, Speer, Fennell P. Turner, Burton St. John, E.C. Lobenstine, Harlan P. Beach, Charles R. Watson, W.I. Chamberlain, J. Lovell Murray? And the biggest of these men were the most willing to give us all the time we needed to place our problem before them."[72]

---

[70]   The Englewood church was one of the strongest mission-supporting churches in the denomination. In part, no doubt, this was due to the pastors who served there, including De Korne, Huizenga, and John Dolfin (1904-1909), who later served as the secretary of the Board of Missions for more than thirty years. The Englewood church had come into the CRC from an earlier split with the RCA in the 1820s, and, as a church already more sensitive to issues in the larger Protestant world, this background, too, may have contributed to the congregation's interest in missions. John De Korne's work as a military chaplain suggests that military and YMCA chaplaincy was another avenue for members of the CRC to connect with the wider American Protestant world, and especially for those interested in missions. Of the fourteen CRC men who served as chaplains to military bases and camps in the U.S. between 1917 and 1918, four were engaged in the missions debate in the denomination, three of whom went on to serve in China (John De Korne, Harry Dykstra, and Richard Pousma). See Richard Harms, "The First Chaplains," *Origins* 23:1 (2005): 9.

[71]   The library claimed in 1918 to have a total of 1,674 volumes of bound reports and periodicals and 4,823 pamphlets on missionary subjects. This information comes from a Missionary Research Library pamphlet in De Korne, personal folder.

[72]   De Korne to Henry Verduin, Nov. 22, 1918, De Korne, personal folder. De Korne's list of missionary statesmen includes Samuel Zwemer, RCA missionary to Islam, widely-regarded expert on the subject and an important contributor at Edinburgh 1910; Karl Kumm, founder of the Sudan United Mission and popular missionary speaker in both Europe

Though the synod gave them a mandate to investigate the feasibility of both locations, from the start both men leaned in favor of Central Africa, more specifically the "Greater Sudan."[73] The synod of 1918 had chosen Central Africa as a potential location for establishing a mission because, it noted, "There are lately in our church voices calling for opening a mission field in Central Africa; a very favorable report was received recently concerning a field there, and even one member of our church already has been named to work there."[74]

The member alluded to was Johanna Veenstra, who played an important role in drumming up interest in Africa. After accepting an altar call as a teenager in a Baptist church in New Jersey, Veenstra had become interested in missions. While a student at Brooklyn's Union Missionary Training Institute, she was chosen in the summer of 1915 to represent the school at a Student Volunteer Movement conference in Lake Geneva, Wisconsin. There she heard missionary speakers from all over the world, including Karl Kumm speaking about the Sudan. As Kumm spoke, Veenstra related a decade later, "I sat spellbound! Not a word of this message escaped my attention! I was profoundly impressed and deeply moved! I went to my tent and retired, but sleep refused to still my thought! I spent three days in meditation."[75] Before she left the

---

and the United States; Robert Speer, a leading Presbyterian missionary spokesperson; Fennell P. Turner, Foreign Missions Conference secretary and author of the 1914 SVM report; Burton St. John, also with the FMC and a compiler of missionary statistics; E.C. Lobenstine, a member of the Presbyterian Church in the U.S.A. (North), a leading expert on China, and the executive secretary of the China Continuation Committee; Harlan P. Beach, missions professor at Yale University, contributor to the mission data generated from Edinburgh, 1910, and voluminous author of mission titles; Charles R. Watson, secretary of FMC, chair of the committee overseeing the Missionary Research Library, and expert on mission work in Egypt; William I. Chamberlain, chair of the FMC, corresponding secretary of the RCA's Board of Missions; and J. Lovell Murray, author of student materials on missions.

[73] In the following section, the term "Sudan" refers not to the present nation state of Sudan but to the large swathe of territory, sometimes called the "Greater Sudan," stretching from the west coasts of Nigeria and Cameroon across central Africa through Chad east to Anglo-Egyptian Sudan (present-day Sudan). For a detailed description of the region of the Sudan as used by the CRC in this discussion, see John De Korne, *To Whom I Now Send Thee* (Grand Rapids: Eerdmans, 1945), 21.

[74] *Acta Synode CRC*, 1918, 86.

[75] De Korne, *To Whom I Now Send Thee: Mission Work of the Christian Reformed Church in Nigeria* (Grand Rapids: Eerdmans, 1945), 23.

conference, Veenstra sought out Kumm, the head of the Sudan United Mission, and volunteered for missionary service in Africa. Although Kumm readily accepted her application, as a health precaution, he told her, she would have to wait three years until she reached the age of twenty-one.

Karl Kumm was a peripatetic missionary-circuit speaker during the first two decades of the twentieth century. Born in Germany to a deeply pietistic Lutheran family, Kumm had studied at Heidelberg, Jena, and Freiburg, earning a Ph.D. and studying Arabic in Egypt, all for the purpose of doing mission work among Muslims. Through marriage to the daughter of a British missionary working there, Kumm had found his life's passion: the Sudan. His interest in the Sudan developed into a "veritable obsession" that he channeled into a mission organization founded with his father-in-law in 1902, the Sudan United Mission.[76] The "whole *raison d' etre* of the SUM" was to construct a bulwark of mission stations across the Greater Sudan in order to prevent the growth of Islam south.[77] Kumm, who had only lived in Africa for a short time, spent the bulk of his time crisscrossing Europe and America recruiting mission organizations to plant stations in the Sudan. By all accounts, he was a highly charismatic speaker, who, when he spoke at Edinburgh in 1910, was able to "hold the audience in his hand and turn it any way he wanted."[78]

Kumm certainly had that effect on Johanna Veenstra, as well as others in the Christian Reformed Church. Determined to go to the Sudan with the Sudan United Mission, Veenstra moved to Michigan in 1915 and began taking classes at Calvin College. She also joined the Girls Mission Society, convincing Student Volunteer Band president John De Korne to bring Kumm to Calvin as a guest missionary speaker in 1917. Writing two decades later, De Korne recalled Kumm as standing head and shoulders above the crowd, with a fine head of bushy, iron gray hair, and "giving stirring addresses so that a number of church leaders were ready to overture synod to take over one of the sections of the Sudan in order that the advance of Islam might stop."[79]

[76]   Jan Harm Boer, *Missionary Messengers of Liberation in a Colonial Context* (Amsterdam: Rodolphi, 1979), 114.
[77]   Ibid. According to Boer, though Kumm thought of himself as a visionary and a pioneer in the "bulwark strategy," his was only a more ambitious version of an approach already accepted by his predecessors.
[78]   Quote by Samuel Zwemer in the introduction to Kumm's biography. I.V. Cleverdon, *Pools on the Glowing Sand* (Melbourne: Specialty Press, 1936), viii. Quoted in Boer, *Missionary Messengers*, 119.
[79]   De Korne, *To Whom I Now Send Thee*, 23.

Inspired by Kumm, Henry Beets published a series of Kumm's articles on the Sudan in the *Banner* just before the synod convened in 1918.[80] After the synod, Beets ran two more articles about mission work in Africa, this time about the United Presbyterian Church's mission work in Ethiopia, adjacent to the Egyptian Sudan.[81]

The synod of 1918 had affirmed this growing enthusiasm for the Sudan by selecting Africa as one of two possible sites in which to begin mission work. Though De Korne and Huizenga were given a mandate to explore *both* China and Africa as possible mission locations, from the start their interest was clearly in Africa; on the cover of their final report, which appeared in mid-December of 1919, they quoted Psalm 68:31: "Ethiopia shall haste to stretch out her hands unto God" (68: 31).[82] They believed the Sudan to be the best location for the Christian Reformed Church's first overseas mission.

They gave a host of what they considered weighty reasons for why the church should choose the Sudan. First, they claimed, the Sudan was virtually without missionary presence, with only one church working there (the United Presbyterians) and three missionary societies (the Sudan United Mission, the Sudan Interior Mission, and the Church Missionary Society). "The need is extremely great," they argued, and "it is possible to block out forty squares, having an average population of a million, not one of which has a missionary."[83] Second, they noted, the African people are emotional but impressionable, which makes their conversion to Christianity more likely than other, more sophisticated,

---

[80] See Karl H. Kumm, "The Christian Reformed Church and Foreign Missions," *Banner* 53 (May 9, 1918): 341; and "If Foreign Mission Work—Then Where?" *Banner* 53 (May 16, 1918): 358-59.

[81] See Stephen Trowbridge, "The Sudan as a Mission Field," *Banner* 53 (May 2, 1918): 321-22; James Kruidenier, "Ethiopia as a Mission Field," *Banner* 53 (June 20, 1918): 457-58; and Kruidenier, "Ethiopia as a Mission Field," *Banner* 53 (July 4, 1918): 473-74.

[82] The English version appeared in December 1919, but the official Dutch version (a word-for-word translation of the English, or *vice versa*) was published in the agenda for the synod of 1920. See "Report of the Synodical Committee for Mission Extension in Sudan or China," Grand Rapids, Mich., Dec. 19, 1919, De Korne, personal folder; and Report 11: "Rapport van de Synodale Commissie voor Uitbreiding van de Zending in Midden Afrika of China," in *Agendum voor de Synode der Christelijke Gereformeerde Kerk* (Grand Rapids: Christian Reformed Church, 1920), 81-151.

[83] De Korne and Huizenga defined the Sudan as "that part of Africa which stretches from Abyssinia in the east to the Senegal and the Niger in the west and from the Sahara in the north to the tributaries of the Congo." "Report," English ver., 25.

people. Third, the United Presbyterian Church, a church with which the Christian Reformed Church was on friendly terms, was urging Christian Reformed people to take up work there.[84] Fourth, in recent years the results of mission work had been considerable. Fifth, and finally, it was strategically important because, according to a number of experts on Islam, most notably Samuel Zwemer, a Reformed scholar of missions held in very high esteem in the Christian Reformed Church, the conversion of even one tribe might be enough to swing the whole region over to Christianity.[85]

These reasons outweighed some potentially serious drawbacks for choosing the Sudan. Transportation difficulties loomed large, they noted, since the Egyptian Sudan was located fifteen hundred miles from Port Said, making both travel to the field and the education of missionary children a challenge. They would have to buy a steam-launch, which would cost somewhere between two and ten thousand dollars. The climate of the Sudan was also far from ideal, with temperatures reaching a scorching 116°F in the hot season. British colonial control could make obtaining permission to work in the area difficult. Finally, the report explained that although there were some disadvantages in the African character for developing a Reformed church, these could also be seen as positive. They wrote:

> African tribes are usually said to belong to the emotional type of people, and we Reformed people usually belong to the intellectual type as contrasted with the emotional type. There is, no doubt, some truth to the statement that these peoples would take more readily to the teachings of Methodist missionaries than to the sterner teachings of Reformed missionaries, but that statement would hold good in some degree at least, for any type of people. And this objection loses its force largely when we remember that the Africans belong to the "child races," and that their further

[84] The UPC was a Scottish Presbyterian church with some Dutch connections. Between 1888 and 1898, the two denominations had considered merging. The union failed, however, because the UPC wanted an "organic" merger, which the CRC rejected, fearing it would lose its distinctive identity. See Zwaanstra, *Reformed Thought*, 19ff.

[85] About Zwemer, the committee wrote: "Dr. Samuel M. Zwemer, well known among our people as missionary to the Mohammedans, and heralded by the Laymen's Missionary Movement as 'probably the world's greatest living missionary,' permitted us to confer with him on several occasions, and after having given our problem some thought, he said tersely, 'Africa, of course.'" "Report," 15.

development depends largely upon the kind of teaching they receive.[86]

To add at least an aura of objectivity to their recommendation for the Sudan, De Korne and Huizenga examined China as a field as well. They noted some significant reasons why China would be a good choice. First, they pointed out, China had its own language and a body of rich literature, which could "be of great value to the missionary." Second, the community life of China was well organized, "which would provide safety and comfort to our missionaries." Third, in contrast to the Sudan, they pointed out, the "climate is healthful—suitable in every way for Americans." Fourth, there were good transportation and communication facilities as well as facilities for educating the missionary children. Fifth, China was growing in world importance, which made the "Chinese of great strategic significance from the missionary point of view." Sixth, the church had a "splendid opportunity" to work with the Reformed Church in America, a sister church which had played no small part in "awakening missionary interest" among Christian Reformed people. Seventh, a number of Christian Reformed Church members were already working in China, supported by their congregations.[87] Last, the committee stated: "The conservative spirit and intellectual qualities of the Chinese people give us many points of contact with them."[88]

But China also had drawbacks as a potential mission field. Among these, De Korne and Huizenga noted the difficulty of the Chinese language. The rising nationalism, fanned by the "various Oriental exclusion acts," resulted in strong anti-American sentiments and contributed to a political situation that was highly fluid. Cultural reasons also made mission work with the Chinese difficult. They wrote:

> The character and temperament of the people makes it extremely difficult to reach them with a Christian message. They have a civilization and a culture of their own; they are well satisfied with themselves; and they feel a contempt for these poor, ignorant

[86] "Report," 20.
[87] Because the CRC did not have overseas missions, CRC young people were forced to go with other denominations. One example is Tena Holkeboer, who went to Xiamen (Amoy) with the RCA in 1920. See Edward Van Baak, "Dr. Tena Holkeboer," *Banner* 100 (Dec. 10, 1965): 10-11.
[88] "Report," 15-17.

foreigners who come to them to tell them of a Christ who was born 500 years later than their own Confucius.[89]

These factors would make mission work in China difficult, but the most compelling strike against China had nothing to do with that country itself. De Korne and Huizenga reported that they had found that "the missionary leaders of China do not seem to be very anxious to have another, very small, church commence missionary operations alongside of the well-organized work that is found there now." Specifically, they mentioned their conference with E. C. Lobenstine, the executive secretary of the China Continuation Committee, who, they noted, was "referred to by several missionary leaders as the greatest authority on China missions." While not exactly discouraging them from opening a mission, Lobenstine, they reported, "Did not encourage us to open a mission in China." They could only conclude that his reasons for not doing so were that there were already so many different boards operating in China that the contribution of another small board to the "evangelization of China would be very slight—almost negligible compared to the extended work now going on there."[90]

In addition to their published report, De Korne and Huizenga used other "propaganda" to convince the church to select the Sudan. When their original plan to visit both locations fell through, they organized a barnstorming crusade to raise money to finance the new field, and, no doubt, to push for the selection of the Sudan.[91] Between the spring of 1919 and the end of the year, they visited all of the churches in the denomination except those in California and Canada. They also enlisted Band members to write articles in the *Chimes* and to visit churches during the summer holidays and give illustrated talks using a stereopticon presentation on the Blue and White Nile regions of the Egyptian Sudan. De Korne, Huizenga, and Band members had forced the denomination to open a foreign field; now they were determined that the field should be the Sudan.

---

[89]   Ibid., 22.
[90]   De Korne, personal folder.
[91]   Though the synod of 1918 had mandated the investigating committee to travel to both Africa and China, the Mission Board balked at the trip when it realized how much it would cost in time and money. For details on this misunderstanding, see De Korne to "Fellow volunteers, who are also newspaper reporters," Nov. 27, 1918, De Korne, personal folder.

The Arguments

De Korne and Huizenga's efforts to marshal support for Africa did not convince everyone in the church. Some were already strongly in favor of going to China. Support for China had been building steadily for a number of years. In fact, the first mention of mission work made in a church paper was in reference to China in 1872 in *De Wachter*, when a reader wrote to stress the great needs of Chinese children. At the turn of the century, another correspondent in *De Wachter* stressed the pressing need for preaching the gospel in China and asked, "What are you doing for China, reader?" [92] Over the years other articles had appeared in church papers suggesting China as a location for the denominational mission work. Thus, it was no surprise when, in the spring of 1918, Harold Bode's minority report from the synodical committee appeared in the *Banner*, recommending China as a site for the first overseas mission.

Bode, pastor of the First Christian Reformed Church in Wellsburg, Iowa, a church belonging to Classis Ostfriesland, made up of a cluster of German immigrant churches, recommended China over South America, for what he termed "eminently practical reasons."[93] Among these reasons were that the Chinese race was homogeneous, the cost of living in China was "ridiculously low," the denomination's work could link up with the China Inland Mission, and the cultural level of China was high.[94] Bode's argument obviously played well in the denomination, for just a month later, the synod of 1918 rejected South America, narrowing the choice to either Africa or China.

After China was chosen as a site for investigation in 1918, however, it slipped behind Africa as the location of choice, mostly because De Korne and Huizenga were more interested in Africa. But once they published their report in the fall of 1919 recommending Africa, China quickly came back into focus. Articles soon began appearing in church papers criticizing De Korne and Huizenga for how they had carried out their mandate and arguing that China was a better choice for the denomination's first mission.

---

[92] Both letters are cited in John Bratt, "Missionary Enterprise," 69 and 130.

[93] These German Reformed churches, made up of immigrants from Lower Saxony, had strongly supported missions in Europe and carried this enthusiasm into the CRC, organizing some of the earliest mission fests in the denomination. Herbert J. Brinks, "Ostfrisians in Two Worlds," in *Perspectives,* 21-34.

[94] H. C. Bode, "Extension of Mission Work," *Banner* 53 (April 18, 1918): 281.

Writing in the December 1919 issue of *De Wachter*, the Reverend Peter Hoekenga, a home missionary on the West Coast, questioned the committee's failure to provide more information on China, which, he said, effectively hindered the synod from making an informed decision. "If the synod receives full and complete information on one field and incomplete on the other," he suggested, "it will be difficult to make a definite decision and clearly choose for one and against the other."[95] One could only conclude, Hoekenga said, that the committee appointed to investigate fields had misunderstood its mandate in recommending to the synod which field to choose. Before giving his reasons for preferring China, Hoekenga mentioned that the fact that "a member of our church has already been named for work there" was not alone a strong enough reason for choosing the Sudan.[96]

Hoekenga went on to argue the case for China. Among the "seven facts of great importance" for why the church should choose China over the Sudan, Hoekenga listed its openness to the gospel, its receptivity to American influence, the pliability of the Chinese people, the vast number of "heathens" in proportion to the number of missionaries working there, and the relatively low cost of doing mission work there. The most important reason for doing mission work in China, he argued, was based on the instruction that Classis Sioux Center had given the synod for deciding on a venue: Preference should be made for work "among a nation which has world-historical significance (*volkerenleven*)."[97] It went without saying, Hoekenga concluded, that this was more true of China than it was of the Sudan.

Other denominational leaders also spoke in favor of China. In January of 1920, the Reverend John Dolfin, a pastor in Muskegon, Michigan, and secretary of the Board of Heathen Missions, had attended a Foreign Missions Conference in New Haven, Connecticut. Reporting in the *Banner*, he said he had enjoyed discussions with several Reformed Church missionaries (Zwemer, Warnhuis, Pieters) and drew the following conclusion:

[95] Peter J. Hoekenga, "Aan de Synodale Commissie voor de Buitenlansche Zending," *De Wachter* 52 (Dec. 24, 1919): 6 (trans.). For help with translating this and following *De Wachter* articles, I am indebted to Prof. Henry Zwaanstra, professor emeritus of church history, Calvin Theological Seminary, Grand Rapids, Michigan.

[96] This is, no doubt, a reference to Johanna Veenstra's commitment to work with the SUM. Band members occasionally threatened to work with other churches or organizations if their church did not respond to their desire for a mission. See *Agendum*, "Report," 157ff.

[97] Hoekenga, "Aan de Synodale Commissie," 6 (trans.).

From personal and private conversations with men whom we had the pleasure of meeting for the first time or anew at this Conference we were strengthened in our opinion that of the two fields, China or Africa, the former is to be preferred above the latter as the opening scene of our Foreign Mission activity. Africa may appeal strongly to sentiment and emotion but China to reason and judgment.[98]

Attacking from another angle, Henry Beets also entered the fray. Instead of promoting China, Beets took issue with Africa. He lamented the fact that De Korne and Huizenga's report did not mention the work of the Netherlands Reformed Church mission in the Sudan. "These people," he wrote, "are so much like us, psychologically, historically and religiously, that it would pay us to ascertain how they feel about work in the Sudan, what their experiences are, their prospects and fears."[99] Using excerpts from a series of articles in *De Kerkbode*, the paper of the Dutch Reformed Church, Beets went on to suggest some reasons for caution in choosing the Sudan.[100]

He cited the political complications the Boers had experienced in gaining permission from the British colonial government to enter the Sudan and suggested that it was already too late for staving off the "Mohammedan peril."[101] Furthermore, he argued, the church would do well to find a field where it had to deal with paganism only, and not

[98] John Dolfin, "Report on Foreign Missions Conference," *Banner* 55 (March 25, 1920): 187. Abbe Warnhuis had been working with the RCA's China mission since 1900. Though they did not mention it, De Korne and Huizenga had also met with him while investigating locations.

[99] Beets, "The Sudan and the Work of the Boers in It," *Banner* 55 (Jan. 15, 1920): 36. Throughout the article, Beets refers to the Netherlands Reformed Church (*Nederduitse Gereformeerde Kerk*) and the missionaries of the Dutch Reformed Church mission as the "the Boers." Beets's use of the "Sudan" refers specifically to that part of the Greater Sudan located in the northern region of Nigeria where members of the Tiv tribe live. The DRCM had established mission work with the Tiv in 1911.

[100] The seven articles that Beets used from *De Kerkbode* are found in De Korne's personal folder.

[101] Because there had been a number of Islamic revolts against British rule in the Greater Sudan, the colonial administration treated Islam with a sensitivity that included prohibiting Christian mission work in the northern Sudan. The British encouraged missionaries to concentrate on the mainly animistic societies in the southern part of the region. See Peter Woodward, *Sudan, 1888-1989: The Unstable State* (Boulder: Lynne Rienner, 1990), 33.

paganism *and* Islam, as it would have to do in the Sudan. Finally, he mentioned the difficulties the Boers had found working with Africans:

> Three young Tivi [Tiv] people were enrolled as converts, Dec. 1918, after seven years of labor among them. Alas, all three had to be disciplined because of sin against the 7th commandment [adultery]—the great sin in Africa as well as elsewhere. These young men were already assisting in missionary work, yet they fell, although they seem to show signs of repentance.[102]

At the end of his article, Beets said that though he did not want to "knock the Sudan proposal," he thought "our Church ought to know just what it is facing," in order to avoid the kind of discouragement and disillusionment "in view of the comparatively little lasting fruit produced so far on our Indian field."

In the months leading up to the synod of 1920, Beets refrained from supporting China publicly, but he had been interested in mission work there for some time. As noted above, Beets regarded the Chinese people highly, but his high estimation had another side as well. In 1910, he had challenged Christian Reformed audiences with the following warning: "Think of China with its 400,000,000 yellow men. All bright, all capable of high civilization. Capable of defeating hosts of white people. Woe if China awakens unchristianized! Our white race will not only lose its supremacy, but may be enslaved."[103] Expanding on this theme, in a 1916 *Banner* article about the importance of China, Beets wrote:

> If we understand our Bible, the Far East has not completed its role in the world's drama. Napoleon in his days, speaking about China, said: "Woe unto the white race if that sleeping giant awakes." We believe ultimately the struggle will be between the white race and the yellow—the great struggle of the last days for the world's supremacy.[104]

---

[102] Beets, "Sudan," 36.
[103] Beets, "Some Reasons for Pushing the Cause of Missions Harder than We Have Ever Done," speech given at Broadway Avenue CRC Laymen's Society, April 24, 1910; LaGrave Avenue CRC Men's Supper, May 16, 1910; and Zeeland, Sept. 2, 1912, Beets, personal folder.
[104] Beets, "The Yellow Peril," *Banner* 51 (Aug. 10, 1916): 497. For Beets's most extensive public comments on both the superiority of the Chinese and the threat they posed to the white race, see his speech to a Calvin College Alumni meeting, June 2, 1930, Beets, personal folder. There is nothing

In the spring of 1920, the tide for choosing China was clearly rising among established church leaders. De Korne and Huizenga responded to the criticism they were receiving by publishing additional materials about China as a potential mission field, but not before one last voice weighed in on the choice.

Throughout the spring of 1920, Barend K. Kuiper, editor of *De Wachter*, the most widely read denominational periodical of the time, and former professor of Calvin College, revealed his strong bias against Africa and in favor of China. Kuiper thought the synod should also bear some of the blame for the problems with De Korne and Huizenga's report, since the synod had been "caught sleeping" on the issue of where to pursue missions and thus only very quickly and perfunctorily, without discussion, narrowed the field to Africa and China.[105] About what he termed as their "cooked and dried" report, Kuiper said that De Korne and Huizenga had made two mistakes: first, they had failed to fulfill their mandate by only giving information about Africa; and then they had compounded their failure by giving their own opinion about choosing Africa instead of letting the church decide based on the facts.[106]

Known as a player in church politics, Kuiper waited until just before the synod met to convey his strongest opinions about where to establish a mission.[107] In a detailed discussion, he took issue with De Korne and Huizenga's argument that Africa should be chosen over China. Though he did not deny the importance of the issues their

---

particularly original about Beets's ideas; he was repeating sentiments common in missionary discourse of the time. Even Chinese Christians expressed these sentiments. At the 1920 SVM conference in Des Moines, Iowa, for instance, James Yen, a Chinese church statesman noted for his literacy programs, said: "It is for you, Christian men and women of western lands, not to say only, but to determine if the coming, rising China will be to the world an eternal, golden blessing to fulfill God's mission for her to the whole world, or whether she will to the world be a yellow peril." Quoted in Albert Smit, "The Significance of the Student Volunteer Movement," *Chimes* 14 (Jan. 1920): 18.

[105] Barend K. Kuiper, "De Zending," *De Wachter* 53 (May 26, 1920): 1 (trans.).

[106] Kuiper, "Het Buitenlandsch Zending Rapport," *De Wachter* 52 (Feb. 25, 1920): 1-2.

[107] For Kuiper's propensity for playing church politics, see John Dolfin to De Korne, April 3, 1920. Dolfin suggests to De Korne that Kuiper got his editorship of *De Wachter* "in a rather shady way," and that he "is holding up his last articles until just before the synod when he can have his say and no one to answer him," De Korne, personal folder.

report raised in favor of Africa (i.e., cost, climate, transportation), he declared these issues to be "accidental," and not so important in themselves. Kuiper then related what he believed was the most important consideration in choosing a mission field. "When the matter is looked at from the great Reformed principle of the honor of God," he stated, "then the main question should be, which field has the greatest **strategic** significance?"[108] If people would be guided by this principle, Kuiper concluded, then the obvious choice was China.

To support his argument, however, Kuiper did not tout the superiority of the Chinese; instead, he underlined the inferiority of Africans. "No one," he said, "can deny that the Chinese in the future shall be of much more importance than the Negroes." De Korne and Huizenga had argued that as the "child races," blacks would be more easily swayed by proselytization. Kuiper, on the other hand, believed this was a sign that the African race would not make much of a contribution to world history. In fact, Kuiper pointed out, the specific individuals whom De Korne and Huizenga had held up as examples of what the Negro race could achieve were without exception born out of a mixture of blacks and whites.[109] "Full blood negroes," he concluded, "had not yet gone very far. It is highly improbable that the Negro races will ever have world historical significance."[110]

Just before the synod of 1920 convened, Kuiper offered the last word. Before doing so, perhaps in response to criticism he had received, he assured readers of his own love for missions, stating, "We, too, are very deeply convinced missions is one of the most significant tasks of the church. We, too, consider it a very lovely affair, full of significance for our church's mission work. It should as soon as possible become one of the highest ideals."[111] He went on to list all of the places that he considered worthy of mission endeavor, and then he gave his own preference for China, because of its "world historical significance."

In the rest of the article, Kuiper urged the church to "think more deeply into the issues of missions," and offered several suggestions for doing mission work. He advised the church to send only the very best candidates to the mission field. Missionaries should be ordained men, he argued, who had received an exceptional amount of training in

---

[108] Kuiper, "Het Buitenlandsch," 2. The bold text is Kuiper's.

[109] De Korne and Huizenga had written that they believed "the African people will bring forth in the future their Crowther, their Booker T. Washington, their Lewis...." Quoted from "Report," 32.

[110] Kuiper, "De Zending," *De Wachter* (May 26, 1920): 1 (trans.).

[111] Kuiper, "Nog Eens Zending," *De Wachter* (June 2, 1920): 1 (trans.).

philosophy and the history of religion. They should also be well versed in the history and culture of the people to whom they went. Too often, he noted, missions are only superficially understood because missionary education is frequently superficial. Poorly educated missionaries, Kuiper warned, run the risk of "awakening the natural antipathies" of the people with whom they work.[112]

Though Kuiper had the last word in denominational publications, Lee Huizenga had the last public word. Citing him as the person "who is credited with doing more than any other person to interest the Christian Reformed church in foreign mission," the June 12 issue of the *Grand Rapids Herald* ran the headline, "Favors Africa as Missionary Field: Lee S. Huizenga, pastor and doctor, will so inform synod." John De Korne, too, was determined that the church should decide on Africa, stating in a personal letter to a Band member, now pastoring a church, "My own opinion remains that Africa offers by far the bigger appeal," though he conceded China was looking stronger than it had, and that "they are both good fields, and the synod cannot go wrong on either one of them."[113] Both men planned to attend the synod, setting up a display of maps and artifacts from both mission fields and making their pitch on the floor of synod.

Arriving at China

When it met, the synod of 1920 appointed a subcommittee to present a proposal to the full body for selecting Africa or China. Writing some years later, Henry Beets, who chaired the committee, recalled, "After lengthy discussions, synod accepted the advice of this committee to the effect that not the Sudan, but *China* should be the country in which our first foreign missionary enterprise should be undertaken."[114]

Beets's account did not reveal details of the committee's "lengthy discussions," but the *Acts of Synod* for 1920 laid out the salient reasons

---

[112] Ibid.

[113] De Korne to Simon Dykstra, May 5, 1920, De Korne, personal folder. In the same letter, De Korne comments, "Your classis must have been pretty much under the influence of the editorial of Prof. Kuiper or similar influences at the time you decided on that instruction to synod [about China]." In addition to lobbying from the home front, those supporting Africa made sure that Johanna Veenstra's first letter from Africa, "First Impressions," appeared serially in the *Banner*. See Johanna Veenstra, "First Impressions," parts 1-3 (of 10), *Banner* 54 (Dec. 25, 1919): 804; 55 (April 15, May 13, 1920): 237, 301.

[114] Beets, *Toiling and Trusting*, 222.

for the selection of China over Africa. Those making the decision wanted to make sure the location was suitable for the health of the missionaries and their families. Thus, the church was committed to sending a doctor with its first mission party, both to do mission work, and, just as important, to provide care for the missionaries. Moreover, because China had a "wholesome climate" and "relatively good means of transport and communication by telegraph," it seemed more suitable for the missionaries and their families. The synod was also concerned about money. It wanted to make sure that the cost of a mission was commensurate with the denomination's ability to finance it *and* that converts would eventually be self-supporting and independent. Equally important was the church's commitment to educating the missionaries' "covenant children." Here again, the synod claimed that China offered better possibilities, though it never spelled out exactly why.

The reason given for selecting China over Africa also involved "strageticity," the word Henry Beets coined to mean "world strategic significance." In the racially charged sentiments expressed in the discussion leading up to the final decision—a discussion in which racially denigrating comments were leveled at Indians, Africans, and Chinese—the consensus of the leadership of the denomination was that the Chinese had a longer, more sophisticated history and that if converted would make more of a contribution to world history. Moreover, the elders of the church believed that they had natural affinities with the Chinese. The most important affinity they noted was China's long history and sophisticated culture, most apparent in their "rich language and literature." Although this gave the Chinese a sense of cultural superiority which tended to make them resistant to Christianity, it also held out the possibility and potential for them to accept and appropriate a more "sophisticated" version of the Christian faith—the Christian Reformed faith, in other words. In fact, some leaders saw a connection between the Chinese and themselves. As the synod noted in its list of reasons for selecting China, "The conservative, intellectual spirit of the Chinese is more in harmony with our people than the emotional nature of the African natives."[115] Even while advocating Africa as a field, De Korne and Huizenga had to admit these "qualities" would provide "many points of contact."

Adding up practical considerations and strategic considerations were important for the church's leaders, but including better opportunity for preserving and propagating the Reformed faith clinched

---

[115] *Acta Synode CRC*, 1920, Art. 34, 2, a-f, 50 (trans.).

the argument for China. As its last, and possibly weightiest, reason for rejecting Africa and choosing China, the synod admitted, "The close cooperation with Churches of less pure confession which belong to the Sudan United Mission, fills us with fear for the maintenance and propagation of our Reformed principles.[116] In China, on the other hand, the synod believed it had a "splendid opportunity" to work with the Reformed Church in America—the same church with which the denomination had broken sixty years earlier. However, working with the Reformed Church was as close as the Christian Reformed Church could get to working with a like-minded church with a similar (Dutch) background and so provided the best opportunity for preserving a Reformed identity.

Sixty years after its founding, the Christian Reformed Church sent its first missionaries overseas. The nearly ten years of discussion and the politicking leading up to the decision reveal missions as an important window into the process of Americanization taking place in the denomination during this period. Many of the key leaders in the denomination and the young people in the church saw missions as a way to connect to the larger American Protestant world. While both the elders and the youth agreed on the importance of missions, they disagreed on the best place to establish a mission. Ultimately it was the elders who selected China as the more appropriate place to begin because of practical considerations *and* because of that country's "greatest historical significance." What clinched the argument for these church leaders was their belief that because there were "many points of contact" between themselves and the Chinese, China offered the better possibility of establishing a Reformed church.

---

[116] *Acta Synode CRC*, 1920, Art. 2, 49-50 (trans.). It is unclear why the synod believed it had to narrow its ecclesiastical partnership to the SUM, since the United Presbyterians were working there, as was the Dutch Reformed Church.

CHAPTER 2

Practically Virgin Soil:
Claiming Rugao, 1921

Vast Fields

Four months after the synod chose China for the church's first foreign mission, a party of missionaries departed from San Francisco for Shanghai. This pioneer party included three of the strongest advocates for opening a Christina Reformed overseas mission: John De Korne, Lee Huizenga, and Harry Dykstra (a recent seminary graduate who had served the previous year as president of the Student Volunteer Band), and their families—altogether a party of eleven. The steamship *China* carried them and fifty other missionaries to China. Arriving in Shanghai three weeks later, the Christian Reformed party took lodgings at the Shanghai Missionary Home and prepared to begin its first task: finding a location for establishing a mission.

Shanghai was an obvious destination, since in 1920 it was not only China's largest and most important city but also the center of the Chinese Protestant movement. Most missions had their headquarters there, and by the 1920s Shanghai was both a starting place for new missionaries and the center of Protestant work. Four hundred

Pioneer China Mission families disembark from the *S.S. China* in Shanghai, November 1920: (*from top of the ladder*) Lee Huizenga with daughter Ann, Matilda Huizenga with daughter Myrtle, John De Korne holding son Melvin, Harry Dykstra, Florence Dykstra, and Nettie De Korne with son Baldwin.

missionaries lived there, half the total number of missionaries in all of Jiangsu Province on the eastern seaboard, in which the city was located. The earliest missionaries in Shanghai had come to plant churches, but by the early decades of the twentieth century, they had also created a vast network of churches, hospitals, and schools, as well as a host of other organizations supporting missionary work.[1] In 1920, Shanghai was the nerve center for a sprawling missionary enterprise stretching across the country.

Following World War I, the number of new missionaries going to China diminished, but the total numbers continued to grow, reaching a high point of around 9,000 in the mid-1920s.[2] These missionaries, representing 130 denominations and mission societies, had staked out vast tracts of territory for their work. Though most missionaries worked along the east coast of the country and in the treaty ports, by 1920 missionaries had claimed most of the interior as well. Of China's

---

[1]   For a history of Protestants in Shanghai and the work there in the 1920s, see Milton Stauffer, *The Christian Occupation of China* (Shanghai: China Continuation Committee, 1922), 133-34.

[2]   This number includes both Protestant and Catholic missionaries. See Jessie G. Lutz, *Chinese Politics and Christian Missions* (Notre Dame: Cross Cultural Publications, 1988), 2.

1,704 counties, only 106 were unclaimed by missionary groups. Despite the fact that various missions had staked out most of China, however, much of the territory was unoccupied.

Typically, missionaries would take up residence in a county seat and then station Chinese coworkers at outstations and meeting points in a large radius around the center. Through an extensive system of comity agreements, a mission could control the work under its claim by limiting the access of other groups or by stipulating the conditions under which others could work in "their field."[3] Though there were no sanctions to enforce these series of agreements, groups who flouted them were looked down on by the Protestant missionary establishment. This comity system obviously favored the missions that had come earliest.

For missions coming late to China, comity agreements made finding a field a major obstacle, and the Christian Reformed Church's experience proved no exception. De Korne and Huizenga had first bumped up against comity agreements while investigating the possibility of mission work in China. At their meeting in New York in 1918, E. C. Lobenstine, the executive secretary of the China Continuation Committee, had not encouraged the denomination to open a mission in China. If it did decide to work in China, he stressed, it should respect existing comity agreements. To emphasize his point, Lobenstine read them the Continuation Committee's statement calling on new missions to consult with the already existing ones:

> In the event of any church or mission wishing to enter an unoccupied field in any provincial area, consultation with the proper inter-denominational or inter-mission body for that sphere, if one exists, should precede any definite steps for occupation. In determining whether or not a new society should enter, due weight should be given to the resources of that society, and the likelihood of its being able to make its occupation of a given area effective before the other.[4]

3   Stauffer, *Christian Occupation*, 330. For the China Continuation Committee's full statement on comity, see p. lxxxv.

4   John De Korne, Christian Reformed World Mission files (hereafter CRWM), n.d. The statement Lobenstine read is found in *Christian Occupation of China*, lxxxvi. Lobenstine, as a secretary of the Continuation Committee, quite possibly helped draft this statement. The China Continuation Committee came out of the World Missionary Conference held in Edinburgh in 1910. Under John Mott's leadership, a Continuation Committee was formed in an effort to better coordinate Protestant mission efforts. Mott organized the

Furthermore, if the church chose China, Lobenstine said, it should seriously consider working with the Reformed Church in America in Fujian Province. But that could happen only by invitation. When approached in New York, Abbe Warnshuis, a Reformed Church missionary and the national evangelistic secretary of the China Continuation Committee, was enthusiastic, even offering to appear before the CRC synod to plead the cause of beginning work in Fujian Province.[5] As it turned out, the synod did not need Warnshuis's urging, deciding for China on its own, quite likely bolstered by the opportunity to work with the Reformed Church—an established mission, and a Reformed mission at that.[6]

By 1920, the Reformed Church in America had been working in China for more than ninety years. Its first missionary, the Reverend David Abeel, representing the American Seaman's Free Society, had first traveled to China in 1829 with Elijah Bridgman on free passage to Guangzhou (Canton). While Bridgman stayed on, becoming the first American missionary to reside in China, Abeel returned to the United States, becoming instrumental in sparking his own denomination's interest in China. In 1842, Abeel returned to China to establish a mission in Xiamen (Amoy), one of the five treaty ports open to western residency. Originally established as an American Board of Commissioners for Foreign Missions' station, the Amoy mission became fully RCA when the denomination formed its own mission board in 1857. Though independent, the Reformed Church worked closely with English Presbyterians and the London Missionary Society to plant churches in Fujian. With its partner agencies, the mission established a hospital, a theological college, schools for boys and girls, and an orphanage.[7]

China Continuation Committee on a trip to China in 1913. Among other things, out of the effort came a survey showing the "Christian occupation" of the country and suggestions for better coordinating existing work in order to form an indigenous Chinese church. K.S. Latourette, *A History of Christian Missions in China* (London: Society for Promoting Christian Knowledge, 1929; rpt. Taipei: Ch'eng-wen, 1973), 669ff. See also Kevin Xiyi Yao, *The Fundamentalist Movement among Protestant Missionaries in China, 1920-1937* (Lanham: Univ. Press of America, 2003), 186.

[5]   De Korne to Henry Beets, March 30, 1920, De Korne, CRWM folder.

[6]   Responding to an overture from one classis, the synod had issued the following instruction: "Our missionaries should work for at least the first two to four years with a church of Reformed confession." *Acta*, 1920, Art. 34. num. 4, 50.

[7]   For the RCA's mission in China, see Gerald De Jong, *The Reformed Church in China, 1842-1951* (Grand Rapids.: Eerdmans, 1992).

Even with a well-established Reformed Church mission in Fujian, there was room for the Christian Reformed missionaries, especially since in 1919 the Reformed mission had taken over the North River area of Southern Fujian from the English Presbyterians. This new district, consisting of two thousand square miles and a population of a million, increased the RCA's total territory from six thousand to eight thousand square miles, and the total population from three to four million.[8] In the whole North River district, there was only one Chinese pastor and twenty evangelists, few with theological training. Visiting all of the preaching stations in the North River district meant covering three hundred miles, mostly on foot.

The Reformed Church suggested the CRC open a mission station adjacent to this North River area in the Shaowu district, but that district overlapped with claims by the America Board of Commissioners for Foreign Missions (ABCFM). When De Korne wrote the American Board in May of 1920 formally requesting permission to enter the Shaowu district, the Reverend W. E. Strong turned down the request, stating that there was no room in the province for a new mission to open a station. After the Christian Reformed Church had officially decided on China, Henry Beets wrote Strong again, requesting further clarification about work in Fujian. Strong rebuffed the church again, this time quoting a missionary in the field who said he did "not think it feasible or helpful to introduce a new church factor or mission within the geographical limits now distinctly ours."[9] Because of comity restraints, Strong went on in his letter to Beets, Fujian appeared closed to new missions. In spite of these discouraging letters, the pioneer Christian Reformed mission party had departed in November 1920 for Fujian, via Shanghai. One family, thinking to save on shipping fees, sent its outfit directly to Xiamen.

But after arriving in Shanghai, the mission sent to the board a minute requesting that "Fukien [Fujian] as a possible location for our China Mission be eliminated from further consideration."[10] En route to China, Lee Huizenga had received a letter from Reformed Church missionary Harry Boot explaining the problem with the CRC working in Fujian. Boot wrote that "if the aim of your church and board was to ultimately or even now amalgamate with our mission, we could give you the glad hand at once, and have you become part and parcel

8   De Jong, *Reformed Church in* China, 166-67.
9   W. E. Strong to Henry Beets, Sept. 4, 1920, CRWM folder.
10   "China Mission Minutes," Shanghai, Nov. 26, 1920, CRWM folder.

of our mission," but he did not think there was room in the province for the entrance of a new mission.[11] Moreover, Boot expressed concern that the Christian Reformed Church would not be willing to join the church union that had taken place the year before, joining all of the churches of the province into the Church of Christ in China.[12] Though Boot expressed regret that there was no space for them in Fujian, he believed sending them elsewhere—to one of the "vast fields as yet wholly unentered [sic] by the Messengers of Light"—was ultimately in the best interest of China.

Merging with another mission, even the Reformed Church's mission, was out of the question; the Christian Reformed Church was determined to have its *own* mission field.

Though its plans for Fujian were dashed, another possible field quickly opened up. The Missionary Home in Shanghai was an informal meeting place for missionaries coming and going across the entire country;[13] there the Christian Reformed missionaries met the Reverend Charles Patton, a member of the South China Mission of the Presbyterian Church, U.S.A. In 1912, Patton and his wife, Isabella, had established a mission in Huizhou City (Kochow), Guangdong Province, on the northern part of the Luizhou Peninsula directly across from Hainan Island. After less than a decade in Huizhou, the Pattons were moving to Shanghai because Isabella's health "had broken down," and so that Charles could take up an administrative post with the China Council of the Presbyterian Mission (North).[14] Finding a replacement proved difficult because the post required evangelistic workers and a doctor. When the Christian Reformed missionaries met him in Shanghai in the fall of 1920, Patton had been searching for more than two years.

Learning that the party included two evangelistic missionaries and a doctor and that they were looking for a suitable location, Patton interrogated them "at length about their principles, their history and the present status of their church, its denominational characteristics, and the probable expansion of the China Mission." According to John De Korne, "The upshot of it all was that he [Patton] made us,

11   Harry Boot to Huizenga, Nov. 11, 1920, Huizenga, CRWM folder.
12   Strong in his letter to Beets had also raised this concern.
13   This was almost certainly a Presbyterian-run guesthouse.
14   Attachment by John De Korne to a letter from Charles Patton to A.J. Brown, December 14, 1920, De Korne, CRWM folder. Patton's letter is written to the home secretary of the Presbyterian mission with his arguments for why the Huizhou field should be transferred to the CRC.

Lee Huizenga rests on the ground (*right*) during the spring 1921 scouting trip to Guangdong province, to look at a possible location for establishing a mission.

in an unofficial way, a proposition to take over his former station in Kwantung [Guangdong] Province, now a part of the South China Mission of the Presbyterian Church North."[15]

As the first step in negotiating a transfer, Patton invited the missionaries to visit Huizhou. After making a two-month trip to Huizhou, covering more than two thousand miles by steamer, junk, rickshaw, and on foot, the missionaries recommended taking over Patton's work. In their report to the board, they cited a favorable climate, proximity to both Guangzhou and Hong Kong, excellent transportation facilities, and good telegraphic and postal communications. Even more importantly, the missionaries believed that they could build a superstructure on the solid foundation that the Pattons had laid in Huizhou. Working alone, the Pattons had established a church in Huizhou's county seat, which was now under the care of a Chinese pastor. Isabella Patton had begun a small clinic and hospital for women and children. In the outlying areas, extending in a radius of several days' journey by foot from Huizhou, Patton had also established twenty-two preaching points, now manned by Chinese evangelists. In less than a decade, Patton had baptized twelve hundred Christians, but only a "score" of them in Huizhou, with the rest scattered throughout the district encompassing more than twenty thousand square miles and more than 2.5 million people.

[15] De Korne, "Report of the China Mission for December 1920," CRWM folder, 1.

The Huizhou field appeared ideal, since the Christian Reformed Church could immediately take over evangelistic and medical work. In addition, there was room to grow. If they needed more room, Patton suggested, they could expand to the southern part of the Luizhou Peninsula, which also belonged to the South China Mission. Surrounded by Presbyterian missions, they could draw on the resources of Reformed colleagues. But since there were no other Protestants working the district, the "rules of comity" would make Huizhou "their field."

There was one potential stumbling block. Before returning to Shanghai, the mission party had signed a tentative proposal with the South China Mission. Among other things, the proposal included the Christian Reformed Church's commitment to working in "connection with the Church of Christ in China and the institutions of its Synod."[16] The missionaries had signed, though with a caveat: They would be willing to work with the Church of Christ, they stated, if that meant cooperating with a body adhering to the "fundamentals of Christianity according to the conceptions of the Reformed churches generally, especially in regard to the Inspiration of the Scriptures, the Deity of Christ, the Vicarious Atonement, and the Unity of the Church."[17]

Though they were well aware of the theological issues beginning to roil the missionary enterprise in China—and especially those dividing Presbyterians—the Christian Reformed missionaries were confident about Huizhou because, they stated, "Mr. Patton is a staunch Presbyterian of the Princeton type, a man of principle, and is sternly insistent upon fidelity to the fundamentals of Christian truth and practice. To a large degree he has succeeded in placing this stamp upon the native congregations in his field."[18] The missionary party returned

---

[16]   The Northern Presbyterians (USA) and the Southern Presbyterians (US) took the first steps to organize a Presbyterian and Reformed Chinese denomination in 1906. When it was formally organized in 1922, the union included Chinese Christians from eight different Reformed missions (including the RCA), totaling 77,000 communicant members, with six synods, and twenty-six presbyteries in nine provinces. See G. Thompson Brown, *Christianity in the People's Republic of China* (Atlanta: John Knox, 1986), 211ff.

[17]   De Korne to the Executive Committee, Board of Heathen Missions of the Christian Reformed Church, May 1, 1921, De Korne, CRWM folder. Years later De Korne admitted to Beets that the church union movement was more liberal than the CRC missionaries had been comfortable with, stating, "It is a fact that a number of the leading men in this new organization [the Church of Christ in China] are decidedly of the type that has come to be known as "modern." See De Korne to Beets, May 8, 1928, De Korne, CRWM folder.

[18]   "Report of the China Mission for March, 1921," 4.

to Shanghai confident that God had provided for them an ideal location for establishing a mission.

By the end of April 1921, however, their hopes were dashed again. At a special, day-long meeting, the South China Mission had deliberated whether to keep the Huizhou field or hand it over to the Christian Reformed Church. In a letter written to Lee Huizenga, Charles Patton assured him that the conference had viewed the transfer fairly and thoroughly "from every conceivable angle" and had decided that "if transfer be made at all we could do no better than transfer to the Christian Reformed Mission."[19] The council raised a question about the denomination's limited experience, but, according to Patton, did not consider this a crucial issue. The deciding factor for the Presbyterians, said Patton, was the suspicion that the Christian Reformed missionaries would not be able to work well with other church bodies. In his formal letter informing the Christian Reformed Church about the South China Mission's decision to keep the Huizhou field, the secretary, John Creighton, stated the matter even more bluntly: "There was real doubt as to the possibility of your Mission working in with the Church of Christ in China in such perfect accord as we feel is absolutely necessary. As you know, we put that as absolutely the question of first importance."[20]

The motion to transfer the Huizhou field to the Christian Reformed Church was defeated by a more than two-thirds majority vote. Patton expressed his regret about the rejection, but saw a silver lining in the outcome. The issue had forced the South China Mission to direct its energy away from centralization and institutional work and recommit to evangelism. After the vote was announced, two families and one single woman had volunteered to go to Huizhou. Patton assured the Christian Reformed Church, that by this decision, "All China is the gainer," since now the CRC would go to "equally good and possibly more needy fields."

Shoulder to Shoulder

With Guangdong and Fujian eliminated, the China Mission looked to other fields. Henan (Honan), in central China, was one location. In their report to the synod, De Korne and Huizenga had noted that though the province had fifty-four mission posts and 320 missionaries, there were unoccupied districts within it. The secretary

[19]   Charles Patton to Lee Huizenga, April 13, 1921, De Korne, CRWM folder.
[20]   John Creighton to De Korne, April 11, 1921, De Korne, CRWM folder.

of the Foreign Board of the Augustana Synod of the Lutheran Church, one of the pioneer missions in China, had even extended an invitation to the Christian Reformed Church to enter their province, with a promise of "all necessary assistance."[21] After arriving in China and discussing Henan with E. C. Lobenstine and others on the Continuation Committee, however, Henan did not look so promising. In answer to a letter of inquiry, the Presbytery of the Canadian Presbyterian Mission of North Honan (Henan) wrote: "It was decided after having heard the correspondence from the Christian Reformed Church of America concerning possible opening for their establishing a mission in North Honan, we inform them that in comparison with other parts of China we do not consider any part of our field unoccupied."[22]

With Henan eliminated, the missionaries went on to eliminate another possible location: Yunnan, in the remote southwest, because it was a "needy" province.[23] Through conversations with the Presbyterians in Guangdong, they had discovered there were no blocks of contiguous territory in Yunnan open for developing and no opportunities for working with a church of Reformed confession. Work in Yunnan would be with tribal people, requiring the use of a different language for each group, and the proportion of missionaries to population was higher there than in other provinces.

---

[21] De Korne and Huizenga, "Honan," *Banner* 55 (April 15, 1920): 233. The Dutch version of the committee's information on Hunan mentions that at a "missionary gathering in New Haven" (*in een vergadering onlangs te New Haven gehouden*) the secretary of the Augustana Synod Mission invited the CRC to enter and promised all help. The invitation was probably extended to John Dolfin, who attended the conference. *Agendum 1920*, 150. There is no indication why the CRC missionaries did not pursue work with the Lutherans once they got to China. Perhaps it was because they were eager to work with a Reformed mission.

[22] The China Continuation Committee gave a different picture of Henan. The committee said, "At first glance one is impressed by the large number and fairly general distribution of evangelistic centers [in Henan]. After comparison, however, with such provinces as Fukien (Fujian) and Shantung (Shandong) this impression gives way to a second, namely that there is a sparseness of centers of evangelism in Honan (Henan), and that the Christian occupation of the province is only begun. In Fukien there is one evangelistic center for every 40 sq. mi., in Honan there is one to every 150 sq. mi." Stauffer, *Christian Occupation*, 81.

[23] In their report to the synod, De Korne and Huizenga had included a section on Yunnan, contrasting it with Fujian as "one of the most needy provinces in all of China." See *Banner* 55 (April 15, 1920): 233.

An even more important reason for rejecting Yunnan was a proposal coming from another direction. In May 1921, shortly after the Northern Presbyterians had turned them down, the missionaries received an invitation from Southern Presbyterian missionaries to join them in Jiangsu Province north of the Yangzi River. The missionaries ecstatically informed the board that the "offer by the Southern Presbyterians of North Jiangsu so well satisfies our requirements that it is not necessary to look into the more remote regions."[24] This offer did not quite come out of the blue. As they had met Patton, the Christian Reformed missionaries had also met several Southern Presbyterians while staying at the Shanghai Missionary Guesthouse shortly after arriving in China in the fall of 1920. After discerning the CRC's "position," the Southern Presbyterians had extended the missionaries a "hearty invitation to investigate their field" in northern Jiangsu Province.[25]

The Christian Reformed Church had had some contact with the Southern Presbyterians even before going to China. In the fall of 1918, while researching at the Missionary Research Library in New York, John De Korne had met Dr. J. C. Garritt, president of the Nanjing Theological Seminary and a member of the Northern Presbyterian mission. Garritt suggested he contact the Presbyterian Church in the United States mission board in Nashville about its north Jiangsu field.[26] De Korne then wrote Nashville inquiring about cooperation, since the two denominations were "greatly similar in doctrine and in practice."[27] The Nashville board responded favorably to the idea of cooperation in the "very large and populous territory assigned to its care" in north Jiangsu and suggested De Korne contact the field directly.[28] The matter ended there, however, most likely because De Korne and Huizenga were more interested in Africa.

At the Shanghai Missionary Guesthouse, both Patton and the Southern Presbyterians had extended invitations to the Christian Reformed missionaries to visit their fields. The missionaries immediately

---

[24] "Report of the China Mission for September," 1921, 1.
[25] "Report of John De Korne to the Executive Committee of the Heathen Board of Missions," August 8, 1921, De Korne, CRWM folder.
[26] Though he was a Northern Presbyterian, Garritt had connections to the Southern Presbyterian mission through marriage and his work at the Nanjing seminary. See Brown, *Christianity*, 375, note 2.
[27] De Korne to the Rev. S.H. Chester, Nov. 14, 1918, De Korne, CRWM folder.
[28] S.H. Chester to De Korne, Dec. 18, 1918, De Korne, CRWM folder.

Lee Huizenga (*standing center*) and Harry Dykstra (*standing far right*) travel on the Yangtze River between Shanghai and Rugao in the spring of 1921 during the first scouting trip to Rugao County.

took up the Southern Presbyterian invitation and traveled north of the Yangzi to the North Kiangsu (Jiangsu) mission field. This was their first glimpse of "real China," and they described it with wide-eyed wonder in church papers.[29] No invitation was extended for the group to begin work in northern Jiangsu, however, until the next spring.

After the Northern Presbyterians had rejected the Christian Reformed Church for working in Guangdong Province in April of 1921, the Christian Reformed missionaries received a formal offer from the Southern Presbyterians inviting them to work in northern Jiangsu Province. At a joint meeting in June of 1921, the Southern Presbyterians had "Resolved that the Taichow (Taizhou) and Yencheng (Yancheng) stations strongly invite and urge the mission of the Christian Reformed Church of America to open work in the large unoccupied fields adjoining our territory."[30] The Southern Presbyterians were desperate for help in northern Jiangsu, and especially from a mission with the "right" theological position.

Southern Presbyterians had been working in China since the early 1840s. Before the Civil War, Presbyterians from both the North

[29] See De Korne, "Traveling in China," pts. 1 and 2, *Banner* 56 (Feb. 10 and March 3, 1921): 87; 135, 138; and H. Dykstra, "A Train Ride in China," *Banner* 56 (March 10, 1921): 151; and "A Boat Trip into the Interior of China," *Banner* 56 (March 17, 1921): 167.

[30] The North Kiangsu Mission letter to the CRC China Mission, June 16, 1921, 1, De Korne, CRWM folder.

and the South had worked together in one denomination. They had first established a mission in Ningbo, a treaty port on the East Coast, expanding in the next twenty years south to Guangzhou and north to Shanghai, central Jiangsu Province, Shandong Province, and Beijing. After the Civil War, the Southern Presbyterians, now with their own denomination (Presbyterian Church in the United States) and a newly formed mission board, sent missionary Elijah Inslee, from New Jersey, to open a station in Hangzhou, another treaty port on the East Coast.[31] During the next ten years, as more missionaries came, the Southern Presbyterian mission expanded north along the Grand Canal to Jiaxing (Kashing), Suzhou (Suchow), and to the port city of Zhenjiang (Chinkiang), where the Grand Canal intersected the Yangzi River.

In 1887, Absalom Sydenstricker opened the first Southern Presbyterian station north of the Yangzi River in Huaiyin (Tsingkiang Pu), about seventy miles south of Shandong Province. By 1894, the Southern Presbyterians had ten missionaries in Huaiyin doing evangelistic work, running a clinic that treated six thousand patients per year, and operating two schools, one for boys and one for girls.[32] During the next twenty-five years, the North Kiangsu Mission expanded from Huaiyin in three directions: north along the Grand Canal to Suqian (Suchien) and Xuzhou; south toward the Yangzi to Taizhou; and east along a branch of the Grand Canal to Yancheng on the Yellow Sea. By 1920, North Kiangsu Mission claimed an area of approximately thirty thousand square miles with an estimated population of thirteen million.[33]

The vastness of their field and its huge population were important reasons for the North Kiangsu Mission's invitation to the CRC. The Southern Presbyterian circular letter to rally support for the invitation stated that their "weak force was utterly inadequate to keep up with the work." Nor, they added, did they expect any time soon to receive "enough workers to begin to meet the needs" of their field.[34] To meet

[31] Inslee, who had worked for the Presbyterian mission in China before the denominational split, volunteered to go as the PCUS's first overseas missionary. Brown, 95.

[32] Brown, *Christianity*, 113.

[33] Ibid., 180.

[34] Circular letter by the Taichow (Taizhou) and Yencheng (Yancheng) stations to the North Kiangsu mission stations, June 16, 1921, 1. De Korne, CRWM folder. Ten years later, a committee evaluating the North Kiangsu Mission complained bitterly that the denomination had still not answered its "crying need" for more recruits. The committee reported: "In every station we found all working to the limit of strength while there remain great

these "crying needs," the North Kiangsu Mission proposed turning over the districts south of Yancheng and east of the Grand Canal to the CRC. This region, which belonged to the mission but was unoccupied, included "three magistracies (*xian*), in which," they noted, "there is no resident missionary of any denomination, and scarcely any work has been opened up." All told, the proposed territory had an estimated population of 4.5 million.

The prospect of more workers for this vast space with its dense population was certainly an important reason for the invitation, but even more important was the need for getting the "right" workers. The Southerners feared that "if this class of people [the CRC missionaries] do not take up the work, others of a less desirable kind will step in." "Already," they noted with alarm, "the 'Holy Rollers' and such freak Missions are trying to get a start here."[35] The Southern Presbyterians found the Christian Reformed missionaries impressive for a number of reasons. The Southerners noted the Christian Reformed missionaries' good manners and congeniality, and, they said, it did their "hearts good to see their deep spirituality and consecration." Most attractive, however, was their conservative theology. "The vital urgency for calling this Mission," the inviting committee wrote, "lies in the fact that they are loyal to the Bible."

Almost certainly the Reverend Hugh W. White penned this invitation. White had been stationed in Yancheng since 1910, organizing five congregations in his first decade with a membership roll of over a thousand.[36] White was more than a successful missionary, though; he was also a fierce defender of the fundamentals of the faith in general and Presbyterian orthodoxy in particular.[37] Following a series of

---

untouched fields which it is impossible to enter. This, while true of all mission fields of our church, is true to a far greater extent with us, for we have by far the largest field with proportionately many times the smallest force to meet the need." See "Report of the Evaluation Committee of the North Kiangsu Mission as Amended and Adopted by the Mission," 5 (China Mission folder, Presbyterian Church USA, Department of History, Montreat, North Carolina).

[35] Southern Presbyterian Circular letter, 4.

[36] Brown, *Christianity*, 183.

[37] For the theological controversies among Presbyterians, see Brown, *Christianity*, 207ff.; Yu-ming Shaw, *An American Missionary in China: John Leighton Stuart and Chinese American Relations* (Cambridge: Harvard Univ. Council on East Asian Studies, 1992), 80-81, 85-86. According to Presbyterian historian James Bear, Hugh White, acting as a "self-appointed 'champion of orthodoxy,'" was instrumental in the North Jiangsu Mission's

lectures held on Guling (Kuling) in the summer of 1920 on the dangers of "modernism" given by W. H. Griffith Thomas, a Presbyterian Old Testament scholar, Hugh White had played a leading role in founding "The Bible Union," a block of conservative missionaries committed to holding back the spread of liberal theology in China.[38] A year after its founding, more than seventeen hundred China missionaries had joined the Bible Union.

Their short meeting at the Shanghai Missionary Guesthouse in the fall of 1920 had convinced White that the Christian Reformed missionaries were not only Bible Union material, they would also be ideal for working unoccupied Southern Presbyterian territory in northern Jiangsu. In a personal letter written in December 1920, White encouraged the missionaries to work the seaboard of northern Jiangsu Province, just south of his own station at Yancheng. He stated that this would be a choice location for new missionaries: Since no other group had established a mission there, they would not have to deal with comity issues. The Christian Reformed Church could also contribute to promoting the "true Christian faith." White wrote:

> The great issue in China today is whether the missionaries are going to give China the Bible or give her a nominal Christianity without the essence of truth. Missionaries who discredit the Bible, who deny the virgin birth, the real resurrection, who teach that the death of the Christ was not vicarious but educational, have manipulated matters so that they have placed their men in positions of influence and are seeking to give the whole missionary body the tone of their views. I regret to say that some of the leaders in this matter bear the name Presbyterian. But the Southern Presbyterian Church is practically a unit in standing for the integrity of the Bible. I believe that the best work you can do in China will be to stand shoulder to shoulder with us and with men of similar views in other missions, teaching that man can be saved by faith in the atoning blood of Christ. If you

---

decision to withdraw its support from the Nanjing Theological Seminary and cooperate instead with the North China Theological Seminary in the southern Shandong city of Tengxian. James E. Bear, Jr., *The Mission Work of the Presbyterian Church of the United States in China: 1867-1952.* Quoted in Brown, *Christianity*, 387, note 79. See also Yao, *Fundamentalist Movement*, 208-09, 211-12, 284.

38 For the Bible Union, see Lian Xi, *The Conversion of Missionaries* (University Park: Pennsylvania State Univ. Press, 1997), 144-49. The Bible Union's declaration about the fundamentals of the faith comes from *China Mission Year Book*, 1923, 101. See also Yao, *Fundamentalist Movement*, 101-38.

are geographically situated near us, we can cooperate to better advantage in theological training and other lines of work.[39]

The sense of moral outrage at the missionary establishment's shifting theological views also came clearly through in North Kiangsu Mission's May 1921 circular letter drumming up support for inviting the Christian Reformed Church to work in north Jiangsu.

> It distresses us to see missionaries in other parts of China giving them the cold shoulder. In those sections where they have considered [work], they did not receive a welcome from the missionaries, men of the union-at-any-cost type. This mission stands for the fundamentals—Kuyper, Dosker, and men of that stamp were their leaders. Surely we are not going to see such men shut out of China because they stand for principle.[40]

In August of 1921, Harry Dykstra and John De Korne represented the China mission at the annual Guling meeting of the North Kiangsu Mission. On the agenda was a proposal to formally approve an invitation for the Christian Reformed Church to establish a mission in the territory claimed by the Southern Presbyterians in northern

[39]   Hugh W. White to the Executive Committee, Board of Heathen Missions, Christian Reformed Church in North America (*via* John De Korne), Dec. 22, 1920, De Korne, CRWM folder.

[40]   Circular letter, 2-3. Abraham Kuyper (1837-1920), Neo-Calvinist Dutch theologian, church leader, and statesman, was revered in the CRC and had a huge impact on the denomination's theology. See James Bratt, *Dutch Calvinism*, 14ff. Henry Dosker (1855-1926), RCA pastor, professor, and scholar, introduced Kuyper and Neo-Calvinism to conservative Presbyterians at the turn of the twentieth century and later taught church history at Louisville Presbyterian Theological Seminary. The Southern Presbyterians, who were skeptical about the RCA because of its membership in the Church of Christ in China, appear to have assumed that Dosker was from the CRC. See George Harinck, "Henry Dosker, between Albertus C. Van Raalte and Abraham Kuyper," *Origins* 19:2 (2001): 34-41. In a handwritten statement attached to the North Kiangsu Mission's circular letter, John De Korne noted: "We assume no responsibility whatever for the statement made on page 2, paragraph 4 [i.e., "Missionaries in other parts of China giving them the cold shoulder"]. That is Dr. White's interpretation, not ours." When Henry Beets reported the "cold shoulder" treatment in the *Banner, Wachter*, and *Heidenwerld*, De Korne denied that the RCA had been cold to them, relating, "The Amoy brethren have certainly treated us white," but admitted some truth about the way the Northern Presbyterians had treated them. See De Korne to Beets, August 3, 1921, De Korne, CRWM folder.

Jiangsu. The report of the committee appointed to study the invitation recommended that "our Mission reaffirm unanimously the two resolutions formally passed by circular letter and that we heartily co-operate in every possible way to assist the Christian Reformed Church to begin their work southeast of Taichow in that portion known as the Rukao field."[41] The motion passed unanimously, and the Southern Presbyterians extended an invitation to the Christian Reformed Church to work shoulder-to-shoulder with them in Rugao of the Jiangbei region of Jiangsu Province.

Good manners, standing in the Reformed tradition, and a commitment to conservative Christianity all aside, the theology of the two groups had "different emphasis and shadings."[42] In fact, this resistance to "radicalism" and to "ecclesiastical innovation" may have been the largest mutual appeal between the Christian Reformed Church and the Southern Presbyterians, because other than sharing a mutual affiliation with conservative theology, they never really spent much time working together.

Yet these differences of emphasis and shading were insignificant in comparison with their contrasting understandings of Reformed identity. While the Southern Presbyterians stood in the Calvinistic tradition, their identity had passed through Scotland and had been shaped by the differences between Presbyterians in the United States (theological, political, and cultural). For the Christian Reformed missionaries, on the other hand, being Reformed meant standing in the Reformed tradition that had passed through the Netherlands and through the refining fires of their immigrant experience in the United States. In short, what divided the two groups was, ironically, probably larger than what brought them together on the mission field.

These differences became more apparent as the years unfolded. During the thirty years the two missions shared territory in Jiangbei, they enjoyed congenial relations. They also met upon occasion for joint activities, usually for large meetings or training sessions during holidays, such as Christmas and Chinese New Year. Their most important connection took place in the context of the Huaidong Presbytery of the Jiangbei region. Initially, the Christian Reformed missionaries

---

41   De Korne to Beets, August 17, 1921, De Korne, CRWM folder.
42   For example, John Bratt outlines the subtle differences in soteriology between the PCUS and the CRC. See John Bratt, "The Southern Presbyterian and Christian Reformed Churches of America," M.A. thesis (Decatur, Ga.: Columbia Theological Seminary, 1938), 13-24.

participated in the presbytery as associate members with full privileges, since Rugao did not have an organized church. At first they found the presbytery impressive, but later they found it too dominated by the Southern Presbyterian missionaries, asserting that "the mission holds the purse strings and the Chinese church is showing no tremendous strides towards independence."[43] The Christian Reformed missionaries were also somewhat wary about joining the Southern Presbyterian-sponsored Presbyterian Church in China (organized as a conservative response to the Church of Christ in China), because of what were termed "fundamentalist" elements among the Southern Presbyterians and some tendencies toward loose church polity.[44] Caught between the "fundamentalists" in the PCUS and those with "modern" tendencies in the Church of Christ in China, the Christian Reformed Church never found a comfortable collegiality with an institutional partner.

An "Earthly Paradise"

In late September of 1921, after the intense summer heat had broken, the Christian Reformed missionary party toured the Jiangbei region of Jiangsu Province a second time to explore the Rugao field it hoped to inherit. When the party returned to Shanghai from their second trip to Rugao, it was enthusiastic about opening a mission station there. In an effort to convince the denomination, the missionaries immediately began flooding church papers with information about the Rugao field. In an eight-part series, entitled "An Introduction to Our Mission Field," that appeared in the *Banner* over a two-month period, Lee Huizenga used information gleaned from *The Christian Occupation of China*, conversations with Southern Presbyterian missionaries, and his fourteen-day trip through the field to describe the proposed field of Rugao.[45]

---

[43]   H. Dykstra to Beets, Nov. 9, 1932, H. Dykstra CRWM folder.
[44]   John De Korne, in a presentation to the executive committee of the mission board while on furlough in 1933, mentioned the mission's concern about the "fundamentalist" elements in the Presbyterian Church and what he termed as "some loose tendencies in church government." Executive Committee minutes, Sept. 6, 1933, De Korne, personal folder.
[45]   Huizenga, "An Introduction to Our Foreign Mission Field," 8 pts., *Banner* 57, 58 (Oct. 19; Nov. 2, 9, 23, 30, 1921; Dec. 21, 28, 1922; and July 12, 1923): 646; 678-79, 695, 725, 743, 791, 809; and 421. Between Nov. 1921 and Dec. 1922, Huizenga, De Korne, and Dykstra contributed a total of nineteen articles on Rugao to the *Banner* alone. Dutch articles also appeared in *Wachter* and *Heidenwerld*. Because the missionaries preferred to write in

Huizenga first described the provinces in which Rugao was located. During the Republican Era (1911–1949), Jiangsu Province was the second to smallest of China's twenty-one provinces, covering approximately 38,610 square miles (just smaller than the state of Kentucky).[46] Located in the center of East China, Jiangsu occupied the southern part of the North China plain as well as the delta on the lower reaches of the Yangzi River. To the north of the province was Shandong Province, to the south was Zhejiang Province, to the west was Anhui Province, and to the east was coastline of more than six hundred miles on the Yellow Sea. Formed by the alluvium of the Yangzi River, Jiangsu Province had the lowest altitude of China's provinces, with more than 68 percent of the province rising less than 150 feet above sea level.

Formed as the state of Wu during the Spring-Autumn period (770–746 BC), Jiangsu was one of China's oldest provinces. But because the Yangzi River intersected the province, it was frequently divided as an administered unit between north and south. The region south of the Yangzi has traditionally been called "Jiangnan," literally "river south." With Suzhou at its center, Jiangnan extended north to the Yangzi and south to Hangzhou in Zhejiang.[47] Throughout history, the region has been one of China's wealthiest, both economically and culturally. Jiangbei, on the other hand, stretched from the north bank of the Yangzi to the southern border of Shandong Province. If Jiangnan conjured up images of wealth and culture, Jiangsu north of the river, "Jiangbei," literally "river north," had the opposite effect. One Chinese writer traveling through Jiangsu province in the 1930s observed: "Jiangnan has fertile soil, beautiful rivers and mountains, convenient transportation, sophisticated culture; 'Jiangbei,' in contrast, has poor

---

English and only consented to write in Dutch if Beets would correct their use of the "Holland language," many of these Dutch articles were excerpts from English articles with annotations by Henry Beets.

[46] This is the figure given by Huizenga, which he got from Stauffer, *Christian Occupation of China* (see p. 133). De Korne also reported this figure from Carl Crow's *Handbook for China* (Shanghai: pub. by the author, 1921), 159. Today, as a result of administrative reshuffling, the province occupies more than 100,000 square kilometers. Information about Jiangsu, unless differing from that pertaining to the Republican period, comes from Du Huaijing, *Jiangsu sheng di tu ce* (Jiangsu Provincial Map Handbook) (Beijing: China Map Pub. Society, 1999), iff.

[47] This division follows G. William Skinner's macroeconomic designation of the Lower Yangzi. See G. William Skinner, "Regional Urbanization in Nineteenth-Century China," in *The City in Late Imperial* China, ed. G. William Skinner (Stanford: Stanford Univ. Press, 1977), 212.

soil and poverty-stricken people. Everywhere one looks is a wasteland. Transportation is poor. It is backward culturally. Therefore, old Jiangbei's are looked down on by 'Jiangnan' people."[48]

Though for most Chinese Jiangbei constituted one place, in fact, the designation of Jiangbei was more complicated than merely north and south, rich and poor. The region north of the Yangzi River can be divided into two sub-regions, one closer to Shandong and one closer to the Yangzi.[49] "Suzhong," as this middle region has been called, lies somewhere between the south bank of the Huai River and the north bank of the Yangzi.[50] The 1921 Southern Presbyterian invitation to the CRC was to work in Rugao County, about thirty miles north of the Yangzi. Unlike the poorer regions to the north in Subei, the Southern Presbyterians thought of the Suzhong district of Rugao County as a kind of "earthly paradise."

[48]   Fan Shuping, "Jiangbei yixian" (a route through Jiangbei), *Jiangsu yuebao* (Jiangsu monthly) 42 (Aug. 1, 1935): I. Quoted in Emily Honig, *Creating Chinese Ethnicity: Subei People in Shanghai, 1890-1990* (New Haven: Yale Univ. Press, 1992), 28.

[49]   In her exploration of the prejudice against people from northern Jiangsu, Emily Honig discovered Jiangbei is not an objective, clearly defined place, but rather represents a belief in the homogeneity of a particular region. Depending on whom one asks, that region can include areas in the neighboring provinces of Shandong and Anhui as well as some districts in southern Jiangsu. It can be defined by geography, language, or economics— but each of these produces very different, if not contradictory, definitions. Honig prefers to use the word "Subei," to describe the whole region north of the Yangzi rather than Jiangbei, because, she argues, Subei is a complex noun designating "both a real and imagined place, as both an actual and socially constructed category." Subei, she also argues, captures the ethnicity created by the term. Honig, *Creating Chinese Ethnicity*, xii. For dividing northern Jiangsu in two regions, see the *China Continuation Committee*, Stauffer, *Christian Occupation of China*, 133. Antonia Finnane also divides Jiangbei at the Huai River. See Antonia Finnane, "The Origins of Prejudice: The Malintegration of Subei in Late Imperial China," *Comparative Studies in History and Society* 35:2 (April 1993): 216. Agriculturalist John Buck, writing in the late 1930s, placed the northern section of Jiangbei in the "Winter Wheat-kaoliang," part of his scheme for dividing the agricultural regions of China, and the southern part of Jiangbei, the area below the Huai River, in the "Yangtze Rice-Wheat" region. See John L. Buck, *Land Utilization in China* (Shanghai: Univ. of Nanking Press, 1937), 65. For clarity, I use the term "Subei" for the northern portion of Jiangbei and "Suzhong" for the southern districts closer to the Yangzi.

[50]   "Suzhong," literally "central Jiangsu," is the term used by the Communist Party during the Japanese occupation of Jiangsu to designate the different areas where it had bases close to the Yangzi River.

After describing Jiangsu Province and giving a brief description of the contrast between Jiangnan and Jiangbei, Huizenga turned to Rugao. The Rugao field, which included all of Rugao County, bordered the Yellow Sea to the east and the Yangzi River to the south. To the southeast of Rugao County was Nantong, the largest city in Jiangbei. To the west was Taixing County, with its county seat of Taizhou City, the second largest city in Jiangbei. Despite lying between two prosperous counties, Rugao during the Republican period was something of a backwater. Part of Rugao's problem was limited access: neither the seacoast nor the riverbank boasted a good port. But even if there had been a good port, access to the county seat would have been limited, since the city was located in the north central part of the county with limited canal access. Frequently in the scorching summers, the county's canals dried up, bringing travel virtually to a standstill and cutting the city off from the outside world.

Since its founding during the Eastern Jin dynasty (AD 317–420), Rugao had never been an important county. Between the fifth century and the seventh century, administration of the county had shifted among various outside centers of control, only becoming an independent county during the Tang (618–907).[51] Though designated as a county, Rugao was usually under the jurisdiction of neighboring counties: during the Song, Yuan, and Ming Dynasties under the jurisdiction of Taizhou; and during the Qing dynasty under the jurisdiction of Nantong.

Nor was Rugao an exciting place geographically. Most of the terrain rose just feet above sea level, with only a few places reaching above a hundred feet. Though unexciting, the county was usually spared the floods afflicting other counties in Jiangbei, since Rugao's terrain formed the shape of an "overturned kettle," allowing the numerous canals crisscrossing the area to drain off floodwater quickly.[52] On their fall 1921 trip through the county, the missionary party noted that while Taizhou, where the Southern Presbyterians had a station, was under several feet of water with swift currents making travel by boat hazardous, Rugao County, with the exception of portions to the

---

[51] After 1949, the Communist government divided the county in two, renaming the coastal region Rudong County. For the history of Rugao County as an administrative unit, see *Rugao Xian zhi* ("The Rugao County Gazette") (Hong Kong: New Asia Printing, 1990), 14ff; *Jiangsu ge xian shi zhi liu: Rugao xian* ("Brief description of Jiangsu's counties and cities"): chap. 6. *Jiangsu Wenxian* ("Jiangsu documents") 13 (June 16, 1972): 22, and 124; and Zhao Ruheng, compiler, *Jiangsu Sheng Jian* ("Handbook on Jiangsu Province") (Shanghai: Xin Zhonggui Jiangshe Xuehui, 1935), Sec. 1, 13.

[52] *North China Herald* (April 26, 1932): 132.

east, remained dry.[53] Even in 1931, when most of Jiangbei was hit by a devastating flood, Rugao was spared. If Rugao had little problem with flooding, the same could not be said about drought. During the 1930s, the county was hit hard by several summers of severe, crop-wasting drought.[54]

Problems with drought notwithstanding, Rugao County was remarkably fertile. The soil along the East Coast was poor because of a high saline content. Some of this poor land had been reclaimed for cultivation, but most of it was covered with tall grass cut for fuel. To the west as far as Taixing County, however, Rugao boasted exceedingly fertile soil. Though not the largest county in the province, Rugao had the largest amount of "average quality" land in all of Jiangsu, about 1.5 million mu (approximately 600,000 acres), roughly half the total of the county's land.[55] In this soil, Rugao's peasants could reap two harvests per year: rice in the spring and wheat in the late fall. When drought hit in the 1930s, the peasants switched to a summer crop of cotton. Other local crops included barley, beans, corn, sorghum, and sweet potatoes. Rugao peasants also grew turnips, one of the county's *techan*, or local specialties. But this famous local cash crop often resulted in misery, when many residents washed the turnips in unsanitary canal water and contracted cholera.[56]

The county's fertile soil contributed to a dense population. Following the construction of the Grand Canal in the Sui dynasty (581–618), Rugao's population had grown steadily, spiking twice in the nineteenth century: when Jiangnan refugees crossed the Yangzi during the Opium War of 1839–1842, and during the Taiping uprising of the 1850s. In the words of the North Kiangsu Mission, because of the relative lack of natural disasters and the great productivity of the

---

[53] Huizenga, "An Introduction to Our Mission Field," *Banner* 57 (Nov. 23, 1922): 725.

[54] The assigned correspondent for the *North China Herald* reported on drought in the paper in March 29, 1932: 476; Aug. 10, 1932: 213; Aug. 21, 1932: 331; Jan. 11, 1933: 50; July 4, 1934: 12; July 18, 1934: 91; Sept. 12, 1934: 385; and Nov. 11, 1936: 225. [Incidentally, Lee Huizenga was almost certainly the *North China Herald* correspondent. Though his name never appears on any of the articles on Rugao, almost all of them can be found in Huizenga's CRWM folder. Moreover, the *NCH* is silent during the years Huizenga was on furlough in the States (1927-1930, summer 1936, and after 1937 when he moved to Shanghai.] See Huizenga, CRWM folder.

[55] Wang Peitang, *Jiangsusheng xiangtu zhi* (Local records of Jiangsu province) (Changsha, Hunan, China: Commercial Press, 1938) 288.

[56] *North China Herald* (May 7, 1933): 254; and (Oct. 14, 1936): 54.

Rugao area, "The Chinese flock to this *earthly paradise*."[57] At the end of the second decade of the twentieth century, the China Continuation Committee estimated the county's population to be 872–878 people per square mile, with all but a handful of Han Chinese descent.[58] During the Nanjing Decade (1927–1937), the county's population soared, reaching 1.4 million by 1931 and making Rugao the most populous county in Jiangsu, with 1,042 people per square mile.[59]

Many of the county's residents lived in Rugao's county seat, Rugao City, a walled city located in the north central part of the county. On their first visit to Rugao City, the Christian Reformed missionaries had circled the city wall on foot, a structure built during the Ming dynasty, twenty feet high, fifteen feet wide, and two miles in circumference. From the wall they counted a few two-story buildings—most notably, a Catholic church and several temples; the rest of the city was a close warren of narrow streets and alleys lined with shops and stalls. Seeing the crowded buildings from above, the missionaries estimated the city's population to be between 100,000 and 150,000.[60] Though extremely crowded, the missionaries found the streets swept clean and tidy. In one corner of the city they toured a public park, which, according to the Chinese evangelist guiding them, was maintained by members of the local gentry. These local gentry had also recently imported machinery to build a power plant, providing the city with electricity.[61]

[57]   North Kiangsu Mission, circular letter, June 18, 1921, De Korne, CRWM folder.

[58]   This figure was based on the 1919 Post Office census. See above, note 47. Though no numbers are given, the *Rugao Xian zhi* claims that small numbers of the following minority groups have always lived in Rugao County: Hui, Manchu, Miao, Zhuang, Tu Jia, and Mongols. *Rugao Xian zhi*, 136.

[59]   Ibid., 138. See also Zhao Ruheng, compiler, *Jiangsu Sheng Jian*, sec. 1, ("Jiangsu Provincial Handbook") (Shanghai: Xin Zhongguo Jianshe xuehui, 1935), 10. Cited in Lenore Barkan, "Patterns of Power: Forty Years of Elite Politics in a Chinese County," in *Chinese Local Elites and Patterns of Dominance*, Joseph W. Esherick and Mary Backus Rankin, eds. (Berkeley: Univ. of California Press, 1990), 202.

[60]   For a description of this walk, see H. Dykstra, "Rev. Dykstra writes about China's needs, its towns and villages, its idol worship," part 2, *Banner* 56 (Nov. 10, 1921): 695-96. It is unclear where Dykstra got population figures for Rugao City, since the China Continuation Committee lists Rugao as having a population of 50,000. See Stauffer, *Christian Occupation of China*, 134. The *Rugao Xian zhi*, however, basing its figure on the 1912 *Gao Min Bao* ("census"), lists the population of Rugao as 143,166. *Rugao Xian zhi*, 139.

[61]   For details about the electric plant, see Barkan, "Patterns of Power," 202.

The electric plant revealed the Rugao gentry's aspirations to catch up with nearby Nantong, to the southeast. On the banks of the Yangzi, just north of Shanghai, Nantong was billed as China's "model city" during the Republican period. Zhang Jian (Chang Chien), a *jinshi* degree holder, was the single most important reason for the spectacular development of Nantong.[62] Before the fall of the Qing dynasty, Zhang had resigned his position in the prestigious Hanlin Academy to concentrate on reform in Nantong. He established schools for both boys and girls. Unusual for a Confucian scholar, Zhang also took an early interest in developing Nantong's industry, starting the Da Sheng weaving mill in 1895. When the textile venture proved successful, he cooperated with other local gentry in building two dozen more factories in the Nantong area. At the same time, Zhang and others also created modern systems of transportation, communication, and banking.[63]

Sha Yuanbing, a native of Rugao who had cooperated with Zhang Jian in founding the Da Sheng Cotton Mill, worked to bring Nantong-style reforms to his hometown. Sha, also a *jinshi* degree holder, invested widely in Rugao economic projects, which included a drugstore, an oil pressing mill, a flour mill, an iron factory, a Shanghai steamship company, a local steamship company, a local "old-style bank," and several land reclamation companies along the coast in Dongtai County to the north. One venture, the Kuang Feng Ham factory, laid the foundation for a major local industry, the curing and processing of ham and other types of sausages.[64]

Like gentry in Nantong, Sha Yuanbing also played a key role in developing education in his hometown of Rugao. On their visit, the missionaries found the educational system built by Sha Yuanbing and other gentry impressive. They toured several schools, both for boys and for girls, and addressed the student body at one of them. On the veranda of the old Confucian temple, converted to an education center after the Revolution of 1911, they spoke to four hundred school children through an interpreter, taking the opportunity to present "the Great God to the representatives of the people."[65]

---

[62] Marianne Bastid, *Educational Reform in Early Twentieth-Century China*, trans. Paul J. Bailey (Ann Arbor: Center for Chinese Studies, Univ. of Mich., 1988), 19-20.

[63] Qin Shao, "Tempest over Teapots: The Vilification of Teahouse Culture in Early Republican China," *Journal of Asian Studies* 57:4 (Nov. 1998): 1011.

[64] Barkan, "Patterns of Power," 204.

[65] H. Dykstra, "Writes about China," part 2, 138.

After exploring Rugao City, the missionaries proceeded east on the Yunyan canal, eventually reaching the high dikes built on the Yellow Sea during the Tang dynasty. They passed through a number of densely populated market towns, with populations ranging between 35,000 and 80,000.[66] On trade days the missionaries noted, "These villages look like a beehive. Thousands come to the village with their chickens, ducks, eggs, pigs and produce of the field."[67] Unlike Rugao, which had modernized to a degree, these market towns had not, serving primarily as administrative and market hubs.

As they traveled through the countryside, the missionaries marveled at the "scores of densely inhabited villages" which could be seen from their houseboat. Even in the far-east districts of the county, where their Southern Presbyterian guide told them to expect only swamps and uninhabited land, they found "thousands of villages and hundreds of thousands of people."[68] They noticed that, unlike the peasants south of the Yangzi whose houses were made from brick, the houses north of the river were made of mud with thatched roofs. Yet they were amazed by the apparent prosperity of the peasants in the Rugao countryside: "To our surprise our way passed through village after village, all prosperous."[69]

"No Knowledge of the True God"

As impressive as they found Rugao, the missionaries had no illusions about the difficulty of establishing a mission there. On their first visits to the county, wherever they stopped crowds would gather and their Presbyterian guide would hold "meetings" on their houseboat, or they passed out tracts and the missionary would read to

---

[66] *Rugao Xian zhi*, 139.
[67] Huizenga, "An Introduction," pt. 6, 791.
[68] Ibid.
[69] John Buck's 1930s survey of materials used for the construction of buildings corroborates this observation. Buck adds, however, that there were also a relatively high number of brick walls, and the general observation that the buildings in the area, while not as good as the region south of the Yangzi, were better in the Yangzi Rice-wheat area (of which Rugao was a part) than in the regions further north in the "Winter Wheat-kaoliang" area. See Buck, "Table 5. Construction Materials of Farm Buildings," 433. About 70 percent of the county's population were peasant farmers engaged in agriculture. Though they appeared to be relatively well off, the vast majority of Rugao's peasants were tenant farmers (approximately 74.4 percent), with less than 17 percent falling into the category of owner-cultivators. See Barkan, "Patterns of Power," 378, note 12.

the gathering crowd. At other places along the canals, they addressed customers in teahouses. Some in their audiences had heard the name of "Yesu" (Jesus), but most did not know who he was. "In those hundreds of villages," Harry Dykstra reported, "the gospel never is and, as far as we could find out, never has been preached."[70]

If Rugao County was virtually untouched by Christianity, it was thoroughly steeped in the Chinese religious traditions. With the fall of the Qing dynasty in 1911, Confucianism, the political and social glue that had held the imperial system together, had been uprooted from the formal Chinese religious system. But Confucianism as a social and ethical system remained deeply ingrained in the minds and hearts of the Chinese people. Like most county seats, Rugao had had a Confucian temple where biannual ceremonies had taken place to commemorate the sage Confucius. During the Republican period, Rugao's Confucian hall had been converted to an educational hall, in front of which a modern school had been built.

After the fall of the Qing, the other two streams of Chinese religion, Daoism and Buddhism, continued to be practiced in Rugao. Daoism, based on the philosophy of Laozi and Zhuangzi, had been in Rugao since the Tang dynasty but was strongest during the Ming and Qing dynasties.[71] Though Chuan Zhen and the Zheng schools of Daoism were both practiced in Rugao, most of the Daoist clergy in Rugao practiced the Zheng school or "Celestial Masters," an orthodox tradition which militated against the excesses of popular religion.[72] During the four hundred years of the Ming and Qing, Rugao had thirty Daoist temples under the supervision of a Daoist association of priests and elders. After the fall of the Qing, the Republican government had "done away with" Daoism, though it continued to be practiced in secret and the number of adherents continued to increase. In 1937, with China on the brink of war with Japan, the Daoist church reemerged in Rugao when Song Liangqi, a member of the local gentry, returned from studying Daoism in Hubei and started a training center for Daoist adepts at the Ling Wei Hall, ordaining 256 clergy.[73] By the end of 1943, during the Japanese occupation of Rugao, Song had ordained 510 clergy. Daoism in Rugao was most popular when floods and famine

---

[70] H. Dykstra, "Rev. Dykstra writes about China," part 1, *Banner* 56 (Oct. 27, 1921): 671.

[71] Information about Daoism in Rugao comes from *Rugao Xian zhi*, 163.

[72] Isabelle Robinet, *Taoism: Growth of a Religion*, trans. Phyllis Brooks (Stanford: Stanford Univ. Press, 1997), 63.

[73] *Rugao Xian zhi*, 163.

struck the county and people sought the help of Daoist adepts to restore harmony through their cosmos-righting ceremonies.

During the Republican period, Buddhism was by far the strongest religious presence in Rugao. Buddhism had first appeared in Rugao during the Sui dynasty, and within three hundred years had become an integral part of life in the county.[74] By the end of the Qing, Rugao City had sixty-seven Buddhist temples, halls, and shrines, with 253 other Buddhist sites dotting the countryside.[75] Most of these Buddhist sites were devoted to the Bodhisattva Guanyin, the most important religious figure in the Rugao area. Guanyin, or Avalokiteshvara, as this bodhisattva was called in India, came to exist as a Buddhist figure in China during the Tang dynasty. Later, during the Yuan dynasty, Guanyin was portrayed as a young woman holding a holy vase in her hand, pouring out water to save the multitude, and became known as the "goddess of mercy." Guanyin's name in Chinese means literally "observing the sounds," referring to her attentive ear to the pleas for help from those who worship her. As one of the main figures in the Chinese popular classic novel, *Journey to the West*, Guanyin was claimed by some to be the most revered Buddhist figure in China, and this was particularly true in the South, where she was considered the patron saint of motherhood and seamen.[76]

Buddhism was the faith not only of the common people in Rugao, but of many local gentry as well. In the mid-1920s, after becoming disillusioned with the movement to modernize China, Sha Yuanbing, who had been instrumental in establishing schools and other progressive reforms during the previous twenty years, became deeply involved in the study of Buddhism. Sha invited scholars to Rugao to lecture on Buddhism, and he organized religious ceremonies. Through his promotion of Buddhism, the faith was strengthened in Rugao. By 1929, the county had 2,462 monks and 400 nuns, growth that came despite the local government's efforts to eradicate the faith from the county. Four years later, the Buddhist clergy founded a relief agency to aid the destitute and to respond to local catastrophes. In 1934 another 200 were ordained as Buddhist priests. Buddhism was at the core of religious life in Rugao.

[74] Ibid.
[75] Ibid. For the names and breakdown of the different temples, hall, pagodas, shrines, etc., see *Rugao Xian zhi*, 1931, roll 3, 1-7.
[76] C. K. Yang, *Religion in Chinese Society* (Berkeley: Univ. of California Press, 1961), 11. The popularity of Guanyin in Rugao also supports the cultural affinity of the district with Jiangnan.

In contrast to the highly visible presence of Buddhism in Rugao, the missionaries found only a marginal Christian presence, and that limited to the county seat. Lee Huizenga called the county "practically virgin soil."[77] The first missionaries to arrive in Rugao were French Jesuits in the 1880s, who established a chapel just inside the city's east gate.[78] As an outstation of the Haimen diocese, more than a hundred miles to the southeast, Rugao's small chapel celebrated mass only on weekends and some religious holidays. Catholic priests rarely visited, but when they did they were willing to help converts and "church friends" avoid paying local taxes and to protect them during times of unrest. As in other parts of China, these efforts fostered widespread resentment; in 1891 when anger boiled up, a mob burned the Rugao chapel to the ground and drove the Catholic Church from the city.[79]

The first Protestants came to Rugao at the beginning of the twentieth century. The Southern Presbyterians had first preached in Rugao in 1904. Eight years later, the Southern Baptists, the second largest mission in Jiangsu, opened a chapel in the city, stationing a Chinese pastor there with a helper.[80] With the Baptists' closest station sixty miles away, foreign missionaries seldom visited the city. When the Christian Reformed missionaries visited the chapel in the fall of 1921, they reported only a handful of people in attendance at the weeknight evangelistic meeting, though, they admitted, this was probably because it was raining "and the Chinese refuse to go out in the rain at night."[81] Baptist evangelist Hua Fuquan told the missionaries there were between forty and fifty Christians in the city. Given the meager results in Rugao, he added, it was uncertain whether the Baptists would remain in the city.

By 1921, the Southern Presbyterians also had a small chapel in Rugao, an outpost of the Taizhou station, twelve hours away by steam

---

[77]   Huizenga to the consistory of the LaGrave Avenue CRC, Oct. 1, 1921, Huizenga CRWM folder.

[78]   *Rugao wen shi zhi ci liao* ("Information on the history of Rugao") 8 (Rugao: Guo ying yin shua chang yin shua, 1985): 54-57.

[79]   Anti-Catholic riots took place across the Lower Yangzi region in 1890-91. In many cities mobs burned churches and in one city a priest was killed. Hu Sheng, *Cong ya pian zhan zheng dao wu si yun dong* ("From the Opium War to the May Fourth Movement") (Beijing: ren min chu ban she, 1981): 370. There are conflicting reports about the return of the Catholic church to Rugao. Though the CRC missionaries reported seeing a Catholic chapel there in 1921, the *Rugao Xian zhi* reports that the Catholic Church did not reestablish a presence there until 1926. *Rugao Xian zhi*, 164.

[80]   *Rugao Xian zhi*, 164.

[81]   De Korne, "Traveling in China," part 2, *Banner* (March 3, 1921): 138.

launch. In a rented building close to the north gate, the Southern Presbyterians furnished a small rented chapel and stationed a Chinese evangelist to oversee a flock of not more than twenty. Because of the meager results in Rugao and their vast territory in the rest of Jiangbei, the Southern Presbyterians were eager to turn the Rugao field over to the Christian Reformed mission.

After seeing the field a second time, the Christian Reformed missionaries were eager to take it over. From every angle, the Southern Presbyterians' offer appeared ideal to them. It was close to Shanghai, the center of the Chinese Protestant movement, facilitating transportation to and from the field. It appeared a prosperous place, not subject to the vicious cycles of flood and famine in other parts of northern Jiangsu, increasing the likelihood that churches could become self-supporting more quickly than in poorer locales. The Christian Reformed mission could work in close cooperation with a mission that shared a commitment both to the fundamentals of the faith and to the Reformed tradition.

Above all, the need for preaching Christianity in Rugao was huge. Writing to his home church, John De Korne underscored the immense need in Rugao.

> The population of this *Hsien* (county), according to official statistics, is more than a million and a quarter. Whether there are any Christians in Rugao Hsien outside of Rugao City, we do not know. We have traveled through that territory, and we have seen the people and the conditions with our own eyes. We have seen the depths of heathendom into which they have sunk. We have seen them bow down to idols in their temples, and bump their heads in humiliation upon the ground. We have seen the walls which they have built opposite the doors of their houses in order to prevent the entrance of evil spirits. In that entire Hsien there is no knowledge of the true God, and our Church has been asked to take upon itself the responsibility of bringing them this knowledge.[82]

Conservative and Safe

The missionaries' conviction about Rugao included a sense of relief. Critics at home had put them on the defensive for taking so

---

[82]   De Korne to his home church, Nov. 1, 1921, De Korne, CRWM folder.

long to find a field.[83] Their flurry of letters and articles following their second trip to Rugao aimed not only to stem this criticism, but also to lobby for the church's approval for Rugao. Their recommendation had to be approved by the synod, scheduled to convene in June 1922. Before the synod met, however, the missionaries first needed to convince the Board of Heathen Missions, and that meant convincing Henry Beets, now the full-time secretary of the board.

Though supportive of the missionaries, Beets raised some questions about the selection of Rugao.[84] Following a chance conversation at a missionary conference, he had learned that two other missions had claims on the Rugao. Dr. Frank Garrett, a medical missionary with the Disciples of Christ mission in Nantong, had told Beets that both his mission and the Southern Baptists had "claims" on Rugao. In response to Beets's question about other claims, John De Korne wrote that they had mentioned the Baptists' meager presence in Rugao several times. About the Baptists' claim on Rugao, he explained, "We did consult with the Baptist representatives about it [occupying Rugao], but they assured us that there was no use trying to make an agreement with them as to territory as they refuse to accept anything 'but the Lord's leading.'"[85] Of even greater concern to Beets was the Disciples' "claim" on Rugao. According to Garrett, approximately half of what the Christian Reformed Church was proposing to take over as a field belonged to his mission, The Foreign Christian Missionary Society (FCMS).

The FCMS had been one of the earliest Protestant groups to enter Shanghai when it became a treaty port in 1842. During the next sixty years, the group expanded its work throughout Jiangsu Province, both south and north of the Yangzi River. The first missionary to enter

[83]   In a letter to John De Korne, Henry Beets mentioned that some of the ministers in the denomination were complaining about the China mission for taking so long in finding a field. One classis had even passed a resolution asking the synod not to send more workers to China until a work had been established there. See Beets to De Korne, Feb. 28, 1922, De Korne, personal folder.

[84]   In a letter to Lee Huizenga, Beets assured him that it was right to take their time in finding a field: "You cannot hurry. It would be unwise to hurry, and the very people that are now, as you say dissatisfied, would be the ones to condemn you if you people should take any steps which would prove unwise and too hasty. Let me emphasize as strongly as I can that you ought to be very deliberate, considering all kinds of factors." Beets to Huizenga, October 6, 1921, Huizenga, CRWM folder.

[85]   De Korne to Beets, Jan. 24, 1922, De Korne, CRWM folder.

Nantong had arrived in the early 1890s, establishing a station there in 1895.[86] Initially the FCMS promoted evangelistic work in the city and surrounding area, but later the mission focused almost exclusively on educational and medical work. By the 1920s the mission was doing very little outside the city. Thus, Garrett's claim on the southeastern portion of Rugao County irked the Christian Reformed missionaries. Each wrote Beets separately, emphasizing that though the FCMS had a claim on a small slice of Rugao County bordering Nantong, the Presbyterians had a much larger claim on Rugao County. Huizenga added that they had recently "met another man of Garrett's mission, who said that they were unable to work their own little part of the field with all their workers, and [he] was glad we were to be neighbors."[87]

Garrett had also planted doubt in Beets's mind about the size of the Rugao field. Since Beets hoped to send thirty missionaries to China in a decade, he was surprised to learn from Garrett that the coastal section of the county "was largely marshy land with a sparse population." Answering Beets's suggestion that "that field is very limited indeed," John De Korne stressed that the entire county, though not large—even including the coastal areas—was more densely populated than they had initially assumed.[88] Furthermore, he added, if the mission found Rugao County too small, it could expand to the two adjacent counties of Jingjiang (Tzingkiang) and Haimen, both under Southern Presbyterian claims.

Others besides Garrett raised questions in Beets's mind, as well. One board member had asked him why the region had been passed over by other missionaries, being as close as it was to Shanghai, the center of the missionary movement. The most important reason, the missionaries responded, was that the Southern Presbyterians had had a claim on the area already for thirty-eight years. Another reason, they added, was that since the "neglected neck" of northern Jiangsu was not in the sweep of the main routes toward the interior of China, "Missionaries and businessmen entering China at Shanghai, proceeded to the interior by either traveling on the Grand Canal or going west on

---

86 Information on the FCMS comes from Archibald McLean, *The History of the Foreign Christian Missionary Society* (New York: Revell, 1921), 260-64. Hudson Taylor, founder of the China Inland Mission, was the first Protestant to go to Nantong [no date given], but had left after meeting fierce opposition there. See McLean, *History*, 261.

87 Huizenga to Beets, Jan. 23, 1922, Huizenga CRWM folder.

88 Beets to De Korne, Dec. 22, 1922, and Feb. 28, 1922, De Korne, CRWM folder.

the Yangzi." Then, "After the main points on along those two routes were occupied," they speculated, "it seems that the corner that was left untouched was so small in comparison with the big west, that it did not appeal strongly to the adventurous souls of the early pioneers."[89]

Ever conscious about finances, Beets and the board also questioned the cost of Rugao. They had the impression that work there would be "very costly," perhaps because of its proximity to Shanghai. That, the missionaries responded, depended on what was meant by costly. Certainly Rugao would be more expensive than a more remote district, but, on the other hand, they said, it would be less expensive than a large treaty port city. Proximity to Shanghai would give them all of the benefits of a big city but less of the cost. Even if Rugao were more expensive than other areas, this was good, they argued, since "all other things being equal, the church in a more prosperous section will be able to attain self-support much more quickly than in those less blessed in a material way."[90]

Satisfied with their answers, Beets swung his support behind the Rugao proposal, using his considerable bully-pulpit resources to convince his readers and the synod. At its June 1922 meeting, the synod ratified Rugao as the site for a mission station. After the decision, Beets wrote the missionaries that their proposals "were carried unanimously and quickly, everybody seemingly satisfied that they were conservative and safe."[91]

Riding a crest of enthusiasm at home, the first party of overseas Christian Reformed missionaries departed for China in the fall of 1920. They must have experienced a huge sense of disappointment when they arrived in China only to discover what the secretary of the China Continuation Committee, E. C. Lobenstine, had warned John De Korne and Lee Huizenga about during their investigation of potential mission fields: China was already occupied, and the additional help of one more very small mission would not be very welcome. Part of the Christian Reformed missions' difficulty in finding a field, however, had to do with the perception of several "mainline" Protestant missions and denominations that the denomination was "fundamentalist" and

[89] Report of the China Mission, Feb. 10, 1922, CRWM folder.
[90] Answer to questions submitted by the Executive Committee on Nov. 8, 1921, question 2. Report of the China Mission, Feb. 10, 1922, CRWM folder.
[91] Beets to De Korne, June 29, 1922, De Korne, CRWM folder.

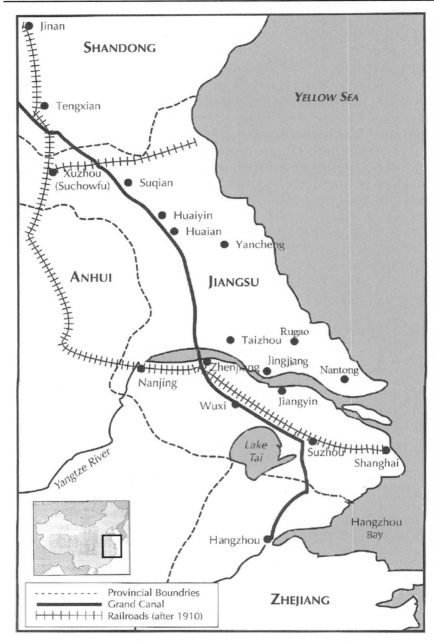

Northern Jiangsu Province, 1930s (Jiangbei).

consequently would not be able to support a church-unifying effort
taking place in some Protestant circles. Even the Reformed Church

in America was wary of the CRC mission's ability to join in a church-unifying effort and only offered to allow the missionaries access to their territory if they worked under that denomination. But the CRC's suspicion of these denominations and efforts, and its determination to establish its own mission field, forced the missionaries to look elsewhere. Finally, despite some reservations about "fundamentalist tendencies" in the Southern Presbyterian mission, the Christian Reformed Church accepted an offer from that mission to take over part of its field in Rugao County of northern Jiangsu Province. The CRC mission was now ready to begin its task of establishing a Reformed church on Chinese soil.

CHAPTER 3

A Stage of Illusion:
Early Mistakes and Conflicts, 1923-1927

Getting Started

Following their visit to Rugao in the fall of 1921, the missionaries had big plans for their prospective location, but another year passed before they could move there. While waiting for the board's formal approval, they continued language study in Nanjing at the Nanjing Language School. Though Rugao had its own dialect, the missionaries studied Mandarin, thinking that once they had mastered the national language, they could fine tune their use of the local Rugao dialect.[1] While John De Korne and Harry Dykstra studied language full time, Lee Huizenga divided his time between language study and work in the University of Nanjing Hospital. After almost two years of study, De Korne and Dykstra were able to lead chapel services and preach in Chinese, which, though "broken," was understood by the people.[2]

---

[1] Rugao is spoken in Rugao and in neighboring counties in Jiangsu Province and is classified as "Jianghuai Mandarin," a subgroup of Mandarin. See *Rugao Xian zhi*, 684.
[2] H. Dykstra to Henry Beets, May 11, 1923, H. Dykstra, CRWM folder.

Before attempting to use their Chinese to preach in Rugao, however, the three men and their families moved to Taizhou (Taichow) in northern Jiangsu Province in the fall of 1922. The move to Taizhou, they believed, would provide "a way to gradually work" toward their own field under exceptionally favorable circumstances.[3] Taizhou was the closest Southern Presbyterian mission station to Rugao, sixty miles away, or about twelve hours by canal steamboat, the usual means of conveyance. Lee Huizenga filled a vacancy in the Southern Presbyterian hospital while the regular doctor furloughed in the United States. The other two missionaries continued their language study, gained experience by helping with the work in the city, and began making preparations for establishing a mission station in Rugao.

Much had to be done before the missionaries could actually move to Rugao. They knew that one of their most complicated tasks would be purchasing property for houses and mission facilities. Shortly after moving to Taizhou, an opportunity suddenly arose for them to purchase a choice piece of property inside Rugao's city walls. Afraid that if they did not seize this opportunity it might be several years before an equally good plot came up for sale, the missionaries pushed the board to approve the land purchase, even before the synod had formally approved Rugao as a field. The multitude of titles and claims for even the smallest parcels made buying any land in China complicated. But land deals made with foreigners could be even more complicated and sensitive, especially in a city such as Rugao where no foreigner had ever resided.[4] To avoid opposition to the transaction, a Southern Presbyterian Chinese evangelist suggested the Christian Reformed missionaries visit the property at night dressed in Chinese clothes.[5]

As it turned out, they did not need to disguise themselves, nor were any of their worst fears realized in securing the property. Completing the transaction took only six weeks, despite having to extend negotiations when some graves were found on the plot.[6] When

---

Because he began medical work soon after arriving in China, Huizenga had not yet mastered Chinese.

[3]   Lee Huizenga to the consistory of the LaGrave Avenue CRC, March 1, 1922, Huizenga, CRWM folder.

[4]   The Southern Presbyterians encountered opposition to their renting property or purchasing land in Jiangyin (1895), Jiaxing (1896), and Yancheng (1910). See Brown, *Earthen Vessels*, 109-10, and 183.

[5]   China Mission Report, December 1921.

[6]   For details of the mission's first land purchase, see H. Dykstra, "Our Purchase of Land in China," 2 pts., *Banner* 58 (May 31 and June 7, 1923): 326-27, and 342-43.

the final terms had been worked out, the two parties met at the mission chapel and divided the money among the various parties: real estate man, middlemen, and family selling the property. At the end, twenty dollars remained unclaimed. After some discussion, one of the Chinese Christians seated at the table suddenly grabbed the money, a move that caused a brawl. When order was finally restored, the missionaries, through their translator, stated that they would not allow quarreling in the chapel and explained that "the money had been contributed by Christians in America, many of whom had given of their poverty, in order that the Chinese might be acquainted with Jesus Christ."[7] After a banquet the next day, both sides concluded the deal. Later that same night, the missionaries delivered a petition to the county magistrate, asking him to inform the citizens of the county that missionaries of the Christian Reformed Church had come to preach the gospel and to open a hospital.

Before moving to Rugao, the mission was also able to purchase property outside the city walls for building residences. Because they believed that living in Chinese housing would be not only uncomfortable but potentially dangerous to their health as well, the missionaries built large brick houses. From all appearances, these houses could have been transplanted from any Dutch-American neighborhood in Grand Rapids, Michigan. Unlike Dutch homes in America, though, the missionaries' Rugao homes had spacious courtyards with lush flower gardens and a tennis court enclosed by high brick walls. All of the houses built by the mission in the early years were built outside the city's east gate, with the exception of Lee Huizenga's house. Huizenga's house, also built according to an American plan but with a Chinese roof, was located inside the city walls, so that he could attend medical emergencies at night after the city gates had been closed. When the construction of their houses had been completed, in the fall of 1923, the missionaries moved to Rugao.

Over the next several years, the China Mission rented or purchased about a dozen more properties in and around Rugao for residences, a hospital, a school, and chapels. With time, no doubt, the missionaries became more adept at making these transactions, but during their entire thirty-year presence in Rugao, buying, building, maintaining, managing, and protecting property consumed a large proportion of their time.

<hr>

[7]   Ibid., 342.

Bird's eye view of the Harry Dykstra home, 1920s. The missionaries built their homes just outside the Rugao City wall across the city moat (*foreground*). Their two-story brick homes would have fit nicely in any Dutch-American neighborhood in Grand Rapids, Michigan.

Even before the completion of their houses, the missionaries began work in Rugao, making occasional trips to the city by steam launch from Taizhou. Following the pattern of Protestant missionaries throughout China, their plan was to make Rugao City a central mission station by "establishing an evangelistic center, a hospital, and a training school for Chinese children" there.[8] As a start, they took over the lease of the Southern Presbyterian's north gate chapel, a renovated storefront, and purchased the chapel's furniture for sixteen dollars. On Sundays, worship services and Sunday school were held, and evangelistic meetings were conducted on weeknights.

Attracting the attention of nonbelievers was the main purpose of the chapel's daily evening services. The organist played "heavenly music," hoping to attract passersby to "turn aside and listen to the gospel" preached by a Chinese evangelist, one formerly employed by the Southern Presbyterians, who was now working for the China Mission.[9] Crowds were greatest at Christmastime, when the festive decorations and a chance to hear American children tell the Christmas story attracted streams of passersby.[10] But on most nights, only a few people trickled in, coming and going throughout the evangelistic service. This trickle of attendees included only men, since "no respected woman could be seen after dark." Nor did Rugao's "long-gowned aristocrats"

[8]   Huizenga, "An Introduction to Our Foreign Mission Field," *Banner* 57 (Dec. 28, 1922): 809.

[9]   H. Dykstra, "Evangelistic Work in Our China Field," *Banner* 59 (July 18, 1924): 453. This was a common method of evangelism in China starting already in the nineteenth century, with the preaching following the paradigm of sin, atonement, and salvation, reinforced by scriptural proof texts. See Andrew Walls, "The Multiple Conversions of Timothy Richard," in *The Cross-Cultural Process in Christian History* (Maryknoll: Orbis, 2002), 245.

[10] Sam Dykstra to his home congregation, Jan. 15, 1926, S. Dykstra, CRWM folder.

This photograph, taken in 1948, peers into the courtyard of the Rugao house converted for use as the first mission hospital in 1925.

attend chapel services, since, as Simon (Sam) Dykstra, an ordained missionary who had arrived on the field in 1924, explained, "A visit would be below the dignity of these folks who do not mingle with the rank and file."[11] In addition to taking over the Southern Presbyterian's north gate chapel, the missionaries opened two more chapels, one at the east gate, and one in the city center, across the street from the city temple. Through these chapels, the missionaries hoped to make contact with the neighborhoods in the city. After a visitor attended a service, someone from the mission (usually an evangelist accompanied by a missionary) would stop by the visitor's home and extend an invitation to study the Bible. From the contacts they made through the city's chapels, the missionaries hoped to form a church.

Soon after their arrival in Rugao, the missionaries saw hopeful signs for that future church. A few of the soldiers quartered near the north gate chapel had shown some immediate interest in their message. Even more significantly, at the east gate chapel were four baptized Christians and nine "registered" inquirers.[12] These Christians and inquirers were under the care of a Chinese evangelist who had

[11]   S. Dykstra to his home congregation, Aug. 21, 1925, S. Dykstra, CRWM folder.
[12]   Report of the China Mission, Oct. 31, 1923.

been trained in a Baptist school. The four baptized Christians came from a range of different backgrounds. There was a postmaster who had become a Christian through the Adventist church, but who did "not seem to have inherited any of their 'Peculiarities.'"[13] There were two other men who had come from the Yangzhou Baptist church and two women, one who had come from the China Inland Mission and another who had come from the Foreign Christian Missionary Society, presumably in Nantong.[14] Not long after their arrival in Rugao, a few local people had also requested baptism, but the missionaries, afraid of accepting them "too soon," did not baptize them.[15]

With this handful of Christians and inquirers, the mission's Chinese workers—evangelists, cooks, gatekeepers, and their baptized children—and their own families, the missionaries believed they had the makings of Rugao's first organized church. Citing their synodical mandate to "organize believers into churches," they wrote the home board requesting permission to form a Rugao church. Since the denomination had never organized churches overseas, no one at home knew how to proceed. Following Beets's suggestion that they research the problem, the mission wrote "friends in China, in Java, in the Netherlands, and in the United States."[16] They also studied the history of church organization of the Presbyterian Church in China (using the Westminster Shorter Confession), their own "Reformed Sending Order" (*Gereformeerde Zendingsorde*), and the fundamental principles and practices of missions in China.[17]

Looking for help closer to Rugao, the missionaries turned to their Southern Presbyterian neighbors and the Huaidong Presbytery. The North Kiangsu Mission had organized the Huaidong Presbytery (*Huai Tong*) in 1910 in order to link the seven Presbyterian congregations in the Jiangbei region.[18] Though it had no ordained Chinese pastors, the presbytery did have twenty-eight Chinese elders and thirty-five deacons, representing more than a thousand Chinese Presbyterians in northern Jiangsu Province. Though elders from the various churches played an important role in the annual presbytery meetings, the Southern

---

[13]   H. Dykstra to Beets, Feb. 15, 1923, H. Dykstra, CRWM folder.
[14]   H. Dykstra to Beets, March 24, 1923, H. Dykstra, CRWM folder.
[15]   For details of the process of being received for baptism, see pp. 00.
[16]   Report of the China Mission, Dec. 1923, p. 2, CRWM folder.
[17]   No copy of their report exists in the mission or missionary folders.
[18]   Brown, *Earthen Vessels*, 186. In the early 1930s, the ecclesiastical body's name was changed to Jiang Bei Presbytery.

Presbyterian missionaries dominated, taking the lead on almost all initiatives and committees.[19]

De Korne and Dykstra attended their first Huaidong Presbytery meeting in October 1923, just before moving to Rugao. Though they did not represent a church and thus could not technically belong to the presbytery, the body gave them "associate status" and allowed them full voting privileges. A year later, in 1924, De Korne and Dykstra attended the meeting again, this time in Yancheng, about one hundred miles northeast of Rugao. At this meeting, the Christian Reformed mission formally requested that the presbytery form a committee to visit Rugao and investigate establishing a church there to join the presbytery. A year later, however, in the fall of 1925, the mission received a letter from the North Kiangsu Mission discouraging the Christian Reformed Church from formally organizing a church in Rugao until there were more baptized members.[20] Adjusting their plans, the missionaries formed a "Preorganization Committee" (*Rugao Chou Pei hui*) to work for the eventual establishment of a congregation.

A decade later, reflecting on their early eagerness to organize a church in Rugao, the missionaries wrote:

> As a mission we have passed through a stage of illusion when we considered the formation of a church organization for Jukao a matter to be completed in the near future. During the years spent in China we have learned much through bitter experience and we are ready to <u>face facts</u>. We admit we were hasty and ill-advised (in 1923). Practically all of those persons there have moved away. The wise elders of the Huai Tong Presbytery were right when they advised against organizing a church unless there were at least fifteen local Christians who could be accepted as charter members. The Lord kept us from making such a serious mistake at such an early stage in our work.[21]

A Small Acorn

The missionaries went to China to establish a church, but they had no clear idea about how to achieve their goal. They knew that first

[19] Figures come from "Zhang lao hui Huaidong chu hui di wu ci ji lu" (Minutes from the meeting of the fifth annual Huaidong Presbytery meeting), held in Yancheng, Jiangsu Province, Oct. 29-Nov. 2, 1924.

[20] "Minutes of Mission Meeting," Nov. 2, 1925, Art. 8, CRWM folder.

[21] "Church Organization Report," Dec. 1933, 4, CRWM folder.

of all they needed to make converts, since there were few Christians in Rugao. There were different avenues open to them to do that, one of them being through educational activities. While they saw education as a way to make converts, even more importantly, the missionaries viewed education as a way to train the children of Christians.

From the earliest days, education had proved to be an important aspect of Protestant missions in China. Initially missions promoted education for some basic reasons: to make converts, to provide a place where Chinese parents could send their children to school to gain literacy without being subject to Confucian indoctrination, and to train Chinese assistants.[22] Later, mission education promoted literacy among the common people, education and equality for women, the abolition of arranged marriages, and student organizations dedicated to advancing physical education and moral instruction.[23] From 1905 on, after the faltering Qing dynasty had abolished the millennia-old state examination system used for selecting government officials in favor of instituting Western-style education as a means to modernize the country, missionary schools enjoyed a measure of popularity. They provided a modern education for Chinese students not able to study overseas. They also provided the best English-language instruction in the country. In the first decade of the twentieth century, there were about two thousand Protestant schools in the country, mostly primary schools, but including forty to fifty middle schools and six institutions of higher learning (i.e., colleges or universities), educating approximately 40,000 Chinese students.[24] In just two decades, the number of Chinese children enrolled in Christian schools jumped from 40,000 in 1900 to 200,000 in 1920. During this period Yanching University (Yenching) was also established by a consortium of mission groups, becoming one of the premier institutions of higher learning in the country during the Republican period.

On their early visits to Rugao, the missionaries had found no Christian school in the city. However, by the time they moved there in the fall of 1923, a member of the east gate chapel, who worked at the post office, had opened a small school and begun teaching twenty boys and girls in grades one through four.[25] Though the postal worker had

[22] Jessie Lutz, *Chinese Politics and Christian Missions: The Anti-Christian Movements of 1920-1928* (Notre Dame: Cross Cultural Pub., 1988), 8.
[23] Philip West, *Yenching University and Sino-Western Relations, 1916-1952* (Cambridge: Harvard Univ. Press, 1976), 6.
[24] Lutz, *Chinese Politics*, 8.
[25] According to Lenore Barkan, this kind of "old-style" education was quite common in Rugao County. In 1930, of the 400,000 people who "recognized

a limited education himself, the missionaries noted, he did his "best to train his pupils in the use of the Chinese language, especially with a view to enabling them to read the Bible."[26]

Though laudable, this small effort by a poorly educated chapel member clearly did not meet the mission's goals for educational work. The missionaries had much higher views of education than merely as a means for evangelism or even for teaching literacy for the purpose of reading the Bible. Though their original party did not include a missionary specially trained for educational work, De Korne argued in a *Banner* article that in order to do educational work well, the mission would have to proceed on a "high class basis." "Nothing less than an A.B. will do for those who come out for this line of work"; in fact, wrote De Korne, an "M.A. or a Ph.D. would not be wasted upon this field."[27] Education on the mission field was an important task.

Education was important because it was fundamental to Christian Reformed identity. It had even been given as a reason for some of the Dutch immigrants' flight to America in the mid-nineteenth century. Some of those immigrants were determined to start Christian day schools, a freedom they had not enjoyed in the Netherlands.[28] Initially, preserving their Dutch identity was an important aspect of starting schools in America, many parents being concerned that loss of the mother tongue would also eventually result in the loss of religious identity.[29] Later, however, when church leaders began seeing a decline in the religious practice of public schools, there were even more calls for churches to establish schools that were Christian, biblical, and Reformed. In 1898 the denomination's synod weighed in on the subject, stating that "positive Christian instruction was involved in the Bible command about the training of children in the fear of the Lord, as well as in the promise made by parents at the baptism of their children."[30]

---

characters" (probably meaning just barely functionally literate), 40,000 had attended only a primary school and of those 30,000 had attended a middle school. The rest had been taught at the county's many private academies or gentry-led institutions. See Lenore Barkan, "Nationalists, Communists, and Rural Leaders: Political Dynamics in a Chinese County, 1927-1937," Ph.D. diss. (Univ. of Washington, 1983), 45.

[26] John De Korne, "Facing the Educational Situation," pt. 2, *Banner* 58 (Dec. 21, 1923): 780.

[27] Ibid., pt. 1, 764.

[28] Beets, *The Christian Reformed Church in North America* (Grand Rapids: Eastern Avenue Book Store, 1923), 138-39.

[29] Zwaanstra, *Reformed Thought and Experience*, 135.

[30] Beets, *Christian Reformed Church*, 142-43.

As the Christian school movement grew, denominational leaders came to see Christian education as a distinctive element of the Reformed tradition that could be traced back to John Calvin's teaching on covenant theology. Since in the New Testament baptism had replaced Old Testament circumcision as a sign and a seal of God's covenant promises to his people, the leaders argued that the children of Christian parents were included in God's covenant promises. Christian parents thus had a biblical obligation to instruct their baptized, covenant children in the fear of the Lord.[31] Parents had the primary obligation for instructing covenant children, but the church had a responsibility as well. When an infant was baptized in a Christian Reformed Church, the members of the congregation vowed to do their utmost to nurture her and instruct her in the Christian faith. This obligation included establishing Christian day schools, which, though run by parents, were mandated as part of each church's ministry. By 1922, there were seventy-five Christian Reformed schools, with three hundred teachers and an enrollment of eleven thousand children.[32]

Christian day schools performed a number of functions in Christian Reformed communities. They sheltered covenant children from spiritual and moral danger.[33] They also played a role in the salvation of covenant children. In Christian schools, Christian Reformed children learned of their sinful condition, the path of redemption in Jesus Christ, and the necessity of spiritual rebirth. Through the process of inculcation, the children also learned Christian principles (i.e., Christian Reformed doctrine and practice). For these reasons, salvation and indoctrination, Christian schools were important in Christian Reformed communities, but there was also a loftier ideal behind the movement. Christian Reformed schools, in obtaining their highest ideals, strove to interpret "all of learning in the light of God's revelation."[34] That is to say, Christian education attempted to

[31] Kromminga, *Christian Reformed Church*, 125. Kromminga traces Calvin's views on covenantal fulfillment of the Old Testament in the New Testament to book IV, chap. XVI, sect. iii of Calvin's *Institutes of the Christian Religion.*

[32] Beets, *Christian Reformed Church*, 142. Based on membership figures found in Kromminga, in 1920 probably about 31 percent of the 245 CRC churches supported a Christian school, with possibly 20 percent of the denomination's children attending them. See Kromminga, *Christian Reformed Church*, Appendix V, "Numerical Growth of the Christian Reformed Church," 235.

[33] Zwaanstra, *Reformed Thought and Experience*, 133.

[34] Kromminga, *Christian Reformed Church*, 121.

understand God's general revelation in nature and history through the special revelation of the Bible.

The Christian Reformed missionaries took their views of Christian education with them to China. Writing from Rugao, John De Korne called the Christian Reformed vision of Christian education "our distinctively Reformed stamp that we love to put on all our work." The need for Christian education for covenant children was, in his mind, just as important on the mission field as at home:

> The teaching in our chapels may be ever so sound, but what kind of a jumbled-up mind will our converts have if all of their other education is received from non-Christian sources? It is easy enough to affirm in our chapels that truth is from God, but we will never be able to give anything that resembles a demonstration of it unless we or other missions establish schools on a Christian basis. We feel the need of Christian schools for the proper development of our Christian life at home; China demands the same thing.[35]

In keeping with their vision, the missionaries had big plans for Christian education in Rugao, but they believed that they could take care of other tasks and gradually realize their educational plans. By the end of 1924, they had made a start, opening a small school in the west gate chapel, adjacent to the newly established mission hospital where Mrs. Dai, the wife of the hospital evangelist, taught ten students in the afternoon. This small beginning was still far from their grand vision for Christian education; the mission eventually hoped to enlarge the school to eight Chinese teachers with twenty-five students enrolled in the lower primary grades, thirty students in the higher primary grades, and twenty students in middle school. Along the lines of their own schools in the United States, the missionaries wanted their school to be Christian-parent run and primarily for educating the children of Christians.

The missionaries' educational plans took on added urgency the next year, in 1925, when the mission discovered that the Episcopal mission in Yangzhou planned to open a school in the Rugao City in the fall. Members of the Rugao gentry had "urgently" invited the Episcopal mission to open a school and had offered them a large tract of land for constructing a building.[36] Since the Episcopal mission had no other

---

[35]   De Korne, "Facing the Educational Situation in Jukao," pt. 2, 781.
[36]   B. L. Ancell to De Korne, April 25, 1925, De Korne, personal folder.

work in the city, the Christian Reformed missionaries immediately wrote the National Christian Council asking for clarification about comity issues. The Episcopal school never materialized, most likely because of the turmoil that descended that summer on Christian institutions following the May Thirtieth Incident in Shanghai.[37] Despite its own misgivings about timing, the mission appointed a new missionary, Wilhemina (Mina) Kalsbeek, to serve on a committee with one of the Rugao Christians "to investigate the possibility of opening a Christian primary school for the children of Rugao Christians."[38]

In October of 1925, the mission resolved to open a school for the children of Rugao Christians. Following the procedures of Christian Reformed schools at home, the mission's resolution included forming a school board of parents, though with a member of the mission on the board to serve as treasurer, and the approval of a $250 budget to cover the first year's costs.[39] After a Christian school board had been formed, the Christian-parent board asked that Lee Huizenga be appointed to serve as the mission representative and treasurer. To help get the effort off the ground, the mission planned to erect a building on the hospital plot, furnish the equipment, and give the school board use of the facility. Though a humble beginning, Henry Beets admitted to *Banner* readers, he reminded them that "tall oaks from small acorns grow."[40]

The Christians in Rugao, however, were not ready for Christian Reformed-style Christian education. Just one month later the mission received a letter from "the Chinese Christians stating that the School Board appointed by them had resigned because of complications."[41]

---

[37] On May 30, 1925, British police opened fire on student protesters in the Shanghai International Settlement, killing eleven and wounding twenty. The ensuing national outrage brought Christian educational work in the country to a standstill. For details about the May Thirtieth Incident, see Jonathan Spence, *The Search for Modern China*, 2nd ed. (New York: Norton, 1990), 340ff.

[38] On the advice of the National Christian Council, the mission decided in August 1925 to drop the discussion of Christian education policy and discontinue the Christian school committee. Two months later, however, at its October meeting, the mission reversed its decision and appointed Kalsbeek to proceed with opening a Christian school. See "Minutes of Mission Meeting," Aug. 1 and Oct. 5, 1925, Arts. 6 and Art. 12, CRWM folder.

[39] "Minutes of Mission Meeting," Nov. 2, 1925, Art. 8: a., b., and c., CRWM folder.

[40] Beets, "The Educational Situation in China," *Banner* 61 (Jan. 22, 1926): 36.

[41] "Minutes of Mission Meeting," Feb. 1, 1926, Art. 9, CRWM folder. There is

Disappointed but undeterred about the loss of parental backing, the mission appointed Kalsbeek to take charge of the effort to establish a school and gave her permission to provide lodgings for a Bible woman and a schoolteacher.

Mina Kalsbeek, a single woman who had come to Rugao in 1924 after a year of intensive language study in Nanjing, worked hard during the next nine months to get the school off the ground. First, she negotiated the services of a Chinese woman named Wu to help with women's work and teach in the primary school when it opened. Then, both for evangelistic outreach and to recruit children for the primary school, Kalsbeek and Wu organized a summer school for July and August of 1926. The summer school curriculum had five periods and a recess, during which Wu taught the children to play games, hoping that if they could "get a group of children to enjoy wholesome games during the early evening hours it will discourage gambling, which seems to be their only sport."[42]

At the end of the summer of 1926, the school held a closing program attended by more than two hundred, with, according to Kalsbeek, at least one parent per family.[43] At the program all of the children's handiwork was displayed, and each guest received a package of sweets at the end of the program. During September, Kalsbeek and Wu called on the children's homes to get their parents' permission to attend school. In several homes, they had opportunities "to witness for Christ" as well as to talk about the purpose of their visit. They "made it very plain that the children would be taught the Christian religion as well as the regular courses in the government schools, but there seemed no objection on that score."[44]

In the middle of September 1926, a little primary school opened with twenty students: seven in the first grade, six in the second grade, and seven in the fifth grade. More children wanted to attend, but Kalsbeek and Wu deliberately kept the beginning enrollment low to insure they got off to a good start. Wu taught most of the classes, with Kalsbeek teaching the English class and the first two grades of arithmetic. An evangelist from the hospital, Zhou Luqing (Chow Loh

no indication what those complications were. Probably they had something to do with the turmoil of May Thirtieth Incident and the uncomfortable position in which it put the parents in relation to the missionaries.

[42] Wilhemina Kalsbeek to Beets, Aug. 1, 1926, Kalsbeek CRWM folder.
[43] Kalsbeek to Beets, Sept. 1, 1926, Kalsbeek, CRWM folder.
[44] Kalsbeek to Beets, Oct. 1, 1926, Kalsbeek, CRWM folder.

Ching), taught drawing and handiwork. In the mornings the students attended chapel, and in the afternoons they studied the Bible, a class taught by Mrs. Chen, the wife of one of the mission's former evangelists. In addition to providing education, Kalsbeek believed that the school's Christian atmosphere would produce "some fine results in Christian character."[45] She also believed that the mission would have "closer contact for evangelistic work in each non-Christian family represented in the school."

Turnips and Onions

The educational program really had no chance to succeed. The missionaries attempted to start educational work during a period when the tide of Chinese opposition to Christianity reached a climax. After the Qing government had abolished the two-thousand-year-old imperial exams in favor of Western-style education in 1905, missionaries were at the forefront of an educational boom. While maintaining their evangelistic agenda, many missionary-run schools expanded their curricula to meet the needs of the "new" China. In the second decade of the twentieth century, especially during the period of the so-called "New Culture Movement," between 1916 and 1919, many Chinese intellectuals showed a genuine appreciation for Christianity and for missionary-sponsored education. Influenced by the Western liberal tradition, the early reformers of the Republican period supported religious expression as a part of civic freedom. Judging religion on a strictly utilitarian basis, they saw Christianity in a favorable light because Jesus Christ's life was an inspiring example of ideal humanity.[46] This appreciation continued after the watershed May Fourth Movement of 1919, but only for a time.[47]

After 1920, appreciation and sympathy for Christianity was replaced by hostility, when more and more intellectuals, influenced by an all-pervading scientific rationalism, began to regard all forms of religion as superstition and bad for Chinese. Ironically, the first

---

[45] Ibid.
[46] George A. Hood, *Mission Accomplished? The English Presbyterian Mission in Lingtung, South China* (Frankfurt: Verlag Peter Lang, 1986), 207.
[47] The "May Fourth Movement" refers to the student protest that took place May 4, 1919, against the Treaty of Versailles' provisions to hand over Germany's claim of Shandong Province to Japan. The protests sparked a period of iconoclastic intellectual ferment that led to the adoption of the vernacular in Chinese literature and interest in Western cultural and political ideas and models. See Spence, *Search*, 271-72, and 310-19.

organized "anti-Christian Movement" of 1922 sparked more interest in Christianity than hostility. A second "anti-Christian movement" in 1924, however, fanned flames of opposition that burst into a bonfire following the May Thirtieth Incident in Shanghai in 1925. The incident ignited the growing passions in China against the Western presence in the country. Much of the animosity toward religion and missionaries came to be centered in the "Campaign for the Restoration of Educational Rights."[48] This campaign attempted to bring missionary schools under government control and end their compulsory religious education. By 1927, the Nationalist government was promulgating a new set of regulations that made running missionary schools very complicated, if not virtually impossible.

In China's big cities, the anti-Christian, antiforeign sentiments were most virulent, but even cities off the beaten path, such as Rugao, were not untouched by the currents sweeping the country. Until 1925, the Christian Reformed missionaries experienced very little hostility in Rugao and no organized opposition, despite being the first foreigners to live in the city. But in April of 1925, even before the May Thirtieth Incident, the rising tide of opposition showed itself in Rugao. At the beginning of the month, Harry Dykstra mentioned in a letter that a branch of the anti-Christian Movement had been recently organized in Rugao, though he dismissed the movement as "just a bunch of students spurred on from some other source."[49] These students had published "some nasty things" about the mission in a local paper, but Dykstra did not believe the mission's work would suffer because of the opposition. His outlook proved too optimistic.

The same month that an anti-Christian movement was organized in Rugao, children disrupted Mina Kalsbeek's afternoon activities for school children held in one of the city chapels. Attendance at the after-school classes had been growing steadily, and the classes had been going smoothly when one day some of the children had become "rowdy." Finally, "after trying every known method of persuasion without getting the desired result," Kalsbeek asked the disruptive students to leave. Twenty left the chapel but stood outside calling for the remaining fifteen students, who were now behaving, to come outside. The next day the "good" students came but would not enter the building. After questioning the children, Kalsbeek discovered that their teachers in the government school had forbidden them to go into the church school,

48   Lutz, *Chinese Politics*, 5 and 160ff.
49   H. Dykstra to Beets, April 5, 1925, H. Dykstra, CRWM folder.

even threatening not to promote them if they did.[50] The government schoolteachers bribed other students to stay away from the chapel school. Soon no one was coming at all, since, as Kalsbeek reported, some of the "once faithful and enthusiastic children turned spies and made it impossible for the others to attend."

Because their teachers had not forbidden them to attend other church activities, some of the children still attended Sunday school and an open-air gymnastics class held twice per week. Not daring to "come openly for fear of the other students," six older girls came secretly to Kalsbeek's house for private English lessons. These students continued to come, in part, because one of their teachers, a Christian, encouraged them to do so.

A month later, after the May Thirtieth Incident took place, opposition to the mission increased dramatically. Describing the days immediately following the incident in Shanghai, Harry Dykstra wrote, "Mammoth parades were staged through the streets of the city here in which all the students large and small took part....Everyone carried a banner, some with very sensible phrases, others with very obnoxious expressions."[51] The next day, however, when Dykstra went to teach his weekly English class at the high school, he was surprised to find all of his students in attendance. The class spent the first hour going through its English lesson and "the next hour going over the ugly Shanghai situation and its relation to us here in Rugao." After class, on his way to the mission's north gate chapel, Dykstra passed a "mile-long" solemn procession of schoolchildren and met a lecture group gathered on the street denouncing the mission. Some of the students were the same ones whom he had just finished teaching in the high school. When they saw their teacher, Dykstra wrote, they "seemed to lose courage and decided to call a finish for the day."

Arriving at the chapel, Dykstra noticed a student table set up on the porch of the big city temple across the street. Realizing that much of the crowds' invective was directed at the chapel, he crossed the street to listen. When some of his former students from the normal school recognized him, they began firing questions at him:

> [They asked] Whether I expected them to believe that we were spending money in their city for homes, chapels, and hospital with no intention of enriching ourselves.... Whether our preaching of a God of love agreed with our actions of cruelty and oppression.

[50] Kalsbeek to Beets, April 30, 1925, Kalsbeek, CRWM folder.
[51] H. Dykstra to Beets, June 9, 1925, Dykstra, CRWM folder.

Why a fleet of American warships was always hovering around China's coast or anchoring in her harbors. Why we who preached such a fine gospel allowed signs in the Shanghai parks where only dogs and Chinese are expressly prohibited to enter.[52]

Standing on the temple porch, Dykstra answered the students. He noted first of all that the mission deplored the bloodshed in Shanghai. He also commended the students for their mourning. He then launched into an apologetic:

I gave a short resume of the long standing friendship between China and America which was in danger of being utterly destroyed by present day developments; of the insidious propaganda of the Bolshiviks [sic] who are using the Chinese student classes as tools to arouse resentment against America; of the long struggle the missions have already carried on against unequal treaties and leased territories obtained by force; of the difference between governments and missions, and finally, I pointed to the happy relations which had been established between us as American missionaries and the people of Jukao [Rugao] and to the record of our activities for more than one year in their own city with which activities they were all acquainted.[53]

While Dykstra was speaking the crowd grew until the temple courtyard was packed. By the time he had finished speaking, the crowd's tension had been diffused, and "the students made protestations of friendship and assured us [the missionaries] that they had no quarrel with us." That evening the electric wires to the chapel, which had been cut by vandals, were repaired, and a record crowd attended the services. Among those in attendance was the principal of the normal school, along with several other teachers. By the fall of 1925, the anti-foreign, anti-Christian sentiment in Rugao had settled down and student attendance at missionary activities had returned to normal.

A year later, however, mission activities were disrupted again. This time students targeted the mission's Christmas celebrations. In 1924 and 1925, students in the larger treaty ports around the country had disrupted Christmas services, but in Rugao Christmas had remained a curiosity.[54] On the afternoon of Christmas 1926, however, students

[52] Ibid. Beets also recounts this incident in "The Situation in China," *Banner* 60 (July 31, 1925): 484-86.
[53] Ibid.
[54] For descriptions of incidents involving student disruptions at Christmas, see Hood, *Mission Accomplished?*, 239 and 248; Lutz, *Chinese Politics*, 196.

disrupted the mission's festivities in the east gate chapel. When a mob of students appeared at the door, the missionaries quickly blocked the entrance, probably having heard of how students in Wuhan had once burst into a church and had shouted blasphemies from the pulpit.[55] Unable to get inside, the infuriated students hurled projectiles into the chapel, hitting two missionaries in the head with turnips and onions. The students stood outside for about a half hour shouting, "Down with the church," and passing out yellow placards of protest before city officials arrived to break up the disturbance. When they visited the normal school the next day, the missionaries received an apology from school officials and assurances that the disruptions would cease. The normal school officials also expressed their belief that outside influences were behind the disturbances.

The "outside influences" cited by Rugao school officials were very active. Education was a political battleground in Rugao during the 1920s, even without antiforeignism. At the turn of the century, believing that education alone could save the foundering nation, Sha Yuanbing and other local gentry undertook educational reform in Rugao. By the fall of the Qing in 1911, they had established more than 150 schools in the county, most notable among them the Rugao Normal School (with provincial-wide approval), the Rugao Middle School, and the Yizhong Commercial School.[56] Most of the teachers in these schools, like Sha himself, were classically educated members of the local gentry who promoted an "ultra-conservative" education.[57] Following the May Fourth Movement of 1919, Rugao students began increasingly to challenge the local gentry's conservative ideas of education. After the May Thirtieth Incident, the clashes over education turned to open warfare, with both the Nationalist Party and the Communist Party using student agitation to bolster their own agendas. Sha Yuanbing and others of the Rugao gentry withdrew from public life.[58]

---

[55] See S. Dykstra to home congregation, Dec. 29, 1926, and Feb. 12, 1927, S. Dykstra, CRWM folder; Nicholas De Vries to home congregation, Jan. 11, 1927, Nicholas De Vries, CRWM folder.

[56] Barkan, "Patterns of Power," 220. For the dates on the opening of each school, see *Rugao Xian zhi*, 18.

[57] Wang Haoran, "Rugao Xian Xianzheng Gaikuang" (Conditions of Rugao County Government), *Jiangsu Xunkan* (Jiangsu Trimonthly) 5 (Oct. 11, 1928): 64.

[58] Sha Yuanbing became so disillusioned with reforms that he retreated from public life and immersed himself in the study of Buddhism. According to Barkan, this period marked the end of the local gentry's hold on the city. See Barkan, "Patterns of Power," 207.

Given the explosive nature of education in Rugao in the 1920s, and especially in 1925 and 1926, it is hardly surprising that the China Mission's educational experiment encountered difficulties. When the missionaries were evacuated from the city a couple of months later, the mission's attempts to establish Christian Reformed-style education came to a halt. Though Kalsbeek resumed modest educational efforts when the mission reopened in 1929, educational regulations by the Nanjing government in the late 1920s and 1930s made it impossible for the mission to open a school along the lines the missionaries had initially envisioned. Christian education, as the missionaries understood it, was not possible in Rugao. Not until after World War II, with the easing of Nanjing's regulations, would the mission make another serious attempt to promote educational work.

A Staggering Blow

Education was not the only battleground that the mission experienced in the 1920s, nor was it the most heated. During 1926, a conflict between the mission and its church workers developed when several of the evangelists went on strike demanding higher wages, an incident that tore the China mission apart as China teetered on the brink of civil war.

By the mid-1920s, the mission was employing seven evangelists, three Bible women, and two colporteurs. The mission hospital also employed a Chinese doctor and several other workers. Because there was not an established church in Rugao, none of these workers came from the Rugao area. They came to the city through a variety of ways, but usually through letters of introduction from another mission. Though one evangelist came from the Baptist mission, most of the others came from Presbyterian missions in Jiangnan, Jiangbei, and the adjacent provinces of Anhui and Shandong.[59]

With the exception of Song Liansen (Song Lien Sen), the colporteur, all of the China Mission's church workers had received some level of education. The church worker with the lowest level of training had taken the Southern Presbyterian Mission's Bible training class in Yancheng, and the worker with the highest level of training held

---

[59]   The lone Baptist may have been Hua Fuquan, who was working at the Baptist chapel in Rugao when the CRC missionaries visited the city in the fall of 1921. See *Rugao Xian zhi*, 164. The status of the Baptists' presence after the opening of the CRC mission is uncertain.

degrees from both college and seminary.[60] Three of the mission's seven evangelists had graduated from the Southern Presbyterian-affiliated Nanking Theological Seminary.[61] One evangelist had graduated from middle school and had received some training at a Bible school, and the other four workers had only attended middle school.[62] Of the Bible women, one named Chen, the wife of a former evangelist, had graduated from a Nanking Seminary training class and had worked in a church for six years.[63] All of the workers, with the exception of the colporteurs, were probably between their mid-twenties and mid-thirties.[64] With the exception of several women hospital workers, all of the Christian workers were married with children.[65]

Salary issues plagued the China Mission from its earliest days.[66] Part of the mission's problem was inexperience and a desire to be fair to the church workers and to the Chinese church. The mission wanted to pay its workers a fair, living wage, but it also wanted to keep the cost of salaries low enough so that Chinese believers could eventually

---

[60] See "Minutes of Special Mission Meeting," Dec. 8, 1926, 1, Art. 4, CRWM folder.

[61] Wang Aitang, Dai Ruiling, and Chen Fang were all graduates of Nanking Theological Seminary. See "Second Annual Report of the Christian Reformed Hospital, 1925," 1-2, Huizenga CRWM files; S. Dykstra to home congregation, June 5, 1926, S. Dykstra, CRWM folder.

[62] For Zhou Luqing's educational level, see "Minutes of Special Mission Meeting," Dec. 8, 1926, 2, Art. 13, CRWM folder.

[63] Kalsbeek to Beets, Nov. 1, 1926, Kalsbeek, CRWM folder.

[64] This estimate is based on graduation dates of the hospital workers and Wang Aitang's graduation from Nanking Seminary in the early 1920s.

[65] Dec. 1926 salary schedule lists no single male workers.

[66] According to a study of church workers completed by Frank Price in 1930s, compensation was a sensitive topic for many of the church workers in the Jiangsu/Anwei region. In his survey of pastors, evangelists, and Bible workers in the region, sixteen reported having savings while seventeen others reported having debts as large as three to four months of salary. Others complained their salaries were too low, with one worker even reporting that he received his salary irregularly. Many believed they should be compensated at least at the level of other rural social workers, such as primary school teachers, agricultural extension workers, supervisors of cooperatives, or village and county officials. In his conclusions, Southern Presbyterian missionary Frank Price agreed with the respondents' complaints, arguing that Chinese evangelists working in the countryside made a sacrifice and that "an income inadequate for his family needs and for his own advancement and that of his children often causes him worry and impairs the efficiency of his work." See Frank Wilson Price, *The Rural Church in China* (New York: Agricultural Missions, 1948), 123ff.

assume responsibility for their salaries. For the sake of flexibility, the mission initially gave each missionary a "free hand in the matter of salaries and allowances," allowing each missionary employer to pay a salary commensurate to each worker's training, experience, and task.[67] This approach would work, they reasoned, as long as the missionaries conferred with each other in order "to forestall jealousies that would certainly arise among them [the evangelists] if their salaries were not uniform." But when the missionary in charge of the hospital, Lee Huizenga, paid his hospital evangelists more than the church evangelists were receiving, "the disparity caused unhappiness in the minds of the [other] Chinese evangelists, and these, in turn, made it embarrassing for the foreigners who employed them."[68]

To solve the problem of disparities, the mission gathered information from other missions and came up with a salary schedule and a policy "as to the best methods for hiring and dismissing Mission employees."[69] A year later, in early December 1926, the mission drafted a letter to send to its church workers explaining the new schedule. At the heart of the schedule was the mission's belief that "those who preach the Gospel have a right to live by the Gospel." The mission's letter explained that the new schedule was based entirely on level of training, since that, unlike basing salary on ability, was an objective, measurable standard upon which to base an individual evangelist's salary. Moreover, they added, the salary scale was adjusted to the economic crisis facing China, to allow each worker to be able to meet socially all the classes among whom they labored, and with consideration of neighboring pay scales, since, the mission reasoned, there should not be a big discrepancy between the salaries of workers in an area.

The new salary schedule had nine levels. Level one was for workers with only Bible training class education and provided for a monthly salary of fifteen yuan, with annual salary increases up to five years, when a worker would obtain the highest salary for level one, nineteen yuan per month.[70] At the top of the schedule, level-nine evangelists who

67 "Minutes of Mission Meeting," April 21, 1927, 2, CRWM folder.
68 Ibid.
69 "Minutes of Mission Meeting," Nov. 30, 1925, Art. 9. From minutes and letters, it appears that the mission had to release several evangelists and at least one nurse during the early years in Rugao. All of these situations were related to theft (i.e., taking money or items from the mission). See H. Dykstra to Beets, April 20, 1925, H. Dykstra, CRWM folder; Angie Haan to Neland church, Nov. 24, 1925, Angie Haan, CRWM folder.
70 "Minutes," Dec. 8, 1926, 1ff., CRWM folder.

had graduated from college and seminary started at thirty-two yuan per month and could obtain forty yuan per month within five years. Bible women were placed on the same salary schedule as single male workers.

The schedule also provided benefits. The evangelists were entitled to a furnished house, a room or house being considered "furnished" when it contained "the necessary heavy furniture."[71] Workers with children under the age of fifteen were eligible to receive an additional two yuan per month, per child, with an additional amount for each child in school. The mission would cover all medical fees for workers and their families, provided the mission doctor had approved the expenses. The new schedule included paid vacation of up to three weeks and included travel allowances for evangelists whose families lived outside Rugao. If an evangelist did not wish to take a vacation, he could redeem a portion of his vacation for pay.

In explaining the new salary schedule to their church workers, the missionaries admitted that none of them was thoroughly satisfied with every provision, but they stated "that the schedule as a whole is as fair a one we can frame with the information we have and the experience we have passed through."[72] The letter also expressed regret that the new schedule would reduce the salary of some of the mission's evangelists but added that "this reduction" should "not be attributed to lack of appreciation for the splendid service you have rendered. It is due to the fact that we had not previously fully realized the implications of our former financial arrangements." Finally, the missionaries expressed

[71] Ibid., Art. 17, 2, CRWM folder.
[72] China Mission to "our Chinese Evangelists," Dec. 31, 1926; copied in "Minutes of Mission Meeting," April 21, 1927, 5, CRWM folder. On balance, the schedule compares favorably with what Price found in the Yangzi Delta area in the 1930s. According to records of salaries paid to their seven evangelists and one Bible woman in 1930, the lowest monthly pay was twenty-two and the highest was fifty-two. The average for the entire group was almost thirty-eight (37.62), with four receiving between thirty-five and forty-five. The mission's provision of other benefits also compares favorably with Price's survey. While sixty-two of the sixty-eight surveyed by Price received some form of housing, only nine received an extra allowance or stipend for their children, and only four received help with medical expenses. The China Mission deliberately decided to compensate its workers just a bit higher than other workers in the region. See Richard H. Pousma, *An Eventful Year in the Orient* (Grand Rapids: Eerdmans, 1927), 149. For evangelists and Bible woman salaries, see De Korne, Dykstra, Kalsbeek, and Smit "Monthly Reports," March-Nov., 1930, CRWM folders. For comparison with Price, see *Rural Church*, 130ff.

their sincere hope that none of the evangelists would sever his or her relations with the mission over the revision of salaries.

At the end of their letter, listing some of the considerations that had influenced their decision to revise the schedule, the missionaries stated their most important concern:

> The strongest consideration that moved us to revise our schedule is that which looks to the ultimate self-support of the Chinese church. Missions are only temporary organizations, and their success should make them superfluous. The fact that the Church in China is almost entirely financed by foreign money has furnished the anti-Christian movement with one of its strongest arguments. They say they cannot possibly understand why millions of foreign money should be spent in China, if the foreigners have no imperialistic motives. The argument is not sound, but it has taken hold of the minds of many Chinese nevertheless. The most effective answer that the Christians of China can give to such propaganda is to take forward steps at once towards supporting their own Christian work, thus reducing the amount of foreign money that needs to be spent. Now it is evident that the higher the salaries of foreign-supported evangelists are, the more difficult it will be for the Chinese Church to take over this financial responsibility. Thus our strongest motive in revising the salary schedule is the ultimate welfare of the Chinese Church.[73]

After passing a resolution adopting the new schedule, the mission immediately used it to adjust the salary of one evangelist, deciding that Zhou Daqing (Chow Ta Ching), the evangelist working in the north gate chapel, should be "classed under No. 4, i.e., Middle School plus Bible School."[74]

Even before they had received the new schedule, the evangelists reacted against it. On December 28, 1926, at a "special" meeting with nineteen missionaries present, the mission read a letter from its evangelists stating that they had formed an organization called the "Society of Chinese Evangelists" (*hua jia shi hui*) for the purpose of fellowship and to become better acquainted with each other's work."[75]

---

[73] "Mission Minutes," April 21, 1927, 6.

[74] Ibid., Art. 13, 2, CRWM folder. It is unclear whether Zhou's status was elevated or demoted in status on the salary schedule. Since he was one of the four strikers, it is probably safe to assume the latter.

[75] "Minutes of Special Mission Meeting," Dec. 28, 1926, CRWM folder. By

Field meeting, December 1926. With the language students from Nanjing and the Rugao missionaries, this was the largest field assembly in the thirty-year history of the China Mission, and the one during which the Rugao evangelists went on strike demanding higher wages: (*bottom step*) Richard Pousma; (*second step*) John De Korne, Yvonne Pousma; (*third step*) Jacob Kamps, Isabel Kamps; (*fourth step*) Cornelia Dykstra, Trena Selles, Caroline De Vries, Lillian Bode; (*fifth step*) Dora Smit, Nettie De Korne, Wilhemina Kalsbeek, Nicholas De Vries; (*sixth step*) Lee Huizenga, Matilda Huizenga; (*top step*) Albert Smit, Simon Dykstra, and Albert Selles.

The evangelists then requested that the mission announce to the association within three days, "if possible," its decision regarding the salary schedule. They also requested that two of their number be allowed

---

1926 there were twelve CRC missionaries living in Rugao (five families and two single women) and seven missionaries (three families and one single woman) who had recently arrived in China to study Chinese in Nanjing. All of the missionaries and their families gathered in Rugao in December of 1926 for meetings and the Christmas holidays. Ironically, as it turned out, this was the largest meeting of CRC missionaries in Rugao during the denomination's entire thirty-year presence in the city.

to address the whole mission on the matter of the salary schedule, since "a letter, whether Chinese or English, could not express the ideas so fully as a committee could." Finally, the evangelists suggested that a new organization be formed to include missionaries and evangelists from other parts of Jiangsu, specifically Yancheng to the north and Zhenjiang south of the Yangzi, for the purpose of discussing "matters pertaining to the advance of the work."[76]

The mission responded to the evangelists' letter by welcoming the formation of the new society and expressing "hope that it will prove to be a useful organ in promoting the work of preaching the Gospel in the Rugao community." The missionaries also informed the evangelists that the mission stood by its decision to submit a copy of the new salary schedule to all of the evangelists as soon as possible and it welcomed two members to its next meeting, to be held in the home of John De Korne on January 10. At this meeting, the missionaries promised, they would discuss further a conference of Jiangsu workers, something which, they believed, had "splendid opportunities."

Four of their evangelists appeared at the next mission meeting, held January 31, 1927, "to present their case with respect to the revised salary schedule."[77] One of the evangelists, Dai Ruiling (Tai Suei Ling), worked in the hospital; the others, Zhou Daqing (Chow Ta Ching), Zhang Hongqing (Chang Hong Ching), and Wang Aitang (Wang Ai T'ang), all worked in the chapels.[78] After explaining their concerns and suggesting some changes in the new schedule, the evangelists left so that the missionaries could discuss the proposals. The mission decided to raise the limit for children's allowances from fifteen years of age to eighteen years of age, "or when the child goes to work." With respect to vacation, the mission increased the amount of time allowed to one month and retained the travel allowance, but removed the exchange of vacation time for salary.

[76]   According to a report about the Huaidong Presbytery's Oct. 1926 meeting in Dongtai (about sixty miles north of Rugao), two of the CRC mission's evangelists, Dai Ruiling (Tai Suei Ling) and Zhang Hongqing (Chang Hong Ching), had applied to take Presbytery's examination for licensure. After being interviewed about their "personal faith and doctrinal positions," both were accepted as students under the care of the presbytery and given permission to take an admittance examination at the body's next meeting scheduled for the fall of 1927. "Mission Minutes," Dec. 26, 1926, CRWM folder.

[77]   "Minutes of Mission Meeting," Jan. 31, 1927, CRWM folder.

[78]   Perhaps because of differences in dialects, the missionaries spelled Dai's given name Suei (Sui) rather "Rui," the correct transliteration of the Chinese character for his name.

Although the missionaries showed some flexibility on these items, they rejected the evangelists' request for higher salaries, answering that "since they [the evangelists] presented no arguments which we had not previously considered, we shall maintain our schedule as published."[79] The mission also added a policy for severance. If an evangelist or other worker wished to leave, he was requested to notify the mission one month in advance. If the mission wished to "sever connections" with an evangelist, the mission agreed to notify the evangelist and pay one month's salary beyond the month of notification and pay travel expenses back to the location from which he had come to Rugao.

On February 1, 1927, the day before the lunar New Year, the mission met to discuss another salary issue. After handling a few minor items, the missionaries waded into a salary dispute with one of their hospital evangelists, Zhou Luqing (Chow Loh Ching). In December, Zhou had made "charges arising out of treatment he received while in the employ" of the mission.[80] To answer him, the mission had formed a committee to investigate Zhou's claim that he had not been paid during the month of August 1926, when he had suffered an attack of appendicitis. Though divided on some aspects of the case, the committee of three recommended unanimously to pay Zhou his salary for that month, since he had been forced to go to another hospital and had permission to do so from the hospital superintendent, Lee Huizenga. Concerning Zhou's returning late from his vacation in the summers of 1924 and 1925 and during the lunar holiday in the spring 1926, however, the committee ruled that a "deduction of his salary should have been made, but...it should have been done at the time when salary covering the days he was absent was paid, i.e., at the end of the months in which the absences occurred and not from the salary covering the sick leave.[81] The mission instructed hospital superintendent Huizenga to pay evangelist Zhou his back salary.

Two days later, on February 3, the second day of the "Year of the Rabbit," at another "special" meeting, John De Korne presented a

---

[79] Ibid., 8.
[80] "Minutes of Mission Meeting," Dec. 6, 1927, 3, Art. 12, CRWM folder. It is unclear whether or not Zhou was in the employ of the mission when he made these charges. The language suggests that he was not: "A letter was received from Chow Loh Ching containing charges arising out of treatment he received while in our employ." He does not appear to have attended the Jan. 31 meeting, although the vacation policy and the termination policy seem to be in response to his case.
[81] "Minutes of Mission Meeting," Feb. 1, 1927, Art. 7, CRWM folder. Huizenga, to make up for Zhou's taking extra days in 1924 and 1925, decided to dock him for his time off with illness in 1926.

message he had received from four of the mission's evangelists. They informed the group that

(1) The situation in Jukao is very, very dangerous. Foreign women and children should leave immediately. The families of the Chinese evangelists should also leave, as their position is even more dangerous than that of the foreigners.

(2) Unless the mission will raise the salaries, all four of us will resign immediately, and we ask you to balance accounts with us.

(3) Until the salary matter is settled, we will go on strike. We will do no preaching or Sunday School work next Sunday, will not conduct Bible classes, and will not preach in the chapels.[82]

Though stunned, the missionaries decided to call their evangelists' bluff. Strongly expressing their disapproval of the evangelists' actions, especially at "a time like this when the closest possible co-operation between all Christian forces in China is so highly desirable," the mission, believing that its salaries were liberal in comparison with those of other missions, stood by the revised salary schedule and accepted the resignation of all four "to take effect immediately."[83] Taking into consideration the evangelists' concern for the safety of their families, the mission decided to provide all of them with traveling expenses and to pay their salaries for the next two months.

After the mission had accepted their resignations, the four evangelists' solidarity fell apart. Wang Aitang, who had attended the January 31 meeting to discuss the revised salary schedule, claimed that the other three had, unbeknownst to him, included his name on the letter threatening a strike. When he disavowed any association with the strike, the mission "put this on record so as to clear his name of that charge."[84] Another evangelist, Dai Ruiling, who worked with Huizenga at the mission hospital, submitted a written confession stating that the strike had been wrong, but since he would not consent to having his confession made public, the mission severed its relationship with him.[85] The other two evangelists held a farewell service in which they made some "caustic remarks" about the missionaries.

[82] "Minutes of Special Mission Meeting," Feb. 3, 1927, Art. 3, CRWM folder.
[83] Richard Pousma to his family, Feb. 13, 1927, Pousma, CRWM folder.
[84] "Minutes of Mission Meeting," March 9, 1927, Art. 5, CRWM folder.
[85] Five years later, the mission accepted a written apology from Dai and rehired him. See "China Mission Minutes," Dec. 5, 1932, Art. 570, CRWM folder.

Eight or nine of the Rugao inquirers sided with the evangelists and did their best to stir up trouble. All of the missionaries were harassed, but the main target was John De Korne, who the striking evangelists and inquirers believed to be the main force behind the new schedule. De Korne was reviled as "the big devil" and received letters warning him not to go near the chapel, threatening him with a severe beating, with being driven from town, and even with death.[86] One of the agitators sent a letter with De Korne's signature on it and one of his New Year's greetings to the principal of the Rugao high school, calling the man a "dog" and a "devil" and threatening him "with dire consequences if he did not cease his opposition to Christianity in the city." The matter was quickly cleared up, however, after the principal visited De Korne and was convinced "the letter was a forgery." When Albert Smit, an ordained missionary who had also come to China in 1924, discovered who was behind the letters threatening De Korne, the three suspects, perhaps out of embarrassment, fled town.

Soon after the departure of the evangelists, Wang Aitang, who had been exonerated of all connection to the strike, went to John De Korne and another missionary and told them that Lee Huizenga had encouraged the evangelists in their bid for higher salaries. Wang reported that Huizenga had even suggested that the best moment to present their claims would be at the large mission meeting in December 1926, when all of the new missionaries from Nanjing would be in Rugao for the holiday, and "thus giving full impact to their plea for higher wages."[87] According to Wang, Huizenga not only encouraged the evangelists to press for higher wages, he even hinted that they should threaten a strike.[88] Based on Wang's information and that of various sources, the other missionaries concluded that Huizenga

> had intimated to the evangelists that he did not whole-heartedly support the revised salary schedule and…that he intimated to the Chinese evangelists that his fellow missionaries were niggardly while he himself was magnanimous to them but powerless to thwart the decisions of the other members of the mission; all of which served as marked encouragement to the preachers

[86] Pousma, *An Eventful Year*, 149-50. See also L. J. Lamberts, *The Life Story of Dr. Lee S. Huizenga* (Grand Rapids: Eerdmans, 1950), 137-38.

[87] See handwritten note in De Korne personal folder.

[88] See "Minutes of Mission Meeting," Feb. 26 to March 2, 1927, Art. 5, CRWM folder.

to continue their opposition to the point where they finally determined to strike.[89]

When confronted with these accusations, Huizenga stated categorically: I "firmly deny instigating opposition to the mission."[90] He did, however, admit during the initial discussions that he had assured the evangelists that he believed in higher wages, that he supported the evangelists' desire for higher wages, and that he looked south [of the Yangzi River] to determine the level of wages while the other missionaries looked north [to Subei] where wages were lower, and that he had promised Dai Ruiling, the hospital evangelist, "that he would offset the disadvantage of the new salary schedule by reopening a school providing employment for Mrs. Dai."[91]

Through his promotional skills, Huizenga was a widely known and admired missions figure in America, but he had a complicated relationship with his colleagues on the field. With his knack for promoting his own work and propensity to manipulate different sides (mission colleagues, Mission Board, and the consistory of his home congregation, the LaGrave Avenue Christian Reformed Church in Grand Rapids, Michigan) to achieve his own objectives, especially related to his medical mission work, Huizenga reaped increasing animosity from his colleagues in China.[92] Though his colleagues

---

89   "Minutes of Mission Meeting," April 11, 1927, 2, Art. 9, CRWM folder. One of the other hospital employees, Liu Shuying, stated that Huizenga had met with the evangelists and told them, "Do not tell the other foreigners." See De Korne's handwritten notes on the charges leveled by the mission against Huizenga, De Korne, personal folder.

90   These charges and countercharges all took place between Feb. 26 and March 2 in Rugao. But the mission decided not to publish the substance of its discussions about what came to be known as "the Huizenga case" until April. By that time they had all been evacuated to Shanghai. See "Minutes of Mission Meeting," Feb. 26 to March 2, 1927, Art. 5, CRWM folder. Later, in the 1930s, after Huizenga had returned to the field from an extended furlough, he led an effort to expurgate all documents relating to the affair from the mission's files. Though new minutes were written for the 1920s, they were not replaced in Board files.

91   Evangelist Zhou Daqing also corroborated Huizenga's promise to start a school to offset the loss of wages. See De Korne's handwritten notes on the charges leveled by the mission against Huizenga, De Korne, personal folder.

92   There are suggestions that tensions arose between Huizenga and De Korne while they were investigating the location of mission fields over issues related to Huizenga's health and over the division of their fundraising

acknowledged that he had many good qualities ("energy, progressive initiative, foresightedness, and his capacity for making friendships"), he also had a number of "peculiar traits" that proved "irritating," "annoying," and "even embarrassing."[93] Although they "always hoped these things would end," Huizenga's quirks seemed to loom larger in 1926.[94] The charge that he encouraged the evangelists' strike, whether explicitly or implicitly, forced the mission to make a painful decision: Because of his "hyper-individualism, his inability or unwillingness to co-operate, and his repeated failures to subordinate his own plans to those of the mission," the China Mission recommended that after a period of furlough he be stationed on a field "where his tremendous talents could shine without having to work with other missionaries."[95]

A Larger Turmoil

As painful as the China Mission found these events in Rugao, they were mild compared with the turmoil engulfing China. By the end of 1926, the country was on the verge of civil war. After taking over the combined forces of the Guomindang (KMT) and the Chinese Communist Party (CCP) in July of 1926, Chiang Kai-shek mobilized his Northern Expedition troops to push north from Guangzhou (Canton) with the twin goals of eradicating the warlords' hold on the various regions and ultimately unifying the country. These troops took Changsha in Hunan Province the second week of July and then pushed further north, routing the notorious warlord Wu Peifu and taking Wuhan in central China by early October. By late 1926, Chiang Kai-shek had set up headquarters in Nanchang in Jiangxi Province, and the Communist and other left-leaning elements of the Nationalist Party had made Wuhan their stronghold. A growing rift developed between the two factions.

If they were divided in pivotal ideology, the two Nationalist factions were united in their anti-foreign, anti-Christian sentiments, putting foreigners in the country on edge. In January 1927, mobs had

---

responsibilities. See correspondence between Huizenga and De Korne between 1919 and 1920.

[93]   "Mission Minutes," April 21, 1927, CRWM folder.

[94]   In a handwritten note outlining a history of "the Huizenga case," De Korne noted the "Christmas program," "Harry Dykstra's experience," and "the Communion affair" as pertaining to the problems with Huizenga, but he does not explain any of the items, De Korne, personal folder.

[95]   "Minutes of Mission Meeting," April 8, 1927, 1, CRWM folder.

broken through the barricades protecting the foreign-concession area of Hankou (a district of Wuhan) and had destroyed foreign property. Foreign women and children were evacuated down the Yangzi to Shanghai. The American consulate in Shanghai advised that all women and children in the interior leave for shelter in the International Settlement of Shanghai. Around the country, missionaries and Chinese Christians came under attack. In the Fujian Province cities of Fuzhou (Foochow) and Xiamen (Amoy), mobs looted the YMCA, churches, hospitals, a girls' school, missionary residences, and an orphanage.[96] In Jiangyin in Jiangsu on the south bank of the Yangzi, students took the principal and two Chinese pastors hostage from Southern Presbyterian Mission's James Sprunt Academy for three days.[97] At the end of March, the Nationalist forces took Nanjing, and in the ensuing chaos of looting and rampage several foreigners were killed. Only by a barrage of British and American shells launched from gunboats on the Yangzi was a path cleared for foreigners to evacuate the city. All of the Christian Reformed missionaries studying Chinese in the city took advantage of these gunboats to flee to Shanghai.

Across the Yangzi to the east, Rugao had remained quiet but tense during February and most of March 1927. With rumors swirling about imminent military action, all but two of the missionaries were evacuated from the city in the middle of March. When the mail stopped because riverboats were not running and telegraph lines had been cut, John De Korne and Albert Smit were stranded and cut off from communication with the rest of China. When Nanjing fell, thousands of Jiangsu warlord Sun Chuanfang's defeated troops wandered freely through Rugao, threatening to loot unless city officials and wealthy citizens met their exorbitant demands. Several of the hospital's single young women employees took refuge in the missionary homes, as did Miss Wu, the Christian schoolteacher. Some of the wealthier families of the city also requested shelter in the missionary compounds. Two days after Nanjing fell, De Korne and Smit piled an old Model-T with luggage, and, with the four hospital employees, the schoolteacher, and three or four other passengers, they negotiated numerous checkpoints on their way to the Yangzi, where they were whisked off to Shanghai by an American gunboat.

[96]   Lutz, *Chinese Politics*, 216. For details about the attacks in Fuzhou, see Ryan Dunch, *Fuzhou Protestants and the Making of Modern China, 1857-1927* (New Haven: Yale Univ. Press, 2001), 192-93.

[97]   Kessler, *Jiangyin Mission Station*, 72.

Huddled as refugees in Shanghai and still wincing from the twin blows of their dispute with the evangelists and conflict among themselves, the China Mission had hit bottom. While chaos enveloped China, the missionaries agonized about what to do next.[98] Finally, the mission decided to repatriate all but two families, who would stay on and monitor events in China, waiting for the day when the Christian Reformed Church could return to Rugao. After a little more than six years in the country, the work of the China Mission was on hold.

After finding what they believed was an "ideal" location for mission work, the Christian Reformed missionaries moved to Rugao in 1923 filled with confidence and optimism. They brought with them resources: sincerity, intelligence, integrity, and diligence. They also had financial backing from the home church for setting up homes, chapels, a hospital, and a school. Despite their commitment, sincerity, and other resources, however, they failed miserably in this first encounter with Rugao. Much of the failure can be attributed to the larger political and social turmoil happening around them. But a share of the blame for their failure has to be laid at their feet: The missionaries were simply unprepared to meet the reality of China. Once in Rugao they also discovered that many of the advantages listed for choosing China over Africa in 1920—climate, children's education, and cost—had not turned out to be the case. Perhaps most significantly, if the Chinese were more in "harmony" with them as Dutch-American immigrant Christian Reformed missionaries, this harmony was not immediately obvious. Out of this bitter failure, however, the missionaries began to make adjustments. During their time away from Rugao, the missionaries worked on understanding China better, and they rededicated themselves to returning to Rugao to try again to plant a Reformed church and a thriving Christian community.

In the face of defeat, the missionaries even appear to have gained fresh resolve for tackling China's resistance to the Christian faith. One striking sign of this resolve is their determination to understand China. During the year and a half they took refuge in Shanghai while waiting for the situation in Rugao to stabilize, John De Korne and Albert Smit

---

[98] On April 12, 1927, Chiang Kai-shek's Green Gang henchmen cracked down on the city's unions in an attempt to eradicate communism from the Nationalist party. There is no mention of this brutal bloodbath in any of the missionaries' correspondence or articles, so preoccupied were they with the "Huizenga case."

spent their days studying Chinese and Chinese philosophy. With the help of his language teacher, De Korne worked through several of the Confucian classics. He also gathered material on religious movements in China, later using it to write a dissertation on a secret society in Rugao County. In the United States, Harry Dykstra spent a year and a half studying Chinese history and philosophy at Hartford Theological Seminary in Connecticut, and Lee Huizenga worked on a degree in public health at Yale, focusing on leprosy, a widespread problem in Rugao County.

From this point on, with few exceptions, Christian Reformed missionaries used their time in the States, while on furlough or after having been evacuated and waiting to return (1927-1929 and again in 1937-1946), to increase their Chinese language proficiency and their understanding of the Chinese tradition, studying variously at Hartford, at the University of Michigan, and at the University of California at Berkeley. The missionaries seemed determined not to fail again, at least not on account of ignorance, and their concentrated studies served to deepen their appreciation of China and its people.

CHAPTER 4

The Sowing Period:
Making Contact, Early 1930s

Returning to Rugao

In the spring of 1927, the two Christian Reformed families remaining in Shanghai, the De Kornes and the Smits, took up residence in the French Concession to wait out the storm engulfing China. The men redeemed this time of waiting by engaging in intense language study and China-watching and by relaying blunt assessments of China's prospects for missionary work back to the United States for publication in church papers.[1] This was also a period of soul-searching

---

[1] Occasionally Henry Beets chose not to publish their articles, especially those he found too blunt for North American sentiments, such as two articles De Korne sent in the summer of 1927, one entitled, "The Bolshevization of China," and the other, "The Educational Crisis in China." In response to De Korne's query about why the articles failed to appear in the *Banner*, Beets explained he was afraid that people "were overfed [with news from China], and things are changing so rapidly that it is hard telling just what the actual situation is by the time the articles appear." See John De Korne to Beets, Sept. 2, 1927, and Beets's reply, Oct. 5, 1927, De Korne, CRWM folder.

about the future of mission work in China in general and Rugao in particular. De Korne wondered if missionaries would be free to move about the country after the dust from the revolution had settled, and he worried about a declaration made by some Chinese church leaders who had welcomed back "to China only those foreign missionaries who are content to work under the control of their Chinese employees."[2]

From Shanghai, De Korne and Smit also monitored the occasional news from Rugao. Initially this news was brought by the servants who carried their goods to Shanghai, sometimes as many as sixty cases at a time. Though there were no reports of armed conflict, the situation in Rugao remained highly unstable throughout 1927. After the troops of Sun Chuanfang—a northern warlord of the Zhili clique who had been in control of the five provinces in the lower Yangzi region—fled north in April 1927, Chiang Kai-shek's Nationalist troops had taken the region in June. Unlike many cities in the surrounding area, including Nantong, just forty miles away, Rugao took the transfer of power smoothly, with little destruction or looting. During the summer months of 1927, the various factions of the local Communist and Nationalist parties struggled to cobble together a county government. Later in the summer, when it was rumored that Sun Chuanfang's troops were about to recapture the city, Rugao's top officials fled.[3] Sun's troops never materialized, but Nationalist troops did arrive in Rugao in September and quickly named a new county magistrate.

John De Korne and Albert Smit made their first return trip to Rugao in the middle of July. The trip upriver was easier than expected, and, though surprised to see foreigners traveling, people treated them well. The missionaries found Rugao in political turmoil, with a group of the leading citizens calling for the ouster of a member of the gentry named He Sen, who was accused of paying off one of Sun Chuanfang's men for personal advantage.[4] But the missionaries were greeted warmly and treated to a banquet by the Standard Oil Company agent in Rugao, also one of the city's leading businessmen. They were glad to be in Rugao, but they sensed some change in attitude toward them: "Outwardly all the people we met were polite as usual...[but] from the undercurrents it was noticeable that the antiforeign feeling which has swept China was also present in Jukao [Rugao]."[5]

---

2   De Korne to Beets, June 25, 1927, De Korne, CRWM folder.
3   Barkan, "Patterns of Power," 204.
4   Ibid., 208.
5   "Mission Minutes," Oct. 3, 1927, CRWM folder.

Taking care of their property was a main focus of this and subsequent trips back to Rugao. Unlike their Southern Presbyterian neighbors in adjacent Taizhou County, who had suffered extensive property losses through looting and damage, the Christian Reformed mission had suffered little property damage, something the missionaries considered surprising, since all of their chapels had been occupied by Nationalist troops for short periods of time. After being used to billet troops for a brief time, the mission hospital had been sealed up by the local magistrate. While the missionaries were visiting the city, the Nationalist party "requested" the use of the mission's schoolhouse. Though the missionaries could not refuse this demand, they gave it on the condition that the party assume full responsibility for the buildings and equipment and return it when the mission was ready to use it again. The owner of another mission-rented property had reclaimed it in their absence and had converted it into an opium den.

City officials had also sealed up the mission houses outside the east gate and taken the keys, threatening to requisition them from the mission if the party's own facilities proved insufficient. The missionaries found only minor damage to their houses. In one of the houses, the caretaker had thrown open the pantry to his friends and family, but the other houses were left virtually untouched, though at one they found that "a partly eaten melon was left on the dining room table" and noted that "weeds higher than a man's head give the yard the appearance of a jungle."[6] They recovered some of their household items from local pawnshops at much higher prices than they had originally paid for them.

One important task carried out from Shanghai was to "settle accounts" with the mission's workers who had suffered losses during the upheaval. The missionaries decided to pay the funeral expenses for the wife of one of the evangelists, amounting to about a hundred dollars. When they had been evacuated from Rugao, four of the young women who worked for the mission hospital had left with the fleeing missionaries. Before letting them go, the mission had given them each two months' salary and travel expenses to return to their homes. For those servants who remained faithful in looking after mission property or carrying the missionaries' belongings and messages to Shanghai, the missionaries made generous gifts, such as the one made to Guo Sifu (K'o Sz Fu) "for the heroic work he did in getting messages through to Rugao during a time of danger."[7]

---

[6] Ibid.
[7] "Mission Minutes," April 7, 1927, CRWM folder.

Not all of the mission employees were so loyal to the mission. One colporteur, Song Liansen (Song Lien-sen), had resigned and joined the army. Harry Dykstra's language teacher, a man named Tang, in collusion with a military officer in Rugao, tried to extort more than a hundred dollars from the mission by claiming he had been imprisoned and needed the money to be released. The hospital employees, who had been the main instigators of the evangelists' strike of 1927, proved the biggest disappointment. Hearing more and more "disquieting reports" about the duplicity of the hospital employees, the missionaries decided to close the facility until a foreign doctor could take control of the work. Once the hospital was closed, the missionaries asked several of the employees, including the Chinese doctor, Qian (Chien), to come to Shanghai to settle accounts. When Dr. Qian could not account for the whereabouts of all of the mission's expensive hospital equipment, the missionaries settled accounts with him and the other workers and let them go, since they saw "no immediate prospects for making use of their services in Rugao in the immediate future."[8]

Some of the Chinese Christian workers, however, remained loyal to the mission after the missionaries' evacuation. After the Nationalist soldiers had vacated mission property, four of the Chinese evangelists had remained at their posts and were carrying on nominal chapel work. John De Korne reported that the mission's work continued "after a fashion" at the north gate and east gate chapels in Rugao and in the outstations of Dingyan (Ting Yen) and Haian (Hai'an), both within twelve miles of Rugao.[9] In other correspondence, the missionaries reported the Christian work in Rugao as continuing with a "fair regularity," as "fragmentary," as continuing in a "very limited way," and as continuing under "great difficulties and financial loss."[10] A Sunday worship service was still held in the city, but it was attended only by mission employees.

The small group of Christians in Rugao had been "decimated," as Harry Dykstra put it, by the upheaval of the civil war.[11] Two of the Rugao church's three full-fledged members had left the city. The third

---

[8] Qian also demanded and received back pay for a vacation that he claimed he had not taken the previous year. "Mission Minutes," May 9, 1927, CRWM folder.

[9] John De Korne, "China Chips," *Banner* 63 (Jan. 6, 1928): 13.

[10] See "Mission Minutes," Dec. 5, 1927, CRWM folder; Pousma to Beets, May 4, 1927, Pousma, CRWM folder; and "Mission Minutes," June 6, 1927, CRWM folder.

[11] H. Dykstra to Beets, Dec. 2, 1928, H. Dykstra, CRWM folder.

member, Zhou Huiwu (Chow Huei Wu), was convicted of political crimes and executed in June 1928. He had been one of Rugao's first baptized converts to enter the church and had continued "to show great interest in the gospel work."[12] The missionaries knew that Zhou, a Rugao native, was an ardent nationalist and deeply involved in local politics, but they were shocked to learn that he had allegedly been involved in "Communist activities."[13] The mission wrote: "It was reported that he had confessed his crimes and the common opinion was that he was guilty of them," but the missionaries were still convinced of the sincerity of his Christian confession and "found it difficult to believe that he could deny his profession of faith to the extent of plotting destruction and murder." According to Zhou's fiancée, who saw him just before he was executed, Zhou said, "Jesus died on the cross for his enemies; I, on the other hand, am not afraid to die on a cross to free the workers from suffering."[14] His head was placed on the city wall as a warning to other political troublemakers.

[12] "Mission Minutes," June 11, 1928, CRWM folder.
[13] According to Communist Party history, after failing as a pharmacist of traditional Chinese medicine, Zhou had taken up residence in the mission's east gate chapel, where he eventually became a Christian. While living in the church, Zhou also began secretly working for the Communist Party and at one point helped a leading member avoid arrest. In the spring of 1927, Zhou joined the local Nationalist Party branch and served on a labor relations committee. In May 1927, Zhou was involved in a clash between rickshaw drivers and police that took place in the mission's east gate chapel (while the missionaries were absent from the city). A year later, in the spring of 1928, Zhou helped organize a peasant revolt but was arrested after the uprising was brutally suppressed. "Zhou Huiwu (1895-1928)," Nantong dang an ju sin xi wang (Nantong Archive Information Network) [www.ntda.gov.cn].
[14] According to Communist Party lore, though he was tortured, Zhou "stood firm and unyielding." On the road to the execution grounds, Zhou and other Communists reportedly sang the "Internationale," and when the executioner pushed him to a kneeling position before executing him he struggled to stand up and denounced Nationalist officials, shouting, "Killing party members only makes the party stronger!" Zhou was posthumously inducted into the Communist Party as a member. *Rugao xianzhi*, 748. Zhou was executed during the "Directorship period" of the Nationalist Party's presence in Rugao. During this period the party, in an attempt to weed out Communists and "left-wingers," forced all of its approximately 500 members to re-register. After carrying out background checks, the party accepted only 159 of the 500, others were given "possibility status," and 93 were rejected outright for party membership. Barkan makes no mention of any executions. See Barkan, "Nationalists, Communists, and Rural Leaders," 129ff.

When the missionaries started returning in late 1928, they found other signs of discouragement, but some signs of hope, too. When he returned in the fall of 1928 after a furlough, Harry Dykstra found that the class of promising inquirers that he had left in 1926 had been disbanded.[15] "Many of them no longer come," he reported, "and others are no longer wanted because of past improper conduct." He did note, however, one inquirer who still came faithfully: a bathhouse owner who appeared to have no ulterior motives and had begun bringing his son to the services. Mina Kalsbeek was also working with the inquirer's wife. While visiting the city in 1928, John De Korne and Albert Smit had attended some of the chapel meetings and several Bible studies. About one, De Korne reported that none of the participants showed any evidence of seeking after truth or "any sense of sorrow for sin."[16] But about the participants at another Bible study, De Korne felt cautiously optimistic, having sensed from the participants "a hunger for the Word of God and a "proper sense of humility as in the awful presence of Almighty God."[17]

A Fresh Approach

The trips De Korne and Smit made to Rugao throughout 1927 were also intended to help gauge the best time for the missionaries to return to their homes and work. Other missions were slowly and cautiously returning to their stations in Jiangbei already by the late summer of 1927, including the neighboring Christian Mission in Nantong and the Southern Presbyterian mission in Taizhou. But the Christian Reformed missionaries had decided to wait for permission from the American consul. In answer to their repeated requests to return, the American consul refused permission because the Nanjing government would not guarantee the safety of foreigners. If the missionaries decided to go back without the American government's approval, the consul advised them to write a letter absolving the government of responsibility for them and to be prepared to receive a "severe rebuke" if they needed intervention.[18]

By early 1928, De Korne and Smit were anxious to move back to Rugao. They were afraid that the American consul was playing too safe

---

[15]   H. Dykstra to Beets, Dec. 2, 1928, H. Dykstra, CRWM folder.
[16]   De Korne, "China Chips: Jukao Bible Classes," *Banner* 63 (Feb. 17, 1928): 132.
[17]   Ibid.
[18]   "Mission Minutes," Oct. 3, 1927, 1, CRWM folder.

and that the waiting might continue for years. Finally, they decided to return without the American government's permission. Since the mission's property neither had been destroyed nor was being occupied and Rugao appeared to be safe, they believed they could return safely; if circumstances did turn for the worse, they would receive enough advance warning to depart quickly. Consequently, in April of 1928, De Korne and Smit requested that the Mission Board send the other missionaries back to China in order to reopen the Rugao station. By the beginning of 1929, most of them had returned, and the mission was set to begin a second period of contact with the people of Rugao.

After resettling in their homes, the missionaries were determined to jump-start their stalled work, but they realized they needed a fresh approach. Since their arrival in Rugao in 1923, the mission's four chapels had been the main points of contact with the local people. Bible classes and prayer meetings were held daily in the chapels, with a city-wide worship service on Sundays for Christians and inquirers. At the center of the chapel ministry were the evening evangelistic services. At these services, a message was preached (usually by one of the mission's evangelists) aimed at converting the citizens of Rugao. However, this chapel approach had proved unsuccessful in achieving the missionaries' primary goal of founding "a native Christian church that [would] be self-supporting, self-governing, and self-propagating."[19] At a mission meeting in November 1929, during a visit by Henry Beets, secretary of the Mission Board, the missionaries decided to implement a new plan for making contact with the people of Rugao.

The approach they adopted was based on methods developed by John L. Nevius, a Northern Presbyterian missionary who had worked in China at the end of the nineteenth century.[20] Nevius had arrived in China in 1857 and had taken up mission work in the port city of Ningbo in Zhejiang Province. While working in Ningbo, Nevius was startled to discover a group of Chinese Christians in the countryside village of San Poh who were carrying on the work of their church by themselves without any financial help from a mission. This discovery was startling because the church's independence contrasted sharply with the churches in Ningbo and other mission stations in the area, where almost all of the converts received some kind of help from the mission.

[19] "China Mission Minutes," Nov. 18, 19, 20, 1929, 2, Item 6, CRWM folder.
[20] The following description comes from John L. Nevius, *The Planting and Development of Missionary Churches* (Grand Rapids: Baker, 1958), and Brown, *Earthen Vessels*, 84-85.

Mission Secretary Henry Beets visits Rugao, November 1929. (*Seated on ground, left to right*) Jean Dykstra, Eunice Smit, Connie Dykstra, Andrew Dykstra; (*first row, seated*) Wilhemina Kalsbeek, Trena Selles, Lillian Bode, Florence Dykstra with son Peter, Dora Smit with son Harvey, Cornelia Dykstra with daughter Dorothy, Nettie De Korne; (*last on right*) Liu Shuying; (*standing*) Albert Smit, Harry Dykstra, John De Korne; (*fifth from left*) Chen Guifan; (*center*) Henry Beets; (*to the right of Beets*) Wang Aitang; (*second from right*) Sam Dykstra; Albert Selles.

Since the nineteenth century, the usual way for a Protestant mission to start a church had been to open a chapel, where it would station a salaried Chinese worker under the close supervision of a missionary. The hope was that eventually the number of attendees at the chapel would increase to the point where the group could be organized into a congregation and eventually weaned of missionary leadership and financial support. But in Nevius's experience this did not usually happen; once Chinese Christians had received missionary support and funds, they found it difficult, if not impossible, to give up that support.

After "many years of experience and bitter failures" in Zhejiang, Nevius determined to make a new start in Yantai, Shandong Province, where he moved in 1861. He decided from the outset that Christians should provide their own meeting place, typically in the home of one of the Christians or inquirers, and also that one of the local Chinese Christians should lead new groups. These local leaders would be trained in the Bible at a training class centrally located in a given district and independent of mission control or financing. The missionary's main task would be to visit Christian groups and offer them encouragement and advice. Nevius himself made it a point to travel to each local group at least twice a year. Using this approach, Nevius believed the Chinese church would flourish in its own setting and avoid the appearance of being "a foreign religion under the control of foreign agents."[21]

Nevius's approach in Shandong was met with stiff resistance from his missionary colleagues. Because he could not convince his colleagues to follow his example, when Nevius became too old to itinerate his approach was discontinued. Although Nevius's methods were not well received or successful in China in the late nineteenth century, they later caught on in Korea. After reading a series of articles that Nevius had contributed to the *Chinese Recorder* in the late 1880s, several Presbyterian missionaries in Korea invited Nevius to visit and talk about his approach in starting independent, self-supporting churches. These Presbyterians were so impressed by Nevius's approach that they made it the guiding principle for the work of both the Northern and Southern Presbyterians in Korea for the next fifty years. Because of its success in Korea, by the second decade of the twentieth century Nevius's ideas were echoing in China once again—this time as the "Korean Plan."

It was this Korean Plan that the missionaries decided to adopt in November of 1929. The mission had considered using this approach earlier but had hesitated because its Southern Presbyterian neighbors were not using it. When the Presbyterians adopted Nevius's plan, however, the Christian Reformed mission followed suit immediately. Before making a formal decision, De Korne and Smit had visited Korea in the summer of 1928 to gain firsthand knowledge of the approach. They discovered that the new approach would require a switch from "intensive" to "extensive" contact with the people of Rugao. In other words, instead of waiting for the people of Rugao to make contact with them (i.e., through its chapels), the mission would go out to meet the people of the county. The mission would concentrate on visiting homes, on street preaching, on outdoor Sunday schools, on evangelistic rallies, and on tent meetings. The ultimate goal of all these activities was to create small groups of believers and inquirers who would study

21   Brown, *Earthen Vessels*, 85.

the Bible and Christian teaching and eventually organize themselves into independent churches.

In order to use the Korean Plan, however, the missionaries had to adapt it to fit their situation in Rugao. Because there were few Christians in Rugao and because the missionaries had not been in the county long enough to cultivate native leadership, they would have to continue to use hired evangelists. The mission divided the field into four sections and stationed an evangelist in each section. Each evangelist was provided a place to live in what was deemed the most promising location in the section, the place where a native group might emerge. If a group did form, it could receive a share of the evangelist's time, but only if group members were willing to provide part of his financial support. The missionaries themselves would continue to reside in Rugao and visit their assigned districts to supervise the work of their evangelists and to oversee the formation of small groups.[22]

While the missionaries had to make adjustments because of the lack of native leadership in Rugao, they were determined to follow another guiding principle of the Korean Plan more closely. Up to this point, the mission had paid all expenses for meeting places: "key" money, rent, furniture, and maintenance. Now the mission would ease out of existing rental arrangements and move toward disposing of all of its property, thereby encouraging new groups to meet in locations they would provide themselves, usually the home of one of their number. The missionaries believed this approach would teach new Christians about "service" and nudge them in the direction of financial independence.

The missionaries decided to implement the "modified" Korea Plan in Rugao for a trial period of three years, after which time they would reevaluate its effectiveness. The missionaries were keen on trying this plan because they were disillusioned with "big meetings" and because they believed that the doors of Rugao's citizens were more open to them than ever before. After almost a decade in China, they believed this fresh approach would finally set them on the path to establishing a church in Rugao.

Sowing in Rugao City

In Rugao City, the mission used a variety of means to make contact with people. One important means was medical work. The missionaries believed that medical work was a crucial aspect of their enterprise for two reasons. First, the denomination was committed to

[22] "Mission Minutes," Nov. 11, 1929, CRWM folder.

A typical street scene in Rugao City during the 1930s.

providing the services of a doctor and adequate medical facilities for the missionaries and their families. Second, the missionaries believed that medical work could provide an entrée for preaching Christianity. About opening a hospital, they stated, "A well-equipped hospital for work in China is of the utmost importance to act as an entering wedge into the hearts and lives of the people."[23]

Prior to the arrival of the missionaries, Rugao County, though one of the most populated in the entire country, had just one hospital.[24] Shortly after moving to Rugao in 1923, Lee Huizenga had opened a small clinic for receiving patients and dispensing medicine. At the end of the first month of operation, the clinic had treated eighty-nine patients. A year later, the mission opened a hospital in a remodeled Chinese courtyard house located on the main street of the city. Under the supervision of Huizenga, the hospital's staff of twelve, including a foreign nurse and a Chinese doctor, provided inpatient and outpatient

[23] Report of the China Mission, Aug. 1, 1922, 1, CRWM folder.
[24] The only hospital in Rugao when the mission arrived in 1923 was a small public facility which had been opened in 1921, *Shi Bao* (Nov. 13, 1926): 4. Quoted in Barkan, "Nationalists, Communists, and Rural Leaders," 76, n135.

care and some free clinics, treating 11,275 patients in its first year of operation.[25] Though the hospital treated a wide variety of ailments, the two most common were hookworm and *broncho spirochaetosis*, an acute bronchial infection that frequently led to a chronic condition. When Rugao's famous turnips were harvested in the fall, the hospital also helped treat the annual outbreak of cholera that invariably occurred when people failed to wash them properly.[26]

The hospital was open for only about a year and a half before the chaos of the 1926–1927 Northern Expedition forced it to close. After the missionaries had been evacuated from Rugao in March 1927, the city government had the building sealed for "protection." While the missionaries waited to return during 1928, there was some discussion in the local newspapers about turning the mission hospital into a government institution.[27] When they returned to Rugao at the beginning of 1929, the missionaries found the facility intact but did not reopen it until 1930, when Lee Huizenga returned from his extended furlough.[28] When he did finally return, Huizenga first opened a clinic in the guardhouse of his residence and then eventually moved back into the former facility on the main street of the city. During the 1930s, the hospital expanded service to include treatment for lepers, another ailment particularly widespread in the Rugao area.

As a doctor and an ordained minister, Huizenga was deeply interested in the evangelistic potential of medical missions. He believed passionately that medical missions were not an afterthought of the Lord

[25] "Second Annual Report of the Christian Reformed Church Hospital," 1925, 4, Huizenga folder.

[26] *North China Herald* (Oct. 14, 1936): 54.

[27] An August 21, 1928, article in the *Rugao ri bao* (*Rugao Daily*) reported that the local Nationalist party had decided to ban the missionaries from preaching in the city. Since no other references are made to this action, it not must have been carried out. Copy of an article found in De Korne, personal folder.

[28] In the spring of 1927, the mission recommended that the Mission Board not allow Huizenga to return to China because of his "personal peculiarities." In the meantime, Huizenga made an extensive trip through Southeast Asia on his way back to North America, and then in the fall of 1927 he accepted a scholarship to study public health at Yale for a year. By the time he had finished his study, the mission had accepted his apology, clearing the way for his return to Rugao. He did not return to Rugao for another year, however, because he had accepted an appointment to travel around the world as the foreign secretary of the American Mission to Lepers. For the details, see L. J. Lamberts, *The Life Story of Dr. Lee S. Huizenga* (Grand Rapids: Eerdmans, 1950): 151-58.

but a "forethought," and, as he said, "Preaching without the healing is as incomplete as healing without preaching."[29] With the help of his two Chinese evangelists and a colporteur, Huizenga put evangelism at the center of the hospital's agenda. Huizenga and evangelist Chen Fang, a Nanking Seminary graduate, provided "special religious instruction" for the other hospital workers. Every morning and afternoon except Saturdays and Sundays, worship services were held in the hospital chapel for patients, and the chapel was open for prayers in the evenings as well. On Sundays, in addition to worship services, the hospital staff ran two Sunday schools, one in the hospital chapel and the other in the hospital itself. The hospital colporteur sold Bible portions and Christian literature and made follow-up calls on patients.

There is no evidence to suggest that the medical work in Rugao resulted in many converts, but it did increase the mission's opportunities for evangelism. Free clinics on Tuesday and Thursday afternoons, as well as baby clinics on Saturdays, brought the mission into contact with many people in Rugao. Through treating the city jailor's family in 1924, Huizenga gained entrance to the city jail to provide a free clinic there. Every Friday afternoon, the mission would set up a clinic in the jail and prisoners would come for treatment, many of them suffering from skin diseases because of the jail's poor sanitary conditions.[30] On average, they saw 180 patients per week there, in both the men's and women's wards. During the early 1930s, when the Nationalist government instituted the "New Life Movement" and tried to suppress opium use, the population of the jail swelled. To meet the medical needs of the rising prison population, the Rugao City government asked the mission hospital to vaccinate all of the inmates and hold an anti-opium clinic, a request that gave the mission even greater access to the Rugao City jail as well as to other jails in the county.

As they had hoped, providing free clinics in the jail opened doors to evangelism. The hospital evangelist held weekly meetings in the jails, with attendance averaging two hundred in the city jail and six hundred in the county jail. Huizenga, a member of the Gideons Society, took advantage of his access to the prisons to distribute free Bibles. Prison officials at the city jail also allowed Mina Kalsbeek and her circle of

---

29 Huizenga, "The Ultimate Need for the Christian Ministry of Medicine," *Chinese Recorder* 69:11(Nov. 1938): 559. In this article, Huizenga gives his fullest articulation of the relationship between medical and evangelistic work.

30 Matilda Huizenga, "Visiting Prisoners in Rugao," *Missionary Monthly* 40:467 (April 1936): 102.

Chinese helpers to spend one hour per week with women inmates. At Christmas, Kalsbeek and her helpers gave the inmates cookies, candy, and peanuts.

As much as they appreciated being able to evangelize in the jails, there is little to suggest that it was a particularly effective way of making converts. In fact, Huizenga himself was pessimistic about it. After more than a decade of contact in the jails, he admitted that the mission could not report a single baptism, though two of the inmates had been baptized by the mission and were members of the church before being sent to prison.[31] Though she could not report any baptisms, Kalsbeek "joyfully" noted that eleven of the women inmates had "decided to follow Jesus and were having a wholesome and helpful influence on all the other women in the prison."

The hospital opened doors to the jail and gave the mission other opportunities for preaching Christianity in Rugao, but it also caused major problems. The mission could not come up with a unified policy about the place of medical work. Before Huizenga had returned to China in 1930, the mission had even raised the question, "Do we really need a hospital for evangelistic work?"[32] Their answer was that medical work in China had evolved from being an "opening wedge" to becoming more an expression of the Christian life and ideal, and, they concluded, "Our evangelistic work in Rugao could be carried on in the future even though we never made a contribution in the way of medical work." This view of the lower priority of medical work caused chronic tension between Huizenga and the other members of the mission, tension that sparked open conflict again in 1936 when Huizenga and Kalsbeek were abruptly recalled to the States to explain the difficulties of coordinating the mission's medical and evangelistic work. Huizenga was allowed to return to China only after a "Basis of Agreement" had been worked out whereby all of the missionaries would cooperate more fully to further the cause of the mission.[33]

---

[31] Huizenga, "Prison Work," *Missionary Monthly* 41:484 (Oct. 1937): 279ff. One of the church members serving in jail may have been Liu Yingqing, who had been baptized by Harry Dykstra in 1925. According to church records, he was a security guard who stopped coming to church in 1934 after he was arrested and put in jail for theft. He left Rugao after his release. See notes made on church records found in Religious Affairs Bureau office June 2, 2002.

[32] "Mission Minutes," Jan. 30 to Feb. 8, 1929, 4, Art. 2, CRWM folder.

[33] Frustration with Huizenga's penchant for working independently of the others, doubts about his medical competence, and his obsession with

The missionaries were determined not to let hospital work or other activities distract from the mission's main purpose in Rugao: to preach Christianity. At times, the missionaries believed that even the citizens of the city wanted to distract them from their commitment to preaching. Harry Dykstra reported that occasionally people asked, "Why don't you people do something for the community instead of just preaching and preaching at people all the time?"[34] But the missionaries were not swayed by this complaint. They not only wanted to keep preaching at the forefront of their agenda, they believed that the city was already doing a good job of taking care of its needy.

Rugao had a long history of charity. One important charitable effort in the city was called the "Promote Virtue Hall," which was started during the reign of the Kangxi emperor (1688–1722) by members of the local gentry. The "Promote Virtue Hall" operated out of an old temple and distributed twenty thousand dollars of aid to the needy in the city annually, providing food for the hungry

leprosy work ("his special hobby," as one colleague put it) all contributed to the friction between him and his colleagues. The tensions reached a crisis in 1936. While on furlough that year, Harry Dykstra (one of the original party of 1920) had resigned from the mission, refusing to return to the field unless the board did something about Huizenga and the hospital. In his letter of resignation, Dykstra cited a potential lawsuit against the mission brought by the wife of Zhou Fengwu (Chow Feng Wu), one of the mission's evangelists, about treatment she had received from Huizenga at the hospital. Huizenga was able to mollify the evangelist and his wife, but a more serious situation, which Dykstra described as "a moral issue," was also roiling the hospital. Rumors were swirling in the city about one of the hospital's female employees, whose father threatened to take the hospital to court. (There are no details or record of the outcome of this case.) Dykstra argued that situations like these made it impossible for the mission to supervise the hospital while Huizenga was superintendent. Summarizing the mission's position about Huizenga and the medical work, he wrote: "The Mission seeks to be relieved from all responsibility for the medical work imposed on it by the Board. It cannot conscientiously relinquish it to Dr. Huizenga alone. We would fail our obligation to the church. Rather close down the hospital." See Harry Dykstra to Executive Committee of the Board of Heathen Mission of the Christian Reformed Church, May 26, 1936, H. Dykstra, CRWM folder. The "Basis of Agreement" advised that the mission begin providing free clinics to be held four days a week at the outstations and vindicated the mission's desire to rein in Huizenga, or at least hold him accountable. See "Basis of Agreement for our China Field," *Acts of Synod*, 1936, 130-31. After he agreed to the terms of the agreement, Huizenga was allowed to return to Rugao.

34 H. Dykstra to Beets, May 4, 1932, H. Dykstra, CRWM folder.

and short-term loans for disaster victims to get back on their feet.[35] Another charity used donations from some of the leading citizens to purchase bales of used clothing for distribution to the poor. The city also had a three-hundred-year-old orphanage that took in abandoned children, aiding, on average, a thousand orphans per year.[36] In addition to these charities, there was a school for the deaf and mute, a home for the "feeble and aged," schools for poor children, trade schools for the poor, and a rice kitchen that opened each winter to feed "hundreds of mouths each day."[37]

Since the city already did quite well at promoting charity, the missionaries did not feel compelled to help; they made exceptions in times of catastrophe, however. During the Nanjing decade, Rugao itself did not experience any flooding, but when a flood ravaged most of the regions north of Rugao (i.e., Subei), refugees poured into the county. The stream of refugees forced the Rugao government to open a makeshift camp that temporarily housed up to fourteen hundred flood victims. Many died of starvation and dysentery. Responding to the local government's desperate plea for help, the missionaries collected money from their churches at home and purchased seven hundred articles of clothing for distribution in the camp.[38] The missionary families also donated food. Helping with the flood victims gave the mission an opportunity to evangelize in the camp. Though willing to help in times of great need, the missionaries remained skeptical about the evangelistic value of such activities. According to Harry Dykstra, "The Chinese are very appreciative of this kind of thing, but I doubt whether it gets us anywhere in the way of bringing people to the Lord."[39]

In addition to medical and a limited amount of relief work, the mission also used the printed word to make contact with the citizens of Rugao. One way was through advertising. In order to teach the citizens

---

[35]   Huizenga, "Two Hundred and Fifty Years of Charity in Jukao," *Missionary Monthly* 37:428 (Jan. 1933):10-11, and "How the Chinese Feed the Hungry and Clothe the Naked," *Missionary Monthly* 39:456 (March 3, 1935): 138.

[36]   Huizenga, "Jukao's Work of Mercy," *Missionary Monthly* 38:442 (March 1934): 78. A shorter version of the article about the orphanage appeared earlier in *North China Herald* 189:3456 (Nov. 1, 1933): 171.

[37]   See *North China Herald*, 193:3513 (Dec. 5, 1934): 370.

[38]   The national flood relief commission also asked the missionaries to help with flood relief in the north of the province, but the missionaries, reluctant "to leave the ministry of the word in order to serve tables," opted to work strictly with refugees in Rugao. De Korne to Beets, Dec. 17, 1931, De Korne, CRWM folder.

[39]   H. Dykstra to Beets, May 4, 1932, H. Dykstra, CRWM folder.

of Rugao about Christianity and extend a broad invitation for them to attend church activities, the mission began posting advertisements around the city in the 1930s. Judging from the one poster in existence, these invitation posters were about three feet long and two feet wide and printed on striking vermilion paper, the color of traditional Chinese banners.[40] At the center of this advertisement is a Bible, with the outline of a star imposed on it. In a radius around the Bible are different graphics with characters imposed on them. Starting at the top right and moving down are pictures indicating proper responses to the Bible: a heart for believing (*xin*), an eye for examining (*cha*), a person thinking (*xiang*), and a leaf indicating passing on the message of Christianity (*chuan*). Starting at the top left and moving down are pictures with characters and images communicating the symbolic power of the Bible: as a seed (*zhong*), as a mirror (*jing*), as a sword (*jian*), as water (*shui*), as milk (*nai*), and as a road (*lu*). At the very bottom of the poster is another, smaller open Bible with two sentences summing up the meaning of the Bible for the citizens of Rugao: "This Holy Bible can help you believe in Jesus" (*zhe ge sheng jing neng bang zhu ne xin ye su*); and "Jesus can save you and give you wisdom" (*ye su neng gou zheng jiu ni yu ci ni zhi hui*). Beside each of the characters on the poster are the national phonetic symbols, a literacy aid used during the Republican period. In the center of the poster, in much smaller characters, is an invitation to visit the mission's "Gospel Chapel" (*qing dao fu yin tang*).

The hospital also used printed mailings to make evangelistic contacts. These mailings included invitations to special mission-sponsored activities and a monthly hospital newsletter. "The Christian Reformed China Mission Hospital Monthly" (*Rugao zhang lao hui yi yuan yue ken*) provided former patients and prospective patients in the county a schedule of the hospital and clinic's services and information concerning relevant health issues.[41] "We want to help all in Rugao who

[40] Poster advertisement in the author's possession.
[41] There are four hospital newsletters extant: Feb. 1 and Dec. 14, 1926, and April 4 and Nov. 11, 1933, Lee Huizenga, CRWM folder. It appears that there were nine newsletters published in 1926, but it is unclear how many were published in the 1930s after Huizenga returned to China. Despite publishing the English name of the newsletter as the "Christian Reformed China Mission Hospital Monthly," the Chinese name of the newsletter was the "Rugao Presbyterian Church Hospital Monthly." In China, the CRC mission identified itself in Chinese as the "American Presbyterian Mission" (*mei guo zhang lao hui*), perhaps because of the complications of translating "Reformed" (in Chinese the word implies "revolution," *gai ge*), or because the mission wanted to associate its work with its Southern Presbyterian neighbors.

have physical ailments and those with heavy burdens, and are seeking ways to serve you," the hospital's first newsletter stated in 1926.[42]

The newsletter's main purpose, however, was to present the "life and words" of Jesus. The first newsletter's meditation raises the question, "What must I do to be saved?" This question, states the author, is a basic question asked by all people everywhere: "Scholars and the uneducated, the rich and the poor, the old and the young" all ask this basic question, even people in "dark Africa."[43] Though all ask the same question, the article states, people answer it in many different ways. Giving an example close to home, the meditation notes, the people praying in Rugao's temples every day answer the question by bowing down to idols. All answers to the question "What must I do to be saved?" are wrong, states the article. The Christian answer, the correct answer, is "believe in Jesus Christ, and you and your whole family will be saved."[44] This is because, the meditation notes, Jesus claimed to be "the Way," the only way to be reconciled to God. The meditation closes with a suggestion for the reader: "If you ask what must I do to be saved, give Jesus' way a try."

Another two-page meditation in 1926 discusses a passage from First Corinthians. The meditation, which Huizenga wrote and Liu Shuying (Mina Kalsbeek's Bible woman) translated, explains the meaning of the following verses from chapter six:

> Flee fornication. Every sin that a man doeth is without the body; but he that committeth fornication sinneth against his own body. Or know ye not that your body is a temple of the Holy Spirit which is in you, which ye have from God? And ye are not your own; for ye were bought with a price: glorify God therefore in your body. (1 Cor. 6:18–20)[45]

This meditation begins by explaining that different people have different views of their bodies. Some people only live for their bodies, "Thinking all day long about questions concerning clothing, food, and shelter." Other people neglect their bodies, since, the author states, "They are so eager for the spirit." Still other people, caught up

---

[42]   *Rugao zhang lao hui yi yuan yue ken* ("Rugao Christian Reformed Mission Hospital Monthly") (Feb. 1926): 1.

[43]   "Wo dang zuo shen ma ke yi de jiu?" ("What must I do to be saved?"), *Rugao zhang lao hui yi yuan yue ken* ("Hospital Monthly") 1 (Feb. 1, 1926): 1.

[44]   Acts 2:39.

[45]   "Ge lin duo qian shu liu zhang shi ba zhi er shi jie" (1 Cor. 6:18-20), *Yi yuan yue ken* ("Hospital Monthly") 9 (Dec. 14, 1926): 1-2.

in lustfulness, "only seek happiness in sin, even though they know this is not normal happiness, that it can harm the body, and that it can kill the spirit." Unfortunately, adds the author, "The universe is truly full of such pitiful people!" But the Bible's view, continues the piece, is that bodies were "created for the work of God, and therefore God wants our bodies and spirits, placed on the highest setting." The Bible passage, continues the author, teaches that our bodies are temples of the Holy Spirit and that we should use them to glorify God. Drawing on a local example, the author notes that just as the city temple building does not bring glory to the building itself but to the city god, so our bodies do not bring glory to us, but to the God who dwells in us, who is "glorious, matchless, everlasting, perfect." The meditation closes by reminding readers that they should take care of their bodies, because they are "living temples," and that people should use their bodies to glorify God in all that they do.

In the 1930s, after the mission's hospital reopened, the newsletter's name was shortened to the "Hospital Newsletter," and the meditations were simplified as well. In 1933, the first issue of the revived newsletter emphasizes that the mission hospital is a very important aspect of the church's work.[46] Through the work of the hospital, Christians demonstrate God's love to the people of Rugao. When Christians trust Christ, the article continues, they want to show their love for other people by healing the sick. Healing the sick, the article adds, is a continuation of the work that Jesus himself did when he was on the earth. The meditation ends with a call for all readers to "call on the name of Jesus," because, "Apart from Jesus," it concludes, "there is no other name under heaven by which men can be saved."

Another meditation appearing several months later reveals not only that the hospital newsletter messages had been simplified but also that the messages were now in touch with the times. On the first page of the November 1933 issue is the Bible verse, "O give thanks unto Jehovah; for he is good; For his loving kindness *endureth* for ever" (1 Chron. 16:34); along with it a meditation appears entitled, "Thrifty" (*jie jian*).[47] The short meditation starts out by encouraging

---

[46]   "Zheng shi fu xing kai ban" ("Formal Reopening of the Hospital"), Yi yuan yue kan (*Hospital Monthly*) (April 4, 1933): 1.

[47]   "Jie jian," ("Thrifty") Yi yuan yue ken (*Hospital Monthly*) (Nov. 1, 1933): 2. Though the newsletter meditations published in 1926 were probably written by Huizenga and translated by one of the hospital's church workers, those appearing in the 1930s appear to have been written by the hospital staff.

readers to be thrifty not only with things that belong to themselves, but also with things that belong to others. Since all things come from the hand of the Lord, the author adds, nothing should be wasted. The article, perhaps anticipating some of the themes criticizing women in the "New Life Movement," then goes on to castigate women who, out of jealousy for people with nicer clothes, "go out and borrow money to buy better clothes."[48] By doing this, the author warns, these women not only lose their peace of mind, they also place hardship on the rest of the family. Women who believe in Jesus Christ, the author contrasts, *never* do such things because they "seek first the kingdom of God and his righteousness."[49] A really virtuous woman, when she sees that other women have better clothes, will not feel shame, the meditation concludes, because she knows that borrowing money for clothes is really shameful and because she remembers the command of the Lord: "Owe no man anything."[50]

In the 1930s the mission also sought contact by buying advertising space in a Rugao newspaper. After three years of negotiating a contract, the paper, with subscriptions of two thousand readers, agreed to run thirty-five advertisements on Christian subjects. After running only five advertisements, however, the paper suddenly quit publishing

[48] "The New Life Movement," which began in early 1934, was Chiang Kai-shek's attempt to create "a new national consciousness and mass psychology" that, "through the revived force of the virtues of etiquette, justice, integrity and conscientiousness," would lead to the "social regeneration of China." According to Jonathan Spence, however, (*Search for Modern China*, 414-16), the movement never managed to move beyond "comparatively minor social peccadilloes." Nonetheless, it did result in a great deal of individual harassment and interference in private lives. Women especially felt the whip of those who resented the changes in female behavior that had occurred since the fall of the Qing dynasty. Chinese women were urged to cultivate the virtues of "chastity, appearance, speech, and work," and by the mid-1930s the identity of the "modern woman" had been transformed into an attack on the self-indulgent consumerism and leisured lifestyle that modern women were supposed to be enjoying. Louise Edwards, "Policing the Modern Woman in Republican China," *Modern China* 26:2 (April 2000): 120. See also Norma Diamond, "Women under Kuomindang Rule: Variations on Feminine Mystique," *Modern China* 1:1 (Jan. 1975): 8ff.

[49] This is a paraphrase of Matt. 6:33.

[50] These words are actually not direct "commands of the Lord" (*zhu de fen fu*), but those of the Apostle Paul, quoted without reference from Rom. 13: 8. This misattribution confirms that this meditation was not written by Huizenga himself and suggests that he had very little actual control over what went into the newsletter.

them, because, the editor said, the local office of the Nationalist party had "ordered" the paper to stop. Believing this to be a violation of the Nationalist government's profession of religious freedom, John De Korne decided to take up the issue in a "friendly way" with local officials. After some investigation, he discovered it was not the party objecting to the notices but an antiforeign terrorist organization in neighboring Tongzhou, which had threatened to throw a bomb through the newspaper office's window and kill the editor unless the advertisements were discontinued.[51] De Korne convinced the paper to continue the advertisements, and eventually the ads became so popular that a competing daily solicited the mission's patronage as well.

In a list of bullet points, one advertisement explains and defends the mission's work in Rugao.[52] The number one point the missionaries wanted to make was that it was out of obedience to God that they were proclaiming, "Jesus is the only savior of the world." But in doing so, the mission rejected the use of "national force," although, the ad adds, the church is definitely in the business of helping the nation promote "peace and stability." In addition to mentioning the mission's commitment to preaching the "correct and orthodox teachings" of the Bible, the ad states that the church is made up of "members from all nations, neither limited to male nor female," and that all who enter the organization do so through baptism. In the church, all enjoy "equal status and place." The ad states that while the church is concerned with "the spiritual care and ethical development" of its members, members should have work and be able to support themselves. In smaller print, the ad invites Rugao citizens to attend church meetings and to visit De Korne and his evangelist Chen Guifan or Mina Kalsbeek and her Bible woman Liu Shuying if they have further questions about Christianity.

Now and then, officials and businessmen would mention that they had read the notices, something that the mission took encouragement from, because, as De Korne noted, the "class of people reached by the newspaper is not the class that will readily show public interest in a religion which is still very unpopular in China."[53] But there is nothing to suggest these advertisements resulted in this "class of people" converting to Christianity and joining the church.

Included in the people reading the newspaper were students. After the disruptions students had caused in the 1920s, the missionaries

[51]   De Korne to Mission Board, Nov. 30, 1932, De Korne, CRWM folder.
[52]   This advertisement is found in John De Korne's personal folder.
[53]   De Korne, Report for Jan. 1933, Jan. 31, 1933, De Korne, CRWM folder.

were wary about making contact with them. In the 1930s, student intensity was still present in Rugao, but it was being put to use by the Nationalist party to push an agenda of modernization.[54] Connected with this push for modernization, many students continued to want to study English. Once again, as they had done in their early days in Rugao, the missionaries had opportunities to teach English in the local public schools, including the normal schools. Some of the missionaries held English Bible study classes in their homes, and Lee Huizenga opened an English class for women students in the hospital. All of

---

[54] One major example of the Nationalist government's drive to modernize was its attempt to do away with the lunar calendar. After 1929, the Nanjing government decreed that the country switch from the lunar calendar to the Gregorian calendar and in doing so effectively abolished the thousands-of-years-old practice of celebrating the lunar New Year. By 1933, however, Rugao citizens were ignoring the government's effort to modernize the calendar and celebrating Chinese New Year as they had always done. For instance, though the post office was open, no one was there except the workers. Also, schools were open, but no students showed up for class. See *North China Herald* (Feb. 17, 1932): 284, and *North China Herald* (Jan. 10, 1934): 47. At the same time as it instituted the solar calendar, the Nanjing government promulgated a *kulturkampf* against traditional religious practices. In one of the local illustrated papers published for the "common people," illustrations show people bowing down before idols with a caption raising the question, "Can idols that don't work give you happiness?" Another illustration shows an idol that has been destroyed and asks, "Does it have any spirit left? Can it still oppose you? Superstitious countrymen, quickly come to your senses, seek your own happiness!" *Min zhong hua bao*, Oct. 16, 1928, De Korne, personal folder. John De Korne gives a vivid account of student iconoclasm in an incident where Rugao students, under the direction of the local Nationalist party, entered the Rugao City temple and began haranguing the crowds on the folly of idol worship. Their zeal reaching frenzy, the students knocked the main idol off from its pedestal and destroyed it with axes. When they had finished, however, some of the students "trembled with fear at the sight of the desecration of images they had been taught from childhood to worship, and during the rest of the process they hid in one of the side rooms of the temple." See John De Korne, "China Chips," *Banner* 63 (Dec. 1928): 928. Eradicating superstitious religious practices proved just as impossible as replacing Chinese New Year with western New Year celebrations: When floods or famines hit the area, religious parades imploring the gods for rain were a common sight, unopposed by the local government. See Harry Dykstra, "The Lid Is Off," unpub. art. 1937, H. Dykstra, CRWM folder. By the mid-1930s a Buddhist revival was taking place in the county, with famous Buddhist preachers holding revival meetings. See *North China Herald* (June 5, 1935): 357.

these activities were geared to making contacts that the mission hoped would eventually produce converts. But the evangelistic results appear to have been minimal. As Huizenga reported about the women students attending classes in the hospital: "They seem interested in information about nursing. They do not seem interested in the Bible."[55]

Sowing among Women and Children

In Rugao, the mission had its best results connecting with women and children. When they had first arrived in Rugao in 1923, the ordained missionaries realized that making contact with Chinese families would be very difficult. Because of strict social mores regulating the contact of men and women, they could not meet with women privately. Children, too, were difficult for the ordained men to contact because they were part of the "women's world." Some of the missionaries' wives made efforts to get involved in work with women and children, but because of their own families and because of health concerns, they were limited in how much they could do.[56]

Because of these difficulties, soon after their arrival in the city the ordained missionaries lobbied the Mission Board to send a Bible woman. The first foreign Bible woman, Mina Kalsbeek, arrived in Rugao in 1924. Though ordained men came with college and seminary training, they had very little, if any, training for mission work. Kalsbeek, on the other hand, came to China with only a high school diploma but with a year of preparatory study at the Kennedy School of Mission. Though "she was rather shocked at the liberalism of the Kennedy Mission School" faculty, she found extremely helpful her classes in general sociology, the "Bible in missionary work," ethnology, the study of the community, missionary practice, Chinese religion, storytelling, missionary sociology, methods of mission, household management, "girl in her teens," guidance of play, the elementary department of the church, principles of teaching, and organization of religious education.[57] Kalsbeek also had an aptitude for Chinese, finishing

---

55   Huizenga to the La Grave Avenue CRC, April 1, 1931, Huizenga, CRWM folder.
56   For the challenges facing missionary wives, see Jane Hunter, *The Gospel of Gentility* (New Haven: Yale Univ. Press, 1984), 90-127.
57   For her views about the faculty at the Kennedy School of Mission, see correspondence of Kalsbeek and Beets, Nov. 12, 17, 21, 1921; Jan. 26, Feb. 2, March 25, April 6, 1922, Kalsbeek, CRWM folder. For her courses at Kennedy, see "Statement of courses and grades for session 1921-1922 of Wilhemina Kalsbeek," Kalsbeek, CRWM folder.

the five-year standard missionary language course through Nanjing University in just over two years. Other Bible women came during the thirty years that the mission was in Rugao, but Kalsbeek was the pillar of the mission's work with women and children for more than twenty-five years.

Kalsbeek had some preparation for her work in China and she was good at Chinese, but her first years in Rugao were far from easy. As with the ordained men, she quickly realized the importance of working with women, "For," as she said, "not until there are Christian women will there be Christian homes, and the home influence is an important factor in all missionary work."[58] But getting into homes to meet women took time. Preaching on the streets was not successful either, since Kalsbeek believed foreign women preaching on the street only created a sensation and not genuine interest in seeking Christianity. Furthermore, the limitations of her Chinese and her uncertainty about the contours of Chinese customs made working by herself almost impossible. About the latter constraint, she lamented: "Things which are not done, must not be done, and by far the heaviest load of 'must nots' fall upon poor womankind. I am kept from doing many things which I think would hasten our work and which I should not hesitate doing at home."[59] She became so discouraged about the prospects for women's work in Rugao that in 1925 she wrote board secretary Henry Beets to inform him that she was seriously considering leaving the mission field, not because she was tired of it but because she was feeling "superfluous." She wrote, "The money which goes to my salary could be used to better advantage in the Kingdom."[60]

Kalsbeek believed that the only way that she could continue working in Rugao effectively would be to find a suitable Chinese helper to serve as her Bible woman. Ideally, a Bible woman would be from the second generation of a Christian family and a native of the place where she worked. Since there was virtually no Christian presence in Rugao before the missionaries arrived in the city, finding a native Christian worker was out of the question; moreover, it would be years before the mission could groom such a worker. The only alternative was to find a Bible woman from another mission, preferably Presbyterian. But finding a woman from another mission did not prove easy, either. They were scarce, in part, Kalsbeek said, because "there seems to be a sort

[58]   Kalsbeek to Beets, Dec. 1, 1924, Kalsbeek, CRWM folder.
[59]   Kalsbeek to Beets, Oct. 1, 1925, Kalsbeek, CRWM folder.
[60]   Kalsbeek to Beets, Aug. 3, 1925, Kalsbeek, CRWM folder.

of 'stigma' on Bible woman work and so all the fine young women go into teaching or business."[61] Until she found a full-time Bible woman, Kalsbeek worked with the wife of one of the mission's evangelists, who, though an experienced worker, had too many family obligations to devote much time to mission work. Kalsbeek then hired a Bible woman from the Northern Presbyterian mission in Shandong, but this woman proved impossible for the work in Rugao because of her inability to master the local Rugao dialect. Responding to Henry Beets's suggestion that she take this woman along to itinerate in Rugao, Kalsbeek replied, "She is repulsive to the people and it would harm our future influence to impress them unfavorably at first."[62]

In 1926, Kalsbeek finally found an ideal partner for her work with women and children. Short of women workers for an evangelistic campaign in the countryside during the winter of 1926, the mission hospital loaned Kalsbeek the services of Liu Shuying, an accountant, who, Kalsbeek said, "gave some splendid messages, and seemed able to reach all classes of women, beggars, peddlers, country women, and the women dressed in gorgeous satins all listened to her with the same eagerness." Liu, or "Ruby," as she was affectionately called, was not a native of Rugao but of Wuhu in Anhui Province, not far from Nanjing.[63] She was a third-generation Christian; her mother was a Bible woman and her father was a Christian schoolteacher. After being spared during the Boxer Uprising in 1900, her parents had dedicated their daughter's life to serving the Lord. Upon graduating from the Seventh Day Adventist school in Wuhu, she and her younger sister, Liu Shufen ("Rose"), both began working at the Christian Reformed mission hospital when it opened in 1924, serving as accountant and

---

[61] For the education and salary levels of rural Bible women, see Price, *Rural Church in China*, 136-37. For some of the "stigma" attached to the position of Bible women, especially related to their low levels of education, see Leung Ka-lun, *Hua ren chuan dao yu fen xing bu dao jia* (*Evangelists and Revivalists of Modern China*) (Hong Kong: Christianity and Chinese Culture Research Centre, Alliance Bible Seminary, 1999): 114ff.; and Kwok Pui-lan, "Chinese Women and Protestant Christianity," in *Christianity in China: From the Eighteenth Century to the Present*, ed. Daniel Bays (Stanford: Stanford Univ. Press, 1996), 202-03.

[62] Kalsbeek to Beets, Oct. 1, 1925, Kalsbeek, CRWM folder.

[63] Liu's dialect or accent must not have presented a problem in Rugao. Growing up in Wuhu, Anhui Province, she may even have spoken a version of the Subei dialect, which was also spoken in both Nanjing and Rugao. See Honig, *Creating Chinese Ethnicity*, map 4, 24.

drug clerk.[64] Liu Shuying became Kalsbeek's "inseparable partner" for the next twenty-five years.[65]

Unlike the ordained men, who were assigned to different sections of the field, Kalsbeek and Liu's work with women and children was spread throughout the whole area. Because there were not enough foreign Bible women to assign to each district, Kalsbeek and her Chinese associates worked in Rugao City and also in the countryside as time and opportunity permitted. Though Kalsbeek and later Bible women were not permitted to baptize converts or celebrate Communion and only had an advisory role on the mission council on issues pertaining to church organization, doctrine, discipline, and the administration of the sacraments, in all other matters related to the work with women and children they were given a free hand.[66]

Much of Kalsbeek and Liu's work involved supervising a group of young Chinese women who helped them in both the city and the countryside. Many of the young women in this group were not from Rugao, but from villages scattered around the county who had originally come to the county seat for study. The girls, ranging in age from thirteen to twenty, came to Kalsbeek and Liu's house inside the city walls to study English and to seek friendship.[67] In addition to teaching them English, Kalsbeek and Liu also provided some of them employment in order to keep them from slipping into prostitution. Because there was very little work for the girls to do in Rugao other than sorting tea leaves and making stockings, some succumbed to prostitution, nevertheless. During the flood of the winter of 1931–32, Kalsbeek and Liu employed six of these girls (four full-time and two part-time) to make clothes for refugees in the city. They hoped to continue this "industrial work" after the flood and sell handicrafts to church people in the United States.

By opening their doors and providing opportunities for them, Kalsbeek and Liu hoped that some of these girls would convert to Christianity. Some did in fact become Christians, and they played an

---

[64]   Later their brother Liu Shuhua (Paul) also moved to Rugao and served the mission, eventually marrying one of the Rugao converts.

[65]   For the relationship between foreign Bible women and their Chinese colleagues, see Hunter, *Gospel of Gentility*, 229-55.

[66]   *Acta Synode CRC, 1926* (Grand Rapids: Christian Reformed Church 1926), Art. 42, 41-42.

[67]   Kalsbeek chose to live inside the city to make herself more available to her Chinese neighbors, friends, and contacts. In 1931 alone, Kalsbeek reported hosting 1,348 guests at her own expense. See Kalsbeek, Annual Report for 1930, Kalsbeek, CRWM folder.

important role in contacting women and children throughout Rugao. This circle of young women participated in a variety of evangelistic activities. They followed the mission's tent through the county as "a sort of evangelistic band," with the specific task of running women's meetings. At these tent meetings, some of them would sing and others would give testimonies as part of introducing the main speaker, usually Liu Shuying.[68] They also fanned out into Rugao's villages, visiting homes and holding simple meetings to communicate the Christian message.

While Kalsbeek and Liu encountered very little opposition in Rugao, the young women who helped them frequently did. Most of the opposition came in the form of rude comments, but on at least one occasion three of the girls were physically mistreated. During the New Year's celebration of 1935, a city policeman struck one of the girls after she reacted to his rude comments. Several policemen quickly came over and grabbed her and her two companions and dragged them through the streets to the mayor's office, a distance of about two blocks. At the office the girls complained, and one showed where she had been kicked and her dress ripped. When they received no satisfaction at the police station, one girl's mother took the complaint to a higher official, where the girls received justice. Though the police officer in question did not lose his job—the official explanation being that he *should* lose his job, but since he came from a poor family losing his job would cause his family untold suffering—he was forced to apologize and spend three days in jail. After the incident, several of the girls dropped out of the band, and several others, "advised" by their families, stopped leading outdoor meetings in order to remain inconspicuous.[69]

Despite the opposition they encountered, this group of young women made an important contribution to the mission's work with children, and especially to the Sunday school. Other churches in the Yangzi River delta also promoted Sunday school, but according to Frank Price's survey of rural churches in the 1930s, less than half of the churches in the region held Sunday school classes, and in those churches the classes were, in Price's words, "merely another preaching

---

[68]   According to sources in Rugao, Kalsbeek and Liu only provided education and English lessons and organized the young women into a "choir" in order to further their evangelistic motives. See Yan Lingsu, "Tian zhu jiao ji du jiao zai Rugao" ("Roman Catholics and Protestants in Rugao"), *Rugao wen shi zhi ci liao* ("Information on the history of Rugao"), 8 (Rugao: Guo ying yin shua chang yin shua, 1985): 56.

[69]   Kalsbeek to Beets, March 7, 1935, Kalsbeek, CRWM folder.

service."[70] These classes met only on Sunday and were primarily for the purpose of educating the children of those attending church. Too often, complained Price, these Sunday schools were of the "orthodox type" imported "from the West—hymn, prayer, Scripture reading, class teaching, assembly, closing exercises."[71] That format would have also been typical of Sunday schools in Christian Reformed churches in the United States.[72]

But in Rugao, as a way to open doors to homes, Sunday school was an important part of the evangelistic program. After a period of "breaking in," Kalsbeek and Liu supervised their group of young women in teaching Sunday school. Sunday school in the city consisted of meetings in either one of the chapels or in Kalsbeek and Liu's home. These indoor Sunday schools were mainly for the children of converts and seekers, while outdoor Sunday schools were primarily evangelistic activities for making contacts with families. These outdoor Sunday schools or "ragged Sunday school," as they were called, were held any time or place where children would gather, including the shade of trees in temple courtyards. The teacher would pound a stake into the ground for displaying illustrations and then sit down to instruct the children.

Whether inside or outside, the mission's Sunday schools followed a simple format that included singing Bible songs, Bible verse memorization, and a Bible story. Though they had trouble with the tunes, the children loved to sing, and occasionally their teachers were "overjoyed" to hear them singing Bible songs in the streets. Bible memorization was also a favorite activity. One of the favorite verses to memorize was John 3:16, but other simple verses were recited and learned by rote as well, a practice that fit very well with the traditional Chinese pedagogy of repeating after the teacher. Some of the children took their verses home and helped their brothers and sisters memorize

[70] Price, *Rural Church in China*, 191.
[71] Ibid., 190.
[72] In the nineteenth century, many Christian Reformed people were suspicious of Sunday school as an "American innovation" that could potentially rival catechism classes ("a Trojan horse, carrying traitors inside," as Henry Beets put it), a distinctively Reformed tradition that emphasized imparting Reformed doctrine to covenant children. By the end of the century, however, Sunday schools—adapted to the CRC—and catechism classes were peacefully coexisting in most churches. Even up to the 1950s, however, the denomination still struggled with the question of whether Sunday school was an evangelistic activity or for educating the church's covenant children. See James Bratt, *Dutch Calvinism*, 15 and 59; and Kromminga, *Christian Reformed Church*, 32 and 131ff.

the scriptures, so that occasionally Kalsbeek would meet children who, though they had never attended Sunday school, could recite all of the Sunday school verses.[73] Following "memory work," one of the young women would tell a Bible story, usually using China Sunday School Union illustrations.[74] The next time the children gathered, the teacher would quiz them on the previous lesson's memory verse and story.

A main attraction of the mission's Sunday schools, both indoors and outdoors, were the picture cards teachers handed out each week. One of the Sunday School Union cards used by the mission suggests the teaching content of this medium.[75] The picture card is about two and one-half inches by four inches and features a colorful picture of Jesus leaning against a rock and surrounded by eleven men.[76] At the bottom of the card is a paraphrase of Matthew 28:19, declaring that Jesus chose twelve men to be with him and commanded them to go into the world and proclaim the "good news." On the back of the card is the theme of the picture lesson: "proclaiming the good news," (*chuan kai hao xin xi*), with several Bible verses spliced together to help explain the theme: Matthew 10:24–39 (which outlines the dangers and risks of spreading the gospel); Exodus 24:7 (a reminder to obey what God commands); and John 20:21, Matthew 28:19, and Revelation 22:17 (all three verses commanding believers to proclaim the gospel).

[73] Kalsbeek to Beets, March 2, 1925, Kalsbeek, CRWM folder.

[74] Price reports that about half of the churches surveyed in Anhui, Zhejiang, and Jiangsu used similar materials. *Rural Churches in China*, 191.

[75] The author has in his possession one of the teaching cards used by the mission. It is likely all of the cards followed a similar size and presentation. With the exception of a few of the main stories from the Old Testament (such as the Flood, David and Goliath, Daniel in the Lion's den, etc.), most of the stories were probably from the gospels and centered on Jesus' teaching. For the China Sunday School Union, see Latourette, *History of Christian Missions*, 642 and 751, and Yao, *Fundamentalist Movement*, 231-39. The mission, believing the CSSU was doing a "splendid" job, made a financial contribution to its work and appointed a missionary to serve on its board.

[76] While the teaching posters for use in churches and more formal teaching occasions appear to have been carefully crafted to reflect Chinese sensibilities, the pictures used on the Sunday school cards seem attuned to Western sensibilities. According to Yao, the methodology used by the CSSU was nineteenth-century educational theory, which stressed "the imparting of information." In the late 1910s and 1920s, the CSSU came under growing criticism for using an outdated methodology that was irrelevant to real life and unattractive to young people. Yao claims that these criticisms were from liberal missionaries who wanted to stress more social and cultural concerns. *Fundamentalist Movement*, 234.

The teaching on these cards was probably too complicated for the children, especially for those in the countryside. But that hardly mattered to the children, and even to some of their teachers, because the cards were highly prized collectors' items.[77] In the chapel Sunday schools, children with perfect attendance who could recite their memory verses received a set of picture cards. Outside, in the "ragged" Sunday schools, picture cards were used to draw children to Bible class. When children heard their teachers singing John 3:16, they would run to class with the hope of getting a picture card.[78] Children who behaved and listened well would receive cards at the end of the lesson.

Sunday school and other children's activities were specifically aimed at making contact with mothers. Kalsbeek, Liu, and their helpers visited the families of as many children as they could. Children's activities, such as summer school or other special activities, included closing ceremonies with an open invitation for sisters, mothers, and grandmothers. Contrary to the stereotype of the "confined" Chinese woman, several hundred women, in both the city and the countryside, could be drawn to these special activities.[79] These special children's activities, in turn, opened still more doors in Rugao and were natural opportunities to extend invitations to activities specifically organized for women. In 1935, the mission took advantage of a Nanjing government literacy campaign to push its own agenda. When the government threatened to impose fines and even hard labor on those who failed to learn a thousand characters, Kalsbeek and Liu sponsored literacy classes for women and girls. While Kalsbeek doubted the government's resolve and ability to enforce the law, she said the movement "offers a wonderful opportunity to form classes for women and older girls."[80] In these literacy classes, the mission typically used the Bible or other Christian literature as texts.[81]

[77]   Kalsbeek to Beets, Oct, 2, 1931, Kalsbeek, CRWM folder.
[78]   See De Korne to Beets, Nov. 15, 1931. Sheng Songru, in his description of the mission's work in Jingjiang, also notes the appeal of the picture cards for attracting children to Sunday school. See Sheng Songru, "Xie le si zai jingjiang" ("Selles in Jingjiang"), *Jingjiang wen shi ci liao* 3 (Aug. 1983): 420.
[79]   Price's data about the movement of women in rural churches also challenges the stereotype of "confined" Chinese women. More than 19 percent of his respondents said they left their villages "very often," and another 45 percent said they left their villages "often." See Price, *Rural Churches in China*, 61.
[80]   Kalsbeek to Beets, Nov. 16, 1935, Kalsbeek, personal folder.
[81]   According to Kalsbeek, the Nanjing government's literacy campaign was pushing for every "man, woman, and child to master a minimum of 1,000 characters."

The mission used activities such as literacy classes "to first win them [Rugao's women] as friends and later as the spirit works, as converts." But making friends was extremely hard work, perhaps the most demanding of all Kalsbeek's work with the women in Rugao. About it, she wrote the following:

> The work which takes the most time and energy is the extra-schedule work—the interruptions by people coming to talk over their troubles, needs or problems; hours given to personal private pleading with women and girls who are facing temptation; entertaining guests—many of them come in groups, mostly out of curiosity but we always cherish the hope that they may be led to seek spiritual enlightenment.[82]

The hope that some would seek spiritual enlightenment drove the effort for making contacts in Rugao with men, women, and children. The situation in Rugao City should have been ideal for doing so. At times there was still opposition, but much of it was muted, and the mission was able to tap into larger movements, such as the New Life Movement, to promote its own evangelistic agenda. Making contact proved much easier than making converts, however. Albert Smit wrote the following in 1937 about their meager progress in Rugao City:

> The people of Jukao have all heard or come in touch with the Gospel in some way. The Gospel has been preached in almost every part of the city, and besides we run tracts in the Jukao daily newspaper and put large posters in various parts of the city. No doubt many realize the Gospel is true, but it's still difficult to openly become a Christian, although we do feel there is a change in the attitude of the people.[83]

In contrast to the slow progress in Rugao, the mission found that its work was "rewarded by the results in the county more than in the city."[84]

Sowing in the Countryside

After they had all returned to Rugao in late fall of 1928, the missionaries divided the county into four sections. John De Korne and

---

[82] Kalsbeek, Annual Report for 1933, Kalsbeek, CRWM folder.

[83] Albert Smit, "Letter of Missionary A. H. Smit," *Missionary Monthly* 41:480 (June 1937): 136.

[84] S. Dykstra to First CRC, Grand Rapids, Nov. 1932, S. Dykstra, CRWM folder.

John De Korne watches as Chinese laborers load the mission's car onto a ferry to cross a local canal. The mission bought the car, "a new Ford," in 1928 to facilitate transportation in the Rugao countryside. In the spring of 1930, the car was involved in a road accident that killed a Chinese pedestrian.

his evangelist took Rugao City and Dingyan (Ting Yen) to the east of the city about eight miles. The three other missionaries established outstations in market towns throughout the county. Sam Dykstra took the territory to the northeast of Rugao along the canal stretching to Juejiang (Chuekiang) and the sea; his brother Harry took the territory to the southeast following the canal to Nantong and the Yangzi River; and Albert Smit took the city of Haian across the county border north in Haian County, as well as the territory stretching south of Rugao City to Shizhuang (Shih Chuang), just north of the Yangzi River. In 1932, Albert Selles, an ordained missionary who had returned to China in 1929, opened a second mission station in Jingjiang, a small county on the north bank of the Yangzi River abutting Rugao County to the southwest.[85] The work with women and children continued throughout the entire county, as time and opportunity allowed.

With the exception of the family in the city of Jingjiang, all of the missionaries lived in Rugao and traveled three to four days per week, visiting the evangelists resident in each district and participating in

---

[85]   Although Albert Selles had first come to China in 1926, he was repatriated in March 1927 along with most of the other CRC missionaries, and he returned in 1929 once the Rugao field had opened again.

activities to make contacts. Making contact in the countryside meant street preaching, "ragged" Sunday schools, tent meetings, and literature distribution.

In the early 1930s, when the mission first started expanding its work in the countryside, street preaching was an important activity for making initial contacts. The missionaries and their evangelists frequently traveled by houseboat on the canals crisscrossing the county, stopping in market towns along the way to preach. Sometimes they preached from their boats, but they preferred preaching in towns with camelback bridges spanning the canals, since these venues gave them the best vantage point for addressing large crowds. Attracting a crowd was usually not difficult. As soon as they opened their mouths to sing, either in Chinese or English, a crowd would immediately gather. One favorite hymn for attracting a crowd, according to Sam Dykstra, was "Stand Up, Stand Up for Jesus." After a crowd had gathered, someone (usually the evangelist) would give a simple gospel presentation using posters with large pictures to illustrate a theme from the Bible. As Chinese anger toward Japan grew in the 1930s, starting with the theme of fighting Japan and making a transition to "fighting for Jesus" proved an exceptionally effective way to rouse a crowd.[86]

The mission's street preaching was not limited to the canals or the bridges and was done in many other places as well. On furlough, Mina Kalsbeek reported to church audiences that she had told the "old, old story of Jesus" in a myriad of places. She had preached in a Buddhist nunnery and on a sacred hill where hundreds of pilgrims were toiling. She had preached in countless homes, both rich and poor—"one so grand that I felt rather awed by the splendor and in homes so humble that all the affairs of home and business were crowded into one small, crowded room." She had told the story in bedrooms, in guestrooms, in ancestral halls, in stores, and in carpentry shops, coffin shops, pewter shops, bakery shops, and silk shops. She had preached in courtyards where ten families lived. She had preached on busy streets, in quiet nooks against the walls of houses, in gardens, in parks, in graveyards, along country lanes, in teahouses, in hotels, and in hospitals.[87]

For making initial contacts, the mission found street preaching useful, but over time the missionaries discovered it produced diminishing returns. When they first began preaching in a new location,

---

[86]   S. Dykstra to First CRC, Grand Rapids, Oct. 12, 1931, S. Dykstra, CRWM folder.

[87]   Kalsbeek, "Lengthen Thy Cords, Strengthen Thy Stakes!" undated ms., Kalsbeek, personal folder.

crowds gathered instantly at the sight of a foreigner, with some even bowing down before them as if they were gods.[88] But if they stopped in the same place too often, "so as to become common," people tended to ignore them. To keep drawing crowds, the mission resorted to various gimmicks. Occasionally, Sam Dykstra brought along his eldest daughter to sing. With her long blonde hair and sweet voice lofting "Jesus Calls You" and "I Think When I Read that Sweet Story," she could instantly draw an enthusiastic crowd anytime, anywhere.[89] Albert Smit also found playing Chinese hymns on a second-hand Victrola an effective way to draw crowds.[90]

In the countryside, the crowds were interested in foreigners, and many also expressed interest in the mission's message. But frequently their listeners' questions revealed just how complicated it was to communicate that "old, old story" in a new setting. In one place, someone in the crowd asked Sam Dykstra if he was Jesus Christ. At another meeting taking place in a Buddhist temple, some in the crowd mistook the figure on the teaching poster to be the Buddha instead of the Christ.[91] When Mina Kalsbeek and Liu Shuying mentioned Jesus' healing of a man with a withered hand as a demonstration of his power, a group of women in the "crowd pulled one of their number forward saying, 'Can God heal this woman? She has a withered hand too!'" Completely nonplussed, Kalsbeek could give no answer. A few weeks later, after telling the story of Jesus' "'healing of the man who had been born blind,' an old blind woman came forward and said, 'Can God open my eyes?'" This time Kalsbeek answered that God could, but that he "usually did not work that way any more."[92]

In addition to street preaching, tent meetings were another effective way for the mission to make contacts in the countryside. In the winter of 1932, the mission purchased a tent in Shanghai for special meetings: a "good-looking affair," as one missionary described it, with benches and a platform; it could be adjusted to seat smaller and larger crowds, up to three hundred comfortably.[93] These tent meetings

[88]   S. Dykstra to First CRC, Grand Rapids, Sept. 1, 1926, S. Dykstra, CRWM folder.
[89]   S. Dykstra to Mission Board, Dec. 31, 1931, S. Dykstra, CRWM folder.
[90]   Smit to Beets, n.d. (probably March 1933), Smit, CRWM folder.
[91]   Matilda Huizenga, "Revival of Chinese Religion," *Missionary Monthly* 38:445 (June 1934): 167.
[92]   Kalsbeek, "Can God?...God Can!" *Missionary Monthly* 42:490 (March 1938): 127ff.
[93]   H. Dykstra, Report, Dec. 1932, 1, H. Dykstra, CRWM folder.

were for attracting crowds in the countryside, where people were more responsive to the gospel than their more "sophisticated brethren of the larger villages and towns."[94] In the spring and the fall, when there was a lull in farm work and the mosquitoes were dead but it was not too rainy or cold, the mission hired coolies and watchmen to rotate the tent through the county. Usually the tent was pitched on the farmyard of a "serious inquirer," but at least once the mission pitched it on a military training ground.

Wherever the tent was pitched, crowds filled it. Locations where the tent had never before been pitched drew especially large crowds. Occasionally, if the audience would not quiet down on opening nights, the meeting had to be cancelled and rescheduled for the next night. The tent meetings usually lasted three days, with three general evening sessions and two afternoon sessions for women and children. In some places, school was let out early so primary-aged children could attend the afternoon meetings.[95] All of the meetings focused on evangelism, usually with very simple content, since most in the audience had little education and knew nothing about Christianity. Generally, the tent meetings opened with singing. Sam Dykstra's blonde girls singing hymns always attracted a crowd. At women's meetings, Kalsbeek and Liu taught simple choruses, which the audience (frequently with as many men in attendance as women) would sing over and over until they were committed to memory. Singing was often followed by a testimony, ideally given by someone recognized in the community, either a Christian or an inquirer. At the afternoon meetings, one of Kalsbeek and Liu's entourage of young women would give a simple talk on why she believed in Christianity.

Frequently, the highlight of the tent meetings was the message given by Chen Yongsan (Chen Iong San), one of the mission's colporteurs. Chen, one of the mission's oldest employees, had been hired as John De Korne's colporteur soon after the missionaries moved to Rugao in 1923. In De Korne's estimation, Chen was an alert fellow

---

94   H. Dykstra, "Almost Persuaded," unpub. art., May 1936, H. Dykstra, CRWM folder. According to Daniel Bays, revival meetings were quite common during the Republican period but usually involved meetings of those who already believed and were for the purpose of rededication. The CRC mission's tent meetings, on the other hand, were primarily for making contacts. See Daniel Bays, "Christian Revivalism in China, 1900-1937," in *Modern Christian Revivals*, Edith L. Blumhofer and Randall Balmer, eds. (Urbana: Univ. of Illinois Press, 1993), 161-69.

95   H. Dykstra, Annual Report, 1933, H. Dykstra, CRWM folder.

but handicapped by a lack of training. As the least educated of the mission's church workers (he had only attended middle school and made the lowest salary level), De Korne had to work closely with him, instructing him in the Bible helping prepare simple messages. When they began using the tent to make contacts in the countryside, the missionaries put Chen in charge of the tent, with the responsibility of overseeing its rotation through the county.

If Chen needed help to prepare his messages, he needed no help to deliver them; he was a "natural-born storyteller" and a major attraction at tent meetings. According to Harry Dykstra, Chen had "the rare gift of clothing Bible stories in the garb Chinese country-folk appreciate. His intimate knowledge of Chinese superstitions and the wealth of funny incidents he marshals to the attack call forth hearty laughter when the hearers see themselves and as others see them."[96] Chen could take incidents from daily life and use them to illustrate his simple gospel messages. At one meeting, Chen told the story of meeting a woman who had spent all of her money worshiping idols. According to Chen, this woman said:

> The idols have just taken every cent I had. They have literally eaten me up. First I spent my savings to buy an image of Kuang-yin (Guanyin, the goddess of mercy). After the idol was in my home, I felt that I could not worship empty-handed. So I saved until I had enough money to buy a few chicks. They all died except one and that one I fed and cared for until it grew big. Then it began to lay eggs. I was so happy to see those eggs. No, I did not eat the eggs myself. They were for my idol. I took them to the store and exchanged them for a few coppers. With those coppers I bought a stick of incense for my idol every day. Every egg of my chicken went for the goddess. Sometimes I was hungry but I did not dare to keep the sacrifice of incense from the idol. I had to feed the chicken and became poorer everyday. Then Chinese New Year came around and I did not dare to offer just one stick of incense. I had to do something big for the special occasion. There was no other way. I decided to sell the chicken. With the money I bought a little tower of incense which burned for several days. After that I had no eggs to sell and the chicken was gone. Everything was eaten by the idol. Now you come here with this message of Jesus who is the only Savior. Had I only known![97]

[96]   H. Dykstra, "Had I Only Known," ms., n.d., H. Dykstra, CRWM folder.
[97]   Ibid.

When Chen's rapt audience heard this conclusion, many in the crowd exclaimed, "Bu cuo! Bu cuo!" "Yes! Yes!"

After more singing, one of the missionaries or one of their evangelists would get up to give a talk with more content than Chen could provide. When Liu Shuying talked, Kalsbeek related, she "spoke with eloquent power that could touch the four corners of the tent and could bring her listeners to tears when she mentions the waiting father and draws audible sighs of relief when she relates the prodigal son coming to his senses and returning home.[98]

In both the countryside and the city, the mission proclaimed a simple evangelistic message aimed at attracting a broad range of people. Though these simple messages might vary in approach and degree of intensity, depending on the audience and the setting, they all orbited tightly around a central theme: "Jesus saves." In other words, in these attempts to make initial contact, the missionaries steered away from the "sterner teachings" of the Reformed faith, presuming that once they had a smaller group of genuine seekers they could begin the process of communicating their Reformed distinctives.

At times some of the missionaries expressed uneasiness about broad evangelism. After addressing one particularly attentive group of forty men, John De Korne was "led to give an invitation" in "rescue mission" style. Afterwards, feeling uncomfortable for having fallen into this revivalist strategy, he wrote Henry Beets for assurance.[99] Beets replied that he had no objections to offering an "invitation." He admitted that he, too, sometimes felt the impulse to do so and lamented that Reformed people "sometimes let hearers go away without coming to some kind of decision."[100]

The simplicity of the mission's message in the 1930s also underscores the missionaries' commitment to conservative Christianity. The mission shied away from anything that had the potential for distracting from their main task: preaching Jesus. Notwithstanding the occasional pleas of some of Rugao's citizens that the mission should do more in the way of serving the people, the missionaries believed that Rugao's spiritual needs far outweighed its physical needs, reasoning besides that there were already numerous charities in the city.[101] The missionaries simply believed that given the situation in Rugao and their

---

[98] W. Kalsbeek, "Lengthened Cords," 8, Kalsbeek personal folder.
[99] De Korne to Beets, Sept. 8, 1930, De Korne, CRWM folder.
[100] Beets to De Korne, Oct. 10, 1930, De Korne, CRWM folder.
[101] According to the *Rugao xianzhi*, there were no major floods or famines during the period 1929-1937. See *Rugao xianzhi*, 116.

own limitations of personnel and resources, their primary focus must be on establishing a church.

Those missionaries and Chinese who lacked fluency or rhetorical powers used posters to illustrate their evangelistic messages. Many of these colorful China Sunday School Union posters illustrated simple themes from the gospels, focusing in particular on the life and ministry of Jesus.[102] Some of the posters depicted scenes from Jesus' parables, among them the parable of the "Ten Virgins," the parable of the "Talents" (both from Matt. 25:13ff), and the parable of the "Growing Seed" (Mark 4:26ff.). Another poster, a bit reminiscent of Buddhist moral-education illustrations, showed the "wide path to destruction" and the "narrow path to eternal life," with various punishments and rewards at both final destinations. Some posters took biblical themes and conflated them with Chinese values, such as filial piety, and illustrated them in Chinese settings. One poster, entitled "Lord teach us to pray," for instance, shows the inside of a traditional Chinese home, with a canopied bed in the background and the words over it, "The Lord is my shepherd." In the foreground is a mother in traditional dress seated on a Qing-style chair with two children kneeling before her, their heads in her lap, as if ashamed. To further emphasize the theme of filial piety, and possibly repentance, the father, dressed in the long robe worn by scholars in the 1930s, stands aloof and off to the side, with a stern look on his face and his arms crossed.

The posters used in the 1930s also tapped into the New Life Movement to promote an evangelistic agenda. One poster featured a heart at the center with the character for heart (*xin*) inside it written in ancient grass-stroke style. On the veins coming out of the heart are Bible verses explaining "new life" in Jesus Christ (John 3:7, John 14:6, 1 Tim. 1:19, and Phil. 2:13). At the bottom of the poster, in smaller print, is an explanation of the relationship between the "new life" of the Bible and Chiang Kai-shek's New Life Movement. The poster's explanation reads:

> Thanks be to Chiang Kai-shek's New Life Movement. Both he and his wife are Christians and they want missionaries in China to help create a new China. What is the relationship between the

---

[102] The author has in his possession thirteen of the posters the mission used. There is a remarkable effort in the posters to make the scenes and stories relevant to their Chinese audience. All of the faces in the posters, including that of Jesus himself, are Chinese. The clothing, furniture, and buildings all reflect Chinese sensibilities as well.

New Life Movement and the "new life" of the Christian? Chiang Kai-shek's purpose is to reform the people's attitudes, customs, and ways of doing things, which is the same purpose as that of Christianity. But in actual fact, this "new life" can only be achieved through the cross of Jesus Christ. [103]

During the 1930s, the tent got plenty of use in the countryside (the original tent, in fact, had to be replaced), but the overall effectiveness of tent meetings was difficult to judge. After the meetings, the mission sold tracts and Bible portions and talked with those who had come. Many of the people attending the meetings claimed to "believe in Jesus," but were reluctant to go beyond attending public meetings. When we try "to induce them to study," one missionary admitted, "they have no enthusiasm. Thus far they don't appear enthusiastic about entering the Christian church."[104]

In contrast to the social and political turmoil of the 1920s, the decade of the 1930s was an optimal time for advancing Christianity in Rugao. Chiang Kai-shek's efforts to unify, develop, and modernize the country brought stability and a period of relative prosperity. Taking advantage of the calm, the Christian Reformed mission attempted to find ways to connect with the people of Rugao for the purpose of planting a Reformed church. One thing the missionaries noticed was the Chinese national obsession with modernization. The mission tapped into this drive by appealing to Chinese desires to understand

[103] An interesting question involves the dating of this poster. While James Thomson draws a strong connection between the missionary movement and the New Life Movement, he fails to show direct involvement with the movement before 1936. See Thomson, *While China Faced West: American Reformers in Nationalist China, 1928-1937* (Cambridge: Harvard Univ. Press, 1969), 152, 162-63. Arif Dirlik, on the other hand, only mentions in passing a connection between the movement and Christianity, and that only through Chiang Kai-shek's wife, Song Meiling, who was a Christian herself. According to Dirlik, missionaries at first ignored the movement and only in 1936, when the *Chinese Recorder* dedicated a whole issue to the subject, did they begin to exploit it for their own use. See Arif Dirlik, "The Ideological Foundations of the New Life Movement: A Study in Counterrevolution," *Journal of Asian Studies* 34:4 (Aug. 1975): 963. If Dirlik is correct, the above poster was not used until 1936. More work needs to be done on the early Christian connections to the New Life Movement and its use by missions and independent Chinese churches, especially in rural areas.

[104] H. Dykstra, Dec. 1933 report, H. Dykstra, CRWM folder.

and participate in the modern world. However, the mission's results in Rugao were mixed at best. In the city, the women's work was the most successful, especially their efforts to create space for young women in Rugao society. Though there was a much wider response to the efforts of the missionaries in the countryside, the interest there appears to have had more to do with the "American-ness" of the missionaries and the aspects of the modern world that they brought than with their message of Christianity. Thus, in spite of the stability and openness of the early years of the Nanjing Decade, no major breakthroughs were made in planting a Reformed church in Rugao in the early 1930s. Thus far, the Christian Reformed missionaries had failed to find any of the perceived "points of contact" they had believed would help them plant a Reformed church in China.

CHAPTER 5

Red Letter Days:
Planting a Church, Mid-1930s

Imparting the Truth

After the missionaries had returned to Rugao and had adopted the "Korea Plan," they used a two-pronged strategy: they reached out to make contact while simultaneously drawing serious inquirers into small groups where the important work was done.[1] In small group settings, the mission taught a wide variety of subjects, making adjustments for different ages and education levels. For those being introduced to Christianity for the first time, the teaching focused on major stories from the Old Testament and New Testament, especially stories from

---

[1]   The term "convert" applied to those who had been accepted for baptism and were considered regular members of the church, with all of its privileges and responsibilities. "Inquirers," on the other hand, referred to those who were "interested" in joining the church. Though nowhere defined, judging from notes in mission records, the term "inquirer" was a formal designation for someone on the path to joining the church. The missionary and his evangelist would record the names of inquirers in the mission's "inquirer book." See notes from a mission meeting of Lee Huizenga and evangelist

The China field missionaries and their workers, early 1930s: (*front row, seated on ground, second from left*) John De Korne; (*seated, second from left*) Liu Shuying, Wilhemina Kalsbeek, Lillian Bode; (*third row, standing*) Albert Smit, Chen Guifan, (*far right*) Simon Dykstra; (*back row, second from left*) Albert Selles, Harry Dykstra, Wang Aitang.

Christ's life and ministry.[2] With converts and more seasoned inquirers, the mission used Bible studies from Genesis and Isaiah, Paul's epistles, and Revelation.

Another important component of instruction was catechism. Since catechism was so important in the Christian Reformed Church, it is no surprise that the mission emphasized it in Rugao. Catechism was used to bring "the children of the Covenant of grace to spiritual and ecclesiastical maturity, to a walking in Covenant ways, to inherit

Chen Guifan, April 1934. These minutes are copied from a church book (Chinese) in the Rugao Religious Affairs Bureau (RAB) office. According to Frank Price, the term was used in the Yangzi delta region to designate those who were willing to have their names enrolled, who regularly attended worship, who joined a class on Christian teaching, and who made sincere efforts to live godly lives. Such inquirers were moving toward baptism and reception as full members in the church. See Price, *Rural Church in China*, 179-80.

2   The list of Bible books and topics studied comes from missionary "monthly reports" for 1930-1931. For each month during 1930, the missionaries filled out a form that laid out in detail their work and the work done under their direction. Under "Bible classes," each missionary listed the topics he or she had taught to employees and in Bible classes.

the blessings of the Covenant, to build up the Church, and to assist in the carrying out of its mission."[3] In the denomination as a whole, "catechism" referred to the indoctrination by oral questions and answers, and to the content of this teaching. Content usually included sacred history (i.e., Bible knowledge), church history, and, above all, the Heidelberg Catechism.

Catechism in Rugao also referred both to pedagogical method and to content. Taking a simple question and answer as a main theme, Mina Kalsbeek and Liu Shuying used a catechetical approach to teaching children's classes and Sunday schools, both indoors and at the outdoor "ragged" Sunday schools. In a setting where children had never been exposed to Christianity, they would base a week's lesson on the question, "Are the idols in the temple true or false?"[4] Catechism was also the preferred method for imparting doctrine to converts and inquirers. Working closely with their Chinese evangelists and language teachers, the missionaries translated several simple catechisms and compendiums, including Borstius's *Primer of Bible Truths*, sections of *Stuart's Bible Course*, the Heidelberg Catechism, *Outline of Reformed Truth*, and *A Compendium of the Christian Religion*.[5]

This last work, *A Compendium*, provides a good example of the content of catechism in Rugao. Apart from conflating the English version's first two chapters dealing with the Bible as God's word, the mission's translation followed the remaining twenty-eight chapters almost verbatim. Like the mission's other translations, the Chinese version summarizes the teaching of the Heidelberg Catechism.[6]

---

3   Henry Beets, *Christian Reformed Church*, 217-18.
4   Kalsbeek to Beets, June 1, 1925, Kalsbeek, CRWM folder.
5   Borstius, a seventeenth-century Dutch pastor, produced several simple catechisms used widely in the Netherlands and the U.S., both in the CRC and the RCA. Taking Borstius as their source, Henry Beets and Menno Bosma, another CRC pastor, produced a series of catechisms. See Beets and Bosma's *Short Questions for Little Children*, *Sacred History for Juniors*, and *Bible Truths*. *A Compendium of the Christian Religion* was written by CRC pastor Herman Kuiper and based on a work by the seventeenth-century Dutch pastor, Herman Faukelius. Faukelius's work, first published in 1608 and promoted by the Synod of Dordt, was used in the Netherlands and the U.S. for more than two hundred years. The one criticism of the Faukelius's work was its brevity, a shortcoming that Kuiper corrected by doubling the size of the original.
6   The CRC had three confessional statements at the core of its beliefs: the Heidelberg Catechism, the Belgic Confession, and the Canons of Dordt. Because of its "warm" and "experiential" tone, the Heidelberg Catechism was the main teaching instrument of the church.

Opening with the question, "What is your only comfort in life and death?" it provides catechumens with the standard Heidelberger answer: "the assurance that he belongs to his faithful Savior Jesus Christ."[7] Like the original, the translation develops three main topics: sin (the root of the human problem), salvation (the work of the triune God in bringing about the redemption of sinners), and service (the believer's life of gratitude). Other topics include teaching on the church, justification by faith, the meaning of the sacraments, and instruction on prayer. At the back of the translation are liturgical forms for adult baptism, profession of faith, and the Lord's Supper.

In addition to translating texts, the mission produced some original catechetical materials. One work concentrates on Old Testament history.[8] In its fifty pages of forty lessons, the booklet covers the historical books of the Old Testament. More than a third of the work deals with Genesis and Exodus and treats extensively the Creation and Fall, the Noah cycle, Abraham and his descendants, and the origin of the nation of Israel. The rest of the booklet quickly covers stories from Joshua, Judges, Samuel, Kings, Chronicles, and Daniel, before treating Malachi, the last book of the Old Testament. The brevity of the work belies its attention to detail, as the following excerpt about King David illustrates:

> *Question*: How did David pass on his religious experience to God's people?
> *Answer*: David wrote many of the psalms—about half of them.
> *Question*: How many psalms are there?
> *Answer*: One hundred and fifty.
> *Question*: What was David's sin?
> *Answer*: He murdered Uriah.
> *Question*: What bad effect did this have on David?
> *Answer*: The sword never left his house.
> *Question*: What did Absalom do?

---

7   The Chinese answer is a word-for-word translation of the English (*you yi ge bao zheng, ta shi shu yu zhe zhong xin de jiu zhu ye su ji du*). The catechism is in the author's possession.

8   Albert Selles and Jin Yage (James Ching), *Bible History Catechism* (Old Testament) (*sheng jing li shi wen da—jiu yue*) (trans.). This translation accentuates one of the distinctives of the CRC's teaching ministry in Rugao: its emphasis on the Old Testament. The catechism is in the author's possession. According to Price, of fifty-three churches responding to the importance of teaching "Old Testament facts," five reported this to receive the least emphasis in their program. See Price, *Rural Church in China*, Table XXI, 198.

Answer: He rebelled against his father David because he wanted to be king.

Question: Later who also wanted to be king?

Answer: David's son Ammon.

Question: While David was still alive, who inherited his throne?

Answer: David's son Solomon.

Another work, *A Simple Catechism of the Christian Religion*, illustrates the missionaries' attempt to adapt Christian Reformed teaching to the Chinese setting. This catechism, written in a deliberately simple style for "the children of believers and those with little education," also follows the Heidelberg Catechism's formula of "sin, salvation, and service," but at certain points it was expanded to address the religious situation in Rugao.[9] In explaining the meaning of the First Commandment, for instance, the catechism asks for a specific response to China's religious practices:

Question: What does the First Commandment forbid?

Answer: The glory due to God must not be given to false gods.

Question: Give a list of the things that this commandment forbids.

Answer: All worship of idols (*bai ou xiang*), magic arts (*xing fa shi*), fortune-telling (*suan ming xiang mian*), astrology (*jian ri zi*), geomancy (*feng shui*), worship of ancestors (*jing bai zu jing*), superstitions (*mi xin*), worshiping heaven or earth (*bai tian di*), praying to nature (*qi qiu di shang de shan chuan shu mu*), or the sun, moon, or stars in the heavens (*tian shang de ri yue xing chen*).

Worship as Instruction

Another important method used for strengthening converts and teaching inquirers was worship. In the 1920s, the mission's main worship service took place in Rugao City.

After the mission reopened in 1929, however, with the mission's new emphasis on making broader contacts, worship services were held at various points throughout the field. In Rugao City, the missionaries and evangelists shared the responsibilities of leading Sunday worship and preaching. When the missionaries were visiting an outstation on Sunday, they led worship (preaching and administering the sacraments); normally evangelists led worship services at the outstations. In the 1930s, worship took place in a variety of settings. At

---

9 Selles and Jin Yage, *A Simple Catechism of the Christian Religion* (*jian ming ye su jiao wen da*), 1941 (trans.). The catechism is in the author's possession.

Albert Smit stands with worshipers at the entrance to the Rugao chapel, waiting for the service to begin, early 1930s.

Albert Smit at the backdoor of the chapel, early 1930s.

the market town of Baibu (Pai P'u) twenty miles southeast of Rugao, for instance, an inquirer closed his bakery on Sunday afternoons so that the mission could hold a worship service in his shop. When business started to decline, however, he reopened his shop, allowing the services to continue in the back, where his family lived.[10] Usually meetings in inquirers' houses and shops proved unworkable, and most worship took place in the rooms provided by the mission for the evangelist and his family, despite being contrary to the original policy adopted with the Korean Plan.[11]

The missionaries patterned worship services after those in their churches at home. Christian Reformed worship at home and on the mission field was based on these liturgical principles:

> [The] essence of public worship lies in the meeting of God with his people...these...exercises should succeed one another in an appropriate logical and psychological order. These exercises should contain nothing which is mysterious and incomprehensible to those who participate in them, lest it be impossible for them to worship the Lord in "spirit and truth." These services should be arranged so that the characteristic simplicity of a Reformed church service be maintained. We must guard against the modern tendency to Ritualism in which aesthetic pleasure is substituted and mistaken for spiritual edification, and formalism takes the place of worship "in spirit and in truth."[12]

The mission aimed for simplicity and clarity in worship. Typically, services followed this order:

Hymn
Ten Commandments
Confession of sin
Apostles' Creed
Hymn
Psalm
News
Prayer
Offering (collection of tithes)
Scripture reading
Hymn
Sermon

[10]   H. Dykstra, Report for Feb., 1935, H. Dykstra, CRWM folder.
[11]   For details of the original Korea Plan, see pp. 117-19.
[12]   *Acta Synode CRC, 1920,* 186.

Prayer
Doxology
Benediction[13]

The order of worship in Rugao varied little from that of the Christian Reformed Church. Whereas a typical Christian Reformed liturgy in America started with a *votum*, or invocation (usually from Psalm 121), and a *salutation*, worship in Rugao opened with a hymn. In the States, a creed was usually recited in the second service; in Rugao every service included the recitation of the Apostles' Creed, no doubt to reinforce basic Christian doctrine. At home, "announcements" came at the end of the service, so as not to interrupt the flow of "communication with God." In Rugao, however, "announcements" were presented in the middle of the service (perhaps to insure that everyone who was coming was there) and included announcements about when the next Lord's Supper would be celebrated, when the next examination session would be held, who was under discipline, and other church information.

The use of hymns was one of the most significant differences between worship at home and in China. In the Christian Reformed Church, the use of hymns was a sensitive issue. Based on the grounds that psalm-singing was the practice of the early church, and because John Calvin favored psalms over the latent Mariology in the hymns of his time, Christian Reformed church order allowed *only* the use of psalms in worship.[14] Church leader Henry Beets argued that psalm-singing was a "command of the Lord," that it followed the example of the followers of Christ, and, above all, that it met "the great requirements of praise: exalting God in creation, providence, and redemption, while containing confessions of our unworthiness, expressions of our faith, our gratitude, our needs, etc."[15] By 1934, however, the denomination's first hymnal, the *Psalter Hymnal*, included 141 "carefully selected" hymns.[16] Though the missionaries were personally committed to

---

[13] This liturgy is translated from a "worship order" (*da li bai cheng xu dan*) on the inside cover of John De Korne's Chinese hymnal. The hymnal is in the author's possession.

[14] John Bratt, "Southern Presbyterian and Christian Reformed Church of America," 43. The RCA's use of hymns in worship was also a reason given by four churches for splitting from the denomination in 1857 and forming the CRC. See Zwaanstra, *Reformed Thought*, 5.

[15] Beets, *Christian Reformed Church*, 210.

[16] The inclusion of hymns in CRC worship was a long and often painful struggle. Theologically and historically the denomination was opposed to hymn singing, but calls for including hymns in worship began to be louder

singing psalms in public worship, their situation did not allow it in Rugao, since very few of the psalms had been put to music.[17] Forced to use what they could find at hand, the missionaries chose *Songs of Praise to the Lord* (*song zhu shi ge*), a generic Protestant hymnal. Compiled in 1918, this collection of more than four hundred hymns consisted almost entirely of European and American Protestant hymns, with only a handful written by Chinese composers, and only four from the Psalms (Psalm 23, 98, 121, and 150).[18]

A missionary, a spouse, one of their children, or a Chinese Christian accompanied singing in worship services on the pedal organ.[19] The missionaries found teaching the Chinese to sing "the foreign way" a formidable task, but one that paid dividends, since songs learned by heart often carried the message of Christianity into homes.[20] The mission used a variety of songs from the hymnal, including many Protestant "old favorites": "A Mighty Fortress Is Our God," "Rock of Ages," "Onward Christian Soldiers," "I Need Thee Every Hour," "Jesus I Come," "Take My Life and Let It Be," "Take Time To Be Holy," "Sweet Hour of Prayer," "What a Friend We Have in Jesus," and "He Leadeth Me."[21] Among those chosen by the Chinese evangelists were "Ho, My Comrades," "See the Signal?" "Who Is on the Lord's Side?" and "My God, My God!"[22]

Other hymns used in worship praised Jesus Christ for his great love and mercy, offered comfort in times of trial and struggle, and celebrated the work of the Holy Spirit and the work of the church. Several songs expressed patriotic sentiments, such as "Savior, Save Our Beloved China" (*jiu zhu jiu wo men zhong guo*), "China Return to the

---

in the second decade of the twentieth century. After more than a decade of informal discussion in the denomination, the synod of 1928 appointed a study committee to look into the matter. In 1934 that committee introduced the denomination's first hymnal, the *Psalter Hymnal*, which contained 327 psalm settings and 141 hymns. See "We Used to Only Sing Psalms—What Happened?" *Reformed Worship* 3 (March 1987): 32-35.

17 On Sunday nights, in their private worship services with their families, the missionaries sang psalms, often in Dutch.

18 See *Song zhu shi ge* ("Songs of Praise to the Lord") (Shanghai: Gospel Joint Publishing Society, 1918) (*Fu yin shua he zi hui she*, 1918).

19 Wang Aitang was among the evangelists who could play the piano.

20 See Sam Dykstra, letter in *Missionary Monthly* 41:478 (April 4, 1937), and Kalsbeek to Beets, Aug. 12, 1925, Kalsbeek, CRWM folder.

21 These hymns are among those annotated with phonetic symbols in John De Korne's hymnbook.

22 Wang Aitang chose these hymns for a service in 1947. Albert Smit to De Korne, Oct. 1947, Smit, CRWM folder.

Lord" (*zhong hua gui zhu*), and "My country Tis of Thee," with words adapted for China (*wo ai zhong hua mei di*). Sometimes services included songs written by Chinese, and these might include "Wisdom and Virtue for the Lord's Servant" (*wei zhu pu ren xu song qi de neng*), "My Heart of Joy and Praise" (*wo xin huan xi song yang*), and "God Established His Law to Command the People of the World" (*shang di li lu ming shi ren*).[23]

Some songs reinforced teaching. One teaching song, "Jesus Is Savior" (*ye su shi jiu zhu*), was probably used in the countryside to indoctrinate converts and inquirers with little education. The song summarizes Jesus' victory over sin and his benefits for believers:

> Jesus is savior, he came down from heaven
> Jesus is savior, he was completely perfect and without sin
> Jesus is savior, he was tempted by the devil
> Jesus is savior, the world is thoroughly sinful
> Jesus is savior, he came to the world to forgive me
> Jesus is savior, his precious blood washed away the corruption of sin
> Jesus is savior, he calls people to worship the heavenly Father
> Jesus is savior, he leads people on the heavenly path
> Jesus is savior, believe in the Lord and receive real blessings
> Jesus is savior, believers enter the heavenly city[24]

Though the missionaries had to use hymns, they remained faithful to other aspects of Christian Reformed worship. As at home, worship in Rugao included use of the Ten Commandments (*shi tiao jie ming*) and a Confession of Sin (*ren zui wen* or *ren zui dao wen*). Reading the Law was considered an essential aspect of Reformed worship. Because its importance had not ended in the New Testament, though its function had changed, the Law had pedagogical value for teaching Christ's followers how to live a life of gratitude.[25] The Christian Reformed Church supported this so-called "third use of the law" with Calvin's statement that the Law was "a perpetual spur that will not allow the spiritual man to loiter," but will help him to press on toward sanctification.[26] In China, the mission's translation of their denomination's liturgical forms included a full version of the Ten

---

[23]   These last three hymns come from notes De Korne made in selecting hymns for an undated worship service.

[24]   Handwritten Chinese song found in De Korne's hymnbook. The song is in the author's possession.

[25]   Not all "Reformed" churches used the law in worship; Southern Presbyterians did not, for example. See John Bratt, "Southern Presbyterian and Christian Reformed Church of America," 40.

[26]   John Calvin, *Institutes of the Christian Religion*, II, vii, 12. Quoted in James Bratt, *Dutch Calvinism*, 41.

Commandments (based on Exodus 20) and a simplified summary. Occasionally church members read the Law, which was likely the only part of the worship service in which lay worshipers participated in leading worship.[27]

Since prayer was another important aspect of worship, the mission compiled "model prayers" for use in services.[28] One model prayer was used before the offering was taken (*feng juan de dao gao wen*).[29] Acknowledging that everything comes from heaven, the prayer asks God to receive back a small token of thanks and "to bless them [the offerings] so that they might be used in an appropriate way to glorify God." Another model prayer was used before the sermon (*da li bai jiang dao qian de yi ge dao gao wen*). The prayer implores God to be with those suffering from floods and famine, those who had lost loved ones, and those in prison.[30] It thanks God for allowing the congregation to gather for worship and for protecting the members throughout the week. The prayer then entreats God to help "his servant," the preacher, speak the truth, plant the Word in the hearts of listeners, and prevent Satan from snatching the truth away from them.

Another model prayer was for the nation (*wei guo jia qi dao wen*). This prayer gives thanks to God for creating all things (*wan wu*) and above all for creating humankind (*ren lei*). It acknowledges the responsibility that humankind has to represent God as a "steward (*yuan fu*) over the garden of creation." Even after the fall, though humankind was spread out over the earth and established different nations, we still have the mandate to tend the creation, with the responsibility "to make the whole world like a heavenly garden." Acknowledging the shortcomings of the nation of China, the prayer goes on to ask God to bless the "party" (*Guomindang*) and to help it return to righteousness.

As at home, the sermon was at the center of worship in Rugao. Sermons preached in the Christian Reformed tradition were not

---

[27] See notes of Huizenga and Chen Guifan meeting, April 1934, in which they decided a member should read the Ten Commandments on Easter Sunday. Rugao RAB files (trans.).

[28] The three undated prayers summarized here are translated by the author from prayers found in De Korne's papers. De Korne, personal folder (trans.). The complexity of the Chinese and the reference to current events suggests they were written by the evangelists and not translated from English.

[29] In only eight of the churches Price surveyed was an offering taken. All but one of these churches reported only receiving offerings from between two and five members. Price, *Rural Church in China*, 158.

[30] The mention of "floods and famines" suggests the prayer was written in 1931, the winter of a catastrophic flood in northern Jiangsu Province.

the energetic, optimistic discourses typical of American Protestant sermons of that time. They were sober, exegetical discourses that first explained a text and its relation to (CRC) doctrine before ending with an application. Though exegetical, the messages tended to turn on a few prominent themes: human sinfulness, God's mercy, Christ's suffering, and sinners' utter dependence on Christ for deliverance.[31] Application of these biblical truths called for the Christian "to cultivate a private intimacy with God; hostility to the lusts of the flesh and lures of the world; direction of good works toward the temporary and remedial; and persistent anticipation of one's heavenly destiny.[32] At least once per Sunday, usually in the second service, one segment (or "Lord's Day") from the Heidelberg Catechism was preached.

In China, the missionaries preached in Chinese, on average three times per month.[33] Scattered references reveal only a few of their sermon themes. Harry Dykstra preached at least one sermon on John 17, entitled "Unity."[34] In January 1931, John De Korne preached a sermon on sanctification, and at Easter one entitled "Christ is Risen Indeed!" Sometimes the missionaries recast their sermons as evangelistic tracts, as De Korne did in 1931 with his sermon, "Jesus as the Only Savior."[35] Albert Selles preached a sermon, "I Am Also a Man" (*wo ye shi ren*), based on a passage in Acts (3:1-10), in which the Apostle Peter heals a lame beggar and a crowd quickly gathers around him in amazement.[36] In the first part of the sermon, Selles explained that though Peter had healed the lame beggar, he was only a "man"; in the second part he explained that though a sinner, Peter had been forgiven by God, and that his listeners could also be forgiven by God. The missionaries and their evangelists frequently worked together on sermons; usually the missionary helped the evangelist with interpretation, and the evangelist helped the missionary with Chinese. During the week in 1931 when John De Korne prepared a sermon on sanctification, evangelist Chen Guifan prepared a sermon on Christ's suffering.[37] Occasionally,

[31] James Bratt, *Dutch Calvinism*, 42.
[32] Ibid.
[33] This estimate is based on missionary reports from 1930-31.
[34] H. Dykstra's text and sermon title were published in the hospital's March 1926 newsletter.
[35] De Korne to Beets, Jan. 29, 1931, and April 2, 1931, De Korne, CRWM folder.
[36] The outline for this undated sermon was scrawled on a bank deposit slip tucked in Selles's Chinese Bible. The Bible and sermon outline are in the author's possession.
[37] De Korne to Beets, Jan. 29, 1931, De Korne, CRWM folder.

evangelists had to be corrected for statements they made in sermons, as when one evangelist hinted in a message that Japanese enforced silence on Independence Day "would be followed by all the greater vengeance in the future."[38]

The few evangelists' sermons on record include one that hospital evangelist Zhou Daqing preached in Rugao, "The Cross" (*shi zi jia*). The message explains Christ's cross as the unity of love, as the way of salvation, as completely miraculous, and as the place where God judges sin.[39] Zhou summed up his sermon with a verse from the Gospel of John: "And I, if I be lifted up from the earth, I will draw all men unto myself" (12:32). The same month that Zhou preached this sermon, Chen Fang, another hospital evangelist, preached a sermon on the same topic. In "The Cross of Jesus," Chen spliced together texts from the Old and New Testaments to illustrate that despite the physical and emotional pain Jesus suffered on the cross, God used it to show love for sinners (John 3:16), and to give them joy (Heb. 12:2) and peace (Isa. 53: 7). Wang Aitang prepared a sermon on the first temptation of Christ, which one missionary reported to be "solid spiritual food."[40]

The most intriguing Chinese sermon on record is one preached by evangelist Dai Ruiling. It is a two-part message, "Jesus' Concept of Sin" (*ye su dui yu zui e de guan nian*), in which Dai raises questions about sin and its consequences.[41] Using a passage from the Gospel of John as a springboard, Dai explains that a proper definition of sin is important for everyone, not just religious professionals.[42] He goes on to explain that there are many definitions of the term. In the past, for instance, to have more than one wife (*nan zi duo qi*) was not considered a sin in China, but, he notes, by contemporary "religious standards...it is considered a sin of great moral lapse." As an example of different conceptions of sin in different places, Dai notes that kissing between men and women in public in the West is an expression of affection, but

---

38 H. Dykstra report, Jan. 1932, H. Dykstra, CRWM folder.
39 The outline of Zhou's sermon was published in the hospital's March 1926 newsletter, in the column, "Rugao's Pulpit," which outlined the sermons for January of 1926 (trans.). There are detailed outlines of the Chinese sermons preached, but only the text and title of the sermon Harry Dykstra preached that month.
40 Smit to De Korne, Oct. 1947, Smit, CRWM folder.
41 The sermon is reprinted in the hospital newsletter, Feb. 1926.
42 Dai lists as his text John 9:1-12, a story about the healing of a blind beggar that raises questions about sin, but Dai never refers directly to the text. Dai was released by the mission following the evangelists' strike of 1927 but rehired in the early 1930s.

that in China it is considered unethical. Dai also points out that sin is different in different religions. While Buddhists consider worshiping the Buddha a virtue, Christians consider it "the ultimate sin." From these examples, Dai concludes that "it is difficult to lay down an absolute concept of sin." His purpose in this message, he said, was to interpret "the Bible's real meaning," something he promised to do the next week in the second part of his message. Unfortunately, there is no record of evangelist Dai's second message.

Several months later, however, he contributed another meditation to the hospital newsletter, "A Study of Jesus' Humanity" (ye su ren xing de yan jiu), in which he discusses human perfectibility.[43] Dai argues that Christians are able to be perfect as Jesus was perfect. Sometimes, he explains, when people read about Jesus' miracles and his perfection, they say, "I can't be a Christian, because Jesus' truth is too high; it's beyond what I can do." But, Dai argues, God does not demand of people what is impossible for them. So when Jesus commands his disciples to be perfect (Matt. 5:48) and says that his followers will do greater things than he did (John 14:12), his words must be true. Dai concludes, in "morals (dao de), character (ren ge), and conduct (pin xing), there is nothing that people cannot obtain, but the highest and lowest (gui jian) of man is what he chooses....[For] as Mencius said, 'What kind of man was Shun? What kind of man am I? He who exerts himself will also become such as he was.'"[44] Dai's implication about human perfectibility clashed with the missionaries' teaching, but there is no indication that they reacted to it.[45]

From Inquirer to Convert

The aim of worship was to bring inquirers to conversion and to strengthen converts in order to establish an independent church. Throughout the year, the mission held meetings at its outstations and worship points to examine candidates for baptism. Being accepted

---

[43] Dai Ruiling, "Hospital newsletter" (Dec. 14, 1926): 2.

[44] The quote from Mencius (Shun yi ren ye, zi yi ren ye, zi he wei bi zai) comes from The Works of Mencius. In this first part of Book III, pt. 1, Mencius begins his discussion of human nature, which he concludes is good but in need of rigorous training. Shun was the second of the three legendary "Sage-Kings" praised in Chinese culture for their wisdom and virtue. See Dorothy Perkins, Encyclopedia of China: The Essential Reference to China, Its History and Culture (New York: Roundtable, 2000), 460.

[45] The failure to react may be related to Huizenga's low level of Chinese (i.e., he was not able to read what Dai had written).

for baptism was not an easy matter. Inquirers were examined on their knowledge of the Bible and Christian doctrine and their faithfulness in living the Christian life. Most candidates were examined three or four times over at least a two-year period before they were finally accepted for baptism.[46]

Some of the candidates, such as farmer Wang Yunqing, age thirty-two, were hampered by illiteracy. Others were hampered by limited mental capacity. John De Korne noted that Cong Luchang, age forty-five and a former landlord of the mission, was "not very bright." Occasionally, candidates impressed the mission at their first examination with the ability to recite portions of the catechism, the Apostles' Creed, the Lord's Prayer, and the Ten Commandments. But one good exam was not enough to assure acceptance for baptism: the mission looked for progress in a second examination before confirming promising candidates. After their first examination, De Korne wrote that Wang Tongqing, age twelve, and his younger brother Wang Tongkang, age ten, had made a "fine start on the catechism." In a second examination, however, he noted about Tongqing, the older boy: "not much progress over last time, even appears...to have forgotten much of what he knew previously." Finally, at a third examination, both boys, as well as their father, Wang Tongkang, age thirty-seven, and a hotelkeeper in Shuangdian, were accepted for baptism.

Inquirers examined for baptism were asked five questions. The first question dealt with belief in the Triune God.[47] The question was more concerned with idol worship than with Trinitarian formulation, however. While many in Rugao were willing to hear the message of Christianity and even accept it as "true," when it came to putting away their idols, some claimed, "We know that what you are saying is true but this is our custom and if we don't do it people will laugh at us."[48] But merely renouncing idols was not enough. In more than one case, the mission rejected a request for baptism when there were still idols

---

[46] The following information comes from notes John De Korne made about examinations which took place between 1930 and 1931 in Shuangdian (Shuang-tien), the mission's oldest outstation, located on a canal about twelve miles east of Rugao. De Korne and evangelist Cao Zizhen (Ts'ao Tsi-chen) examined twenty-one inquirers three times over a year-and-a-half period (Oct. 10, 1930; April 7 and 9, 1931; and Oct. 28, 1931). Most of these inquirers were examined all three times, with only five passing on the third examination. De Korne, personal folder.

[47] The questions are translated from notes found in De Korne's personal folder.

[48] Kalsbeek to Beets, Oct. 1931, Kalsbeek, CRWM folder.

in an inquirer's home, even though the idols belonged to other family members. The mission was afraid that in times of crisis, the convert might be tempted to implore the idol, or, even more likely, be forced to do so by other family members. This happened to one of Sam Dykstra's inquirers, who, after the death of his sister in childbirth, was forced, "as the representative of the family," to burn spirit money for his dead sister and her baby.[49]

For many inquirers, however, giving up idols was easy compared with giving up ancestor worship. At every examination the question was asked, "When was the last time you worshiped your ancestors?" At her first examination in April of 1931, Cong Xinzhen, the forty-one-year-old wife of Cong Luchang, seemed an ideal candidate for baptism. John De Korne noted she was "very bright" (in contrast to her husband), that she was "well posted in Bible truth," and that her family was "determined to follow Christ." She also reported that all idols had been eliminated from the family's house and that no incense had been burned for more than two years. But she failed the examination because, De Korne noted, the family still "remembers" its ancestor, and Cong Xinzhen justified doing so because, she said, this family ritual was "different from the worship of God." Eight months later, she was turned down a second time, even though she had not worshiped ancestors for six months and was eager to receive baptism.

The missionaries' daily experience in Rugao indicated that ancestor worship was at the core of the Chinese religious tradition.[50] Around them everywhere, they saw the homage paid to ancestors at the ubiquitous family shrine in homes, at the gravesites that dotted the countryside, and in the numerous ancestral halls and temples throughout the county. The commonplace sight of tables laden with offerings to the deceased made it difficult to imagine the practice as anything more than worship calculated to cultivate blessing and avoid punishment. But the missionaries were also aware of scholarly discussions that traced the practice in the Chinese classics as important for cultivating filial piety. While appreciating the ethical value of ancestor worship in cultivating virtue, the missionaries rejected its practice in Christian homes as a subtle and thus particularly pernicious

---

[49] S. Dykstra to First CRC, Grand Rapids, June 10, 1931, S. Dykstra, CRWM folder.

[50] The following discussion comes from John De Korne, *Chinese Altars to the Unknown God* (Grand Rapids: Smitter, 1926), 50-56, 99, and 103-04; and H. Dykstra, "Evangelistic Work in our China Field," *Banner* 59 (July 18, 1924): 452-53.

form of idolatry. Indeed, John De Korne called ancestor worship "the greatest single obstacle to the progress of the Christian church in China today."[51]

Though the mission refused to budge on ancestor worship, like most Protestants, it did attempt to accommodate inquirers' respect for the dead.[52] In the 1930s, the mission began holding memorial services for Christians and inquirers. When the mother of one of Mina Kalsbeek and Liu Shuying's young women died of rabies, the mission held a memorial service every seven days after her death, following the traditional custom of the "seven sevens" sacrifices for the dead. The body of Tzan Toh Tzen's mother was placed in a coffin with the characters for "Christian" painted on it in black, and the coffin was placed in the family's house. Although the immediate family's refusal to burn incense angered the extended family and some neighbors, the mission's memorial services for her were well attended, sometimes topping seventy people, and the mission was pleased that so many non-Christians had an opportunity to hear the Christian message at her funeral.

The mission hoped that Christian funeral practices would catch on across the field. Of efforts made by Christians in Libao (Li Pao), a district to the northeast of Rugao, to transform funeral practices, Harry Dykstra wrote the following:

> Church leaders decided to buy a Christian funeral ground. They also decided to seek contact with Christians in other parts of the field in order that they might cooperate in making definite plans for Christian funerals. Standardized coffins are planned which

---

51   De Korne, *Chinese Altars*, 103.

52   For a summary of Protestant resolutions coming out of the Centenary Missionary Conference on ancestor worship held in Shanghai in 1907, see De Korne, *Chinese Altars*, 102-13. Frank Price's survey of the Yangzi Delta region found that only thirteen of the sixty-eight churches surveyed opposed *all* forms of ancestor worship, and that the other churches generally rejected some aspects of the practice. The forms rejected included "kneeling and kowtowing, burning incense and paper money, sacrifices, presenting of sacrificial foods, burning of candles, all superstitious ceremonies at graves, and worship of ancestral tablets." Many of the churches in the region tried to find suitable alternatives for Christians to show respect for their dead by allowing tomb sweeping at the Qingming festival; memorial services in homes, churches, or cemeteries; and observances of birthdays of the deceased parents or ancestors using pictures and photographs, as long as these things were only used for "sincere remembrance but not worship." See Price, *Rural Church in China*, 203.

will be used by Christians for their dead without distinguishing between rich and poor. A burial service will be arranged which will challenge the respect of pagan neighbors. If present intentions can be carried out a heavy burden will be removed from the shoulders of our Christians. The non-Christians will soon learn that Christians do not seek vain-glory in the extravagant funerals because we believe our departed ones have gone to the house with many mansions. At the same time proper respect shown for the body of the departed person will emphasize the truth of our Christian belief that in God's time the flesh will again arise from the humiliation of the grave.[53]

The second question posed to those seeking baptism concerned sin. Inquirers were asked if they believed in original sin and in total depravity and if they hated their own sin. From the missionaries' Calvinist perspective, conviction of sin was the *sine qua non* of being saved. At times, the missionaries found troubling the "conspicuous lack of the conviction of sin" in Rugao.[54] After attending a Bible study upon his return to Rugao in 1928, John De Korne noted, "I didn't notice any evidences of a sincere seeking after the truth: much less did I notice any sense of sorrow for sin; how could there then be any genuine turning to the Lord for salvation?"[55] Even among their evangelists, this sense of sin may have been dubious, as evidenced by Dai Ruiling's sermon on sin mentioned above. When they did perceive a sense of sin in an inquirer, the missionaries noted potential for breakthroughs, as when De Korne sensed in a group "a hunger for the Word of God," and "something of a proper sense of humility as in the awful presence of Almighty God."[56]

The third question posed to inquirers dealt with the life and ministry of Jesus. There is no indication that this question posed a problem for any of the mission's inquirers seeking baptism. But the fourth question, about commitment to the teaching of the church, touched on a troublesome issue in Rugao. The inquirer was asked, "Will you forsake all secret societies, factions, and groups which rebel against orthodoxy, etc.?" Cults and sects were something of a problem in the Rugao area. In his 1932 critique of the mission's "new method" (the Korean method), which prohibited missionaries or their evangelists

---

[53]   H. Dykstra, "Christian funerals in our Jukao field," unpub. ms., H. Dykstra, CRWM folder.
[54]   Kalsbeek to Beets, April 1, 1926, Kalsbeek, CRWM folder.
[55]   De Korne, "China Chips," pt. 3, *Banner* 63 (Feb. 17, 1928): 132.
[56]   Ibid.

from renting chapels in favor of meeting in homes, Sam Dykstra worried it would aggravate "the danger of promoting cliques and secret societies as formerly encountered in Rugao."[57] In Dongchen (Tong-ch'en), on the canal between Rugao and Shuangdian, the mission had met strong opposition from "the most popular religion in China."[58] Christian sects could be a problem, too. After a group of Christians from the outstation of Libao returned to their ancestral home in Haimen in 1937, they joined a group of Seventh Day Adventists who practiced faith healing. Later, Sam Dykstra convinced those who had become Adventists in Haimen to return to the traditional Protestant teachings and practices they had earlier accepted through the mission's work in Libao.[59]

The final question posed to inquirers dealt with issues related to the Christian life. Are you willing to forsake "this world," they were asked, "and the evil desires of the world?" This "forsaking the world" was a sensitive question in the Christian Reformed Church in the States during the twenties and thirties. In the 1920s, the denomination had been roiled by a controversy over the question of "common grace" and its implications for Christian living. Some in the denomination followed the lead of Dutch theologian Abraham Kuyper, who taught that in addition to God's special grace, which only the elect received,

---

[57] S. Dykstra, "New Method of Work, 1929-1932," S. Dykstra, CRWM folder.

[58] There is no mention of the name of this secret society, but it may have been the "Great Harmony Society" (*da tong hui*), China's largest secret movement during the Republican period, a sect which synthesized Daoism, Buddhism, and Confucianism with Islam and Christianity. The presence of secret societies in Rugao sparked John De Korne's interest to write a dissertation on one sect called the "Fellowship of Goodness" (tong shan hui). See John De Korne, "Fellowship of Goodness: A Chinese Secret Religious Society," Ph.D. diss. (Hartford, Conn: Hartford Seminary, 1934).

[59] About this incident and the Adventist group, Sam Dykstra wrote: "They [the Libao Christians] traveled ten miles on Saturday to worship on the Sabbath and fifteen to reach a meeting of an independent, self-supporting church which was held on Sunday. These latter were believers in faith cures and most of them had been brought in through sickness. They pray with the sick and if they be not healed, tell them that they are too guilty to receive the blessing. They must first sell a few boxes of Gospels and then return for more prayer. They are fined if they neglect worship on Sunday. We met with representatives of this sect when we reached our most distant point more than a hundred miles from Rugao. They gave us the evening service and they were surprised by our soberness, contrasting with their own enthusiasm." S. Dykstra to First CRC, Grand Rapids, May 4, 1937, S. Dykstra, CRWM folder.

God extended a "common grace" to all of humankind. While this view provided an expansive vision of Christian action in the world, some argued that Kuyper's view opened the back door to "worldliness."[60] Three of the church's synods, addressing the question of "worldly amusements," categorically condemned gambling, dancing, and the cinema as out of bounds for Christians.[61]

Temptations to "worldliness" were plentiful in Rugao. Gambling—games of chance, almost any use of cards, and dice—was rejected in the Christian Reformed Church, because it "denied God's sovereignty and defied his providence."[62] But gambling was ubiquitous in Rugao, especially the game of mahjong (*ma jiang*), played by people of all ages. The missionaries found the sight of "children gambling furiously in the street" appalling. Part of the rationale for teaching the children games in Sunday school, Mina Kalsbeek wrote, was to "discourage gambling, which," she added, "seems to be their only sport."[63] Although there are no specific cases on record of a conflict between the mission and converts or inquirers over gambling, Sam Dykstra commented, "Gambling and other social sins have a very wide range and we are at times astonished to learn of the connections of those who have become seekers after God."[64]

Attending the cinema was also a temptation in Rugao during the 1920s and 1930s. The synod of 1928 had declared that "those who attended 'innocent' plays or movies supported an industry generally given over to evil, endorsed the conduct of stage and screen personnel,

---

[60]   For details of Kuyper's views about common grace and its implications, see James Bratt, *Dutch Calvinism*, 32.

[61]   For the synodical discussions about "worldly amusements," see *Acts of Synod*, 1924, 148; 1926, 56-58; and the synodical report in *Acts* 1928, 86-89; an abridgment of the report appears in *Banner* 63 (May 4, 1928): 344-45; and *Banner* 63 (May 11, 1928): 359. See also Kromminga, *Christian Reformed Church*, 120ff, and James Bratt, *Dutch Calvinism*, 116-17.

[62]   James Bratt, *Dutch Calvinism*, 117.

[63]   Kalsbeek to Beets, Aug. 8, 1926, Kalsbeek, CRWM folder. Providing activities as a distraction from gambling was a common missionary strategy. See *China Church Yearbook*, 1924, 424.

[64]   S. Dykstra to First CRC, Grand Rapids, April 15, 1926, S. Dykstra, CRWM folder. The missionaries were not the only ones disgusted with gambling in Rugao. Sha Yuanbing, one of the leading gentry in the city, detested mahjong. When people saw him approaching, they would hide their gambling devices in an effort to avoid being scolded. See Barkan, "Patterns of Power," 197. In the late 1920s, as part of their program of social reform, the local branch of the Nationalist Party also tried to abolish all gambling and lotteries. See "KMT Reform Agenda" n.d., De Korne, personal folder.

and developed a habit that would weaken their powers of moral discrimination and lead them to attend wicked shows."[65] Not much is known about the cinema in Rugao, but the missionaries did complain that the theaters drew bigger crowds than their chapel services. Given the city's proximity to Shanghai, it is highly likely that the citizens of Rugao were aware of and enjoyed the burgeoning movie industry there.[66]

Dancing was immoral, the 1928 synod said, because it nourished forbidden lusts.[67] There is no indication that dancing was a temptation in Rugao, but the sexual licentiousness associated (in CRC minds) with dancing was noted by the missionaries. In an oblique reference to some of the temptations and sins that beset inquirers and converts in Rugao, Sam Dykstra mentioned that his supporters should read the lists of sins in the Apostle Paul's letters to the early church.[68] Just so they did not miss his point, he added, "Our hospital report gives you some idea of the diseases that afflict this community and there is so often a direct connection between sin and suffering, so you may often be enabled to estimate the inroads of sin by reading the records of the physician." Dykstra's delicate reference was obviously to sexually transmitted diseases, which at least one hospital report recorded as the clinic's second-most-treated ailment, accounting for 10 percent of total treatments for inpatients.[69]

Gambling, cinema, and illicit sexual relations were all potentially besetting temptations in Rugao, but the biggest stumbling block for inquirers was a sin of omission: weak Sabbath observance. "Keeping the Sabbath day holy" was an issue in the United States as well. In a 1929 *Banner* article, "Sabbath Observance," Henry Beets blamed

---

[65] "Report on Worldly Amusements," *Synodical Agenda*, 1928, 35-36; quoted in James Bratt, *Dutch Calvinism*, 268 n43.

[66] There is some conflicting evidence about cinema in Rugao. The missionaries reported the populace's interest in cinema, but the *North China Herald* reported in 1934 that a movie theater was left unfinished when the builder ran out of funds for completing the project. See *North China Herald* (March 14, 1934): 407 and (July 4, 1934): 12.

[67] James Bratt, *Dutch Calvinism*, 40-41.

[68] S. Dykstra to First CRC, Grand Rapids, April 15, 1926, S. Dykstra, CRWM folder.

[69] The most common ailments of inpatients at the mission hospital in 1925 were hookworm and sexually transmitted diseases. See "Second Annual Report of the Christian Reformed Hospital, 1925," 5, Huizenga, CRWM folder. Price's respondents also reported in the 1930s that illicit sexual relations were "becoming something of a problem in rural communities." See Price, *Rural Church in China*, 61-62.

the increasing lawlessness in the States on "the alarming increase of *Sabbath desecration.*"[70] Moreover, he was afraid that too many people in the denomination, "their consciences dulled by the prevalence of sinful or doubtful practices on the Lord's Day," were breaking the fourth commandment, despite the fact that it was read each Sunday in the morning service. While Beets did not advocate a return to an earlier generation in the church, which applied Sabbath keeping in a "*Puritanic or legalistic*" fashion resulting in a day "of monotony and gloom," he strongly urged the church to get back to the high standards set by the Synod of Dordt, which stated that the purpose of the Lord's Day was three-fold: "*rest, worship,* and *service.*"[71]

If Sabbath observance in the United States was difficult to uphold, it was next to impossible in China. Unlike Americans, with their rhythm of six days of labor and one day of rest, the Chinese labored seven days a week, only taking off during the lunar New Year celebrations. Catholic missionaries had tried to introduce the practice of Sabbath in the sixteenth century but had made accommodations when they were unable to alter the traditional rhythm of life.[72] Protestants, too, when they came to China in the nineteenth century, found it difficult to get Chinese Christians to practice strict Sabbath observance. In the 1920s, as part of its attempts to modernize the country, the Nationalist government had tried to alter this several-thousand-year-old rhythm by instituting a six-day workweek with a seventh day of rest. It, too, was unsuccessful. The idea of Sabbath rest went against deep cultural grooves.

Frank Price's survey of rural churches in the 1930s confirmed the difficulty of Sabbath observance in the Yangzi delta region. Of the fifty-four churches responding to questions about the Sabbath, only ten reported that their members kept "strict Sabbath observance."[73] In the other churches, 69 percent of farm members did farm work on Sundays, and 71 percent of merchant members opened their shops. More than 70 percent of the churches surveyed expressed the view that strict Sabbath observance was impossible, with another 8 percent stating that it was possible but very difficult. Price also found that regular attendance at worship was difficult for a number of reasons, including busy seasons (related to agriculture and commerce), distance

---

[70]   *Banner* 64 (July 12, 1929): 485-86.
[71]   Ibid. Italics are Beets's.
[72]   See Latourette, *Christian Missions in China*, 194. Latourette does not say what accommodations were made.
[73]   Price, *Rural Church in China*, 209.

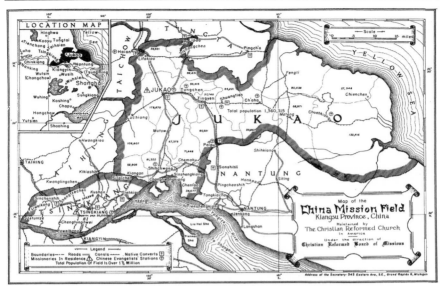

Map of the China Mission field drawn
by the missionaries for use in home churches, 1930s.

from church, sickness, lack of pastoral visitation, lack of emphasis on regular attendance, and lack of Bible teaching on the Sabbath. Price believed that overemphasizing Sabbath observance could even be a bad witness for Christianity in China, since "abstinence from all work would give non-Christians the impression of laziness.[74]

For all of the above reasons, observing the Sabbath was difficult in Rugao; nonetheless, the missionaries were reluctant to alter their idea of proper Sabbath Day observance. Many of those examined for baptism knew their Bible and parts of the catechism, could recite from memory the Lord's Prayer, the Ten Commandments, and the Apostles' Creed, and expressed a strong desire to be baptized, but "resting" on the Sabbath remained a stumbling block for many. In fact, the Sabbath question was usually the final hurdle to cross before entrance into the church. At a 1933 examination of twelve inquirers (which included five soldiers, an official with the local government, a book salesman, two businessmen, a servant, a clerk, and an apprentice), none were accepted for baptism. Some of these inquirers had been studying for more than two years, and it was largely because of issues related to Sabbath observance that they were not accepted.[75]After the examination,

[74]   Ibid., 213.
[75]   De Korne to the Executive Committee, Board of Missions, April 30, 1933, De Korne, personal folder.

when the mission encouraged the inquirers to "continue attention to Christian truth and Christian life," one of the evangelists remarked that though he appreciated the missionaries' caution, at "other places where he had labored in China, most of these men would have been received into the church."[76]

In the early 1930s, the missionaries struggled to formulate a Lord's Day policy that reflected their own commitment to the Sabbath yet was realistic for Rugao. They wrote the neighboring Southern Presbyterian mission and the Reformed Church in America's Amoy mission asking how each handled Sabbath observance.[77] Before making a final recommendation, John De Korne also wrote mission secretary Henry Beets about the issue. There were "a number of inquirers," De Korne wrote, "who could be baptized as far as knowledge of the truth, but who were making no serious effort to keep the Sabbath." Was the mission, he wondered, doing the right thing by withholding baptism from them? Despite his strong feelings about Sabbath-breakers at home, Beets's view of keeping the Sabbath in China was remarkably realistic and flexible:

> I am glad there are a number of inquirers who could be baptized....
> This is a question we discussed also over in Amoy....It is easy for us westerners to pass judgment on that from our standards and with the training of centuries back of us. But if you will study the old church orders and the Acts of our Synod 300 years ago, you will notice that this has been a slow process of education, lasting through centuries, and the process is new with every coming generation, at least to some extent....Perhaps their taking a definite stand might be instrumental in causing them to see that there is such a command as the Sabbath command in God's word. If you think that otherwise they are showing a change of heart and a change of life, it seems to me we should not be too strict on that one thing, in view of the fact that the Chinese are not trained to honor and observe the Sabbath day, like we have been. But if their heart is right with God, that of course is the main thing. Slowly on the other matter ought to improve. There are other commands that the Chinese are frequently very slow in obeying, like things about lying and stealing, and I presume about uncleanness, I mean in the moral sense. But as regarding these points, too, there will have to be a slow persistent training,

---

[76]   Ibid.
[77]   There is no record of either mission's response.

that they may walk in the way of holiness, without which no man shall see Jehovah....But you know how imperfect all of these things are with us too, so I should say do not be too strict with these babes in Christ. If you have only reasons to believe they are in Him, He will perfect that which he has begun.[78]

After seeking advice from Beets and the other missions, the Christian Reformed missionaries formulated a policy for Sabbath observance. At the heart of the decision was the principle that proper Sabbath observance meant joyfully setting aside Sunday as a day for worship and the development of spiritual life. Instead of being a compulsory demand of the law, Sabbath observance should flow naturally out of the heart as a "freely bubbling up expression of the new life within."[79] Based on this principle, the mission decided that the minimum requirement of those seeking admission to the church was a sincere desire to use the day for the worship of God and for the development of spiritual life. Those seeking baptism also had to promise to make a diligent effort to be present at a church service every Sunday, and they had to promise to forgo all unnecessary business and labor on that day "as far as they possibly could."[80] Unless inquirers could promise to meet these minimum requirements, they could not be baptized and received into the church.

Beyond the questions of orthodox belief and the commitment to Christian living, there were other issues which could delay an inquirer's baptism. After the parents of one of Kalsbeek and Liu's young women were accepted for baptism, the sacrament was delayed because of a lawsuit impending on a mortgage they held on some property. They decided to wait to be baptized, Kalsbeek said, because "they thought it might reflect on the good name of the church if they were members and had to go to court."[81] Family opposition also delayed a number of baptisms. Two of Sam Dykstra's inquirers had their books torn up by family members, forcing them to study at night to avoid further conflict.

[78] Beets to De Korne, Oct. 10, 1930, De Korne, CRWM folder. During his trip to China in 1929, Beets stopped in Xiamen (Amoy) to visit RCA missionaries.

[79] This principle and the following points come from an outline John De Korne made, "Observance of the Day of Rest," Dec. 30, 1929, De Korne, personal folder.

[80] Just as at home, however, there were exceptions to the standards set for Sabbath observance, particularly in the case of "special difficulties." The mission appears to have allowed some inquirers to keep their shops open.

[81] Kalsbeek to Westside churches, May 16, 1932, Kalsbeek, personal folder.

During the examination of one of these inquirers, a young man, family members had dragged him out of the meeting and beat him. Though he returned in the afternoon to pass the exam, the mission decided to delay baptism until his situation at home improved.[82] Another inquirer, Chen Shiw Dzen, one of Kalsbeek and Liu's entourage, passed her exam and had obtained her father's consent for baptism, but on the Sunday when she was announced as a candidate for baptism, "some of those present went to her father and filled his heart and mind with fear of the dreadful consequences that would follow."[83] Though she was willing to defy her father's opposition, the mission would not baptize her until she had regained her father's permission.

Occasionally, irregular marital relationships held up baptisms. In one case, when an inquirer began requesting baptism, the mission urged him to end his sinful relations with his concubine. But she refused the five hundred yuan he offered her and then committed suicide.[84] In another case, when Sam Dykstra discovered that a candidate for baptism had more than one wife, he felt compelled to withhold baptism, especially since the government was also opposed to polygamy. The decision was heartrending, Dykstra said, because he was barring "a man who wishes to serve the Lord and professes his faith in him, though the craving for male progeny and the custom of the age have laid him in bondage."[85]

The desire for progeny may have been behind another irregular marital situation in Shuangdian in the early 1930s. In addition to having objections about Cong Qiayun's views of ancestor worship, the mission was slow to baptize the three members of the Cong family because of the daughter's marital situation.[86] Through her mother's urging and negotiations, the daughter, Cong Yuzhen, age twenty-eight, had left her first husband and had taken a second one, a man who was living in another city with a wife and several children. Though he felt compelled to reject both mother and daughter, in his notes John De Korne suggested that she had acted out of filial piety, noting, "She seems to have done it without realizing it was wrong."[87] Later, however,

---

[82] S. Dykstra to First CRC, Grand Rapids, June 10, 1931, S. Dykstra, CRWM folder.

[83] Kalsbeek to West Side churches, May 16, 1932, Kalsbeek, CRWM folder.

[84] S. Dykstra to First CRC, Grand Rapids, April 1937, S. Dykstra, CRWM folder.

[85] S. Dykstra to First CRC, Grand Rapids, Jan. 27, 1940, S. Dykstra, CRWM folder.

[86] "The Cong family case" (in Chinese) is in John De Korne's personal folder.

[87] This would not have surprised De Korne, since in another place he

in a public worship service, her parents, Cong Luchang and Cong Qiayun, admitted that divorcing the first husband was contradictory to the teaching of Jesus, that what they had done was a sin, that they repented of this sin and asked for Christ's forgiveness, and that they promised in future affairs to follow the Ten Commandments and the teaching of Jesus.[88] The mission then baptized all three.

Joining the Church

If an inquirer could demonstrate a solid grasp of biblical and doctrinal truth, showed a commitment to living a godly life, and there were no other impediments, the mission accepted the inquirer for baptism and admission to the church. Baptism of adult believers was the first of five key practices that constituted the translation of Christian Reformed beliefs about joining the church.

For the missionaries, baptisms were events of "great joy and celebration." In some places, baptisms were celebrated by the whole community. In one place priests from a nearby temple blew off firecrackers before a baptismal service to ward off evil spirits. On these occasions, the worship hall was decorated festively and the Communion elements, bread and wine, were set on a table in the front.

For the baptism ceremony, a missionary would read a translation of a shortened version of the baptismal formula used in the Christian Reformed Church.[89] The names of the candidates were read, and they were called to the front of the congregation, where they were asked publicly the five questions used at their examinations. In Rugao City this was an orderly process, but in the countryside the scene could be chaotic. Of a baptismal service he attended in the countryside, Lee Huizenga wrote that the "uncouth lot" pressed forward around the pulpit, and some of the candidates "even scraped and spit on the ground floor," as they were being baptized.[90] In both city and countryside, the missionary sprinkled water from a bowl on the convert's head, pronouncing the name of the triune God: Father, Son,

---

acknowledged that the Chinese desire for progeny was closely linked to ancestor worship. See *Chinese Altars*, 55.

[88] De Korne's records do not explain why the husband, who had previously been accepted for baptism, was also required to make a confession.

[89] Only ordained missionaries were allowed to administer the sacraments.

[90] The city baptism service is recorded on a sixteen-millimeter film Albert Smit made in Haian in the 1930s, Smit film, CRWM folder. The country scene is from a baptism service on the Taizhou field that Huizenga described in "A Native Church," n.d., unpub. ms., Huizenga, CRWM folder.

and Holy Spirit.[91] Some of those receiving baptism were moved deeply by the ceremony. About one elderly woman receiving baptism, Harry Dykstra wrote:

> She is a dear old lady with a radiant face who had come to see her Savior just as her earthly days are drawing to a close. Her Bible knowledge was not extensive but she witnessed of sin, deliverance and gratitude. As she knelt she wanted to bow her head to the ground in Chinese fashion. We gently lifted that dear face upward to administer the sacrament.[92]

A second key practice in the missionaries' understanding of joining the church was infant baptism. Infant baptism was a cornerstone of Christian Reformed theology. Whereas many outsiders viewed *predestination* as the one doctrine that characterized (or caricatured) Reformed or Calvinist theology, the "covenant of grace," with its concomitant practice of infant baptism, was for Christian Reformed people "the distinctively Reformed doctrine, even more so than, for instance, the doctrine of election."[93] The covenant of grace emphasized that salvation was entirely of God, for his glory, and that "the really saved are not to be viewed as a number of wholly separate suddenly converted individuals but as an organism, as a people, as those who belong together both in the church militant and in the church triumphant, as *believers and their seed through their generations*."[94] The covenant of grace was thus viewed as an antidote to the rampant "methodism and individualism, of evangelicalism and revivalism, of religious subjectivism and sensationalism" found in American Protestantism.[95]

The phrase *"believers and their seed"* is at the heart of covenant theology. In the Christian Reformed Church, the idea of covenant theology stems from the Old Testament passage where God makes the following promise to Abraham: "I will establish my covenant between me and thee and thy seed after thee throughout their generations for an everlasting covenant, to be a God unto thee and to thy seed after

[91] While they preferred sprinkling, missionaries were not opposed to immersion. Harry Dykstra believed that the Chinese preferred sprinkling because, as he said, "it is so much easier." See H. Dykstra to Beets, March 24, 1923.
[92] H. Dykstra, Report, April 1934, H. Dykstra, CRWM folder.
[93] William Hendriksen, "The Doctrine of the Covenant of Grace," *Banner* 66 (April 24, 1931): 386.
[94] Ibid.
[95] Ibid.

thee" (Gen. 17:7). Through this covenant, "God dispensed his grace to those with whom he bound himself."[96] This covenant carried over to the people of Israel. In the New Testament, this same covenant with Abraham's spiritual descendents was ratified through the blood of Jesus Christ and extended to all who believed in Jesus Christ. Symbolic of the shift between dispensations, the New Testament sacrament of baptism replaced the Old Testament rite of circumcision.

The central truth here is that the covenant of grace is extended to those who believe in Jesus Christ and to their children. This extension was based on the above analogical thinking about the relationship between the Old Testament and the New Testament and on two proof texts: "For to you is the promise, and to your children" (Acts 2:39); and "For the unbelieving husband is sanctified in the wife, and the unbelieving wife is sanctified in the brother: else were your children unclean; but now are they holy" (1 Cor. 7:14). Because covenantal teaching gave assurance of salvation in cases of infant mortality, it was a source of comfort for Christian parents.[97] It was also a primary reason for Christian education, since parents were obligated by church order to bring their covenant children up in "the fear and knowledge of the Lord."

The implications of covenant theology were important in Rugao. When the missionaries first arrived, however, there was some question about practicing infant baptism. Because he had heard of a Southern Baptist presence in the city, Henry Beets had worried in 1921 about having pedobaptists and "those who reject it" working in the same town. Lee Huizenga had written back to assure him that this would not be a problem, since

> The Chinese know little of the difference between the essential differences of pedobaptism and adult-baptism. In fact, mission converts for years to come are baptized when adult and the children of them (well, tell me what to do?). A father believing, a mother serving idols, a father just converted, among heathen surroundings, etc. Theoretically the child should be baptized;

96 De Korne, "The Certainties of the Covenant of Grace," *Banner* 72 (Oct. 7, 1937): 939. De Korne wrote this article after he left China, while serving as a pastor in Iowa.
97 Until the 1930s, however, "seed" was taken literally, with the result that adopted children of believers were not included as members of the covenant, unless it could be verified that the child's biological parents were believers. See Henry J. Kuiper's editorial, "Discipline and the Welfare of the Church," *Banner* 67 (June 10, 1932): 556-57.

practically it may be better to wait. Up to the present it has caused no trouble.[98]

As they got to know Rugao better, the missionaries began to realize that the covenant of grace, with its ancillary practice of infant baptism, might provide a way to break through a huge impediment in China to Christian conversion: family solidarity. Strong traditional customs, such as ancestor worship, funerary practices, and marriage practices, made it virtually impossible for individuals to break away from family. But when families joined the church together, the mission found there was a greater likelihood that they would remain in the faith. Thus, the Christian Reformed conception of covenant theology lent itself naturally to the task of communicating Christianity in Rugao, especially in the rural districts, where traditional practices and family relationships were still very strong. Sam Dykstra found it a "joy" to testify to the consolation of the covenant promises of God and hoped that his relationship with his own children could communicate "some of the riches of God's promise when he assures us that he will be our God and the God of our children."[99] In the same letter, he added,

> Instead of the individualism that is rampant these truths of the covenant could mean so much for this people that loves to speak of itself not as so many persons but as many families. May the way be opened for us to reach this family unit that the influence of the gospel may radiate through its members.

Covenant theology was also part of the missionaries' justification for switching from the chapel method or intensive approach of the 1920s to the modified Korean, or extensive approach, because of its emphasis on communicating Christianity to family groups.[100] Moreover, this idea of covenant theology was behind the mission's reluctance to baptize individual family members and the preference for baptizing whole families.[101]

---

[98] Huizenga to Beets, April, 1924, Huizenga, CRWM folder.

[99] S. Dykstra to First CRC, Grand Rapids, July 2, 1926, S. Dykstra, CRWM folder.

[100] See H. Dykstra to Beets, Sept. 30, 1930, and H. Dykstra to home churches, Jan. 5, 1931, H. Dykstra, CRWM folder.

[101] Price found that only four churches in the Yangzi delta region required an inquirer "to win his family to Christian faith" before being received into membership. Nineteen other churches urged this to take place but did not consider it a requirement. More than half the churches did not believe it was important. See Price, *Rural Church in China*, 181.

Communicating an emphasis on family was not difficult, but communicating the teaching behind it was a challenge. Sam Dykstra admitted that, since their evangelists were graduates of union institutions, they often had "very hazy ideas of doctrine and no conviction in regard to some of the problems that we consider important."[102] More specifically, Dykstra noted, the evangelists had no idea of baptism's relation to the covenant. The majority of the mission's evangelists came from Presbyterian missions (North and South), where they would have been exposed to teaching about infant baptism (though not the Christian Reformed understanding of covenant theology), but at least two of the mission's evangelists came from Baptist missions. According to Lee Huizenga, these workers were more interested in getting a job than in differences in theology.[103]

The idea of covenant and its relationship to infant baptism was clear in the mission's ceremony for baptizing the children of believers. Unlike children baptized in Christian Reformed churches in the States, who were usually infants, children baptized in Rugao varied in age, depending usually on when the parents had become Christians. At the service, parents stood at front of the church and presented their children for baptism. The missionary (or evangelist) explained that baptism was a "mark of the covenant" (*en yue de yin ji*) that God had made with Abraham and with his believing descendants. This was followed by three questions. First, did the parents believe that their "children were conceived and born in sin and thus suffered from all of the consequences of sin, but that through Jesus Christ their child was made a righteous member of the church?" Second, did they "affirm their belief in the teachings of the Old and New Testament and the doctrines of the church?"[104] Finally, the parents were asked if they promised to take care of their children until they reached the age of maturity by "giving them all of the above teaching, taking care of them, watching over them, helping them or using other ways with all of your strength to take care of them?" If the parents promised, the missionary

---

[102] S. Dykstra to First CRC, July 1926, S. Dykstra, CRWM folder.
[103] Huizenga to Beets, April, 1924, Huizenga, CRWM folder.
[104] This summary comes from the (Chinese) form used by John De Korne and Cao Zizhen in Shuangdian. See De Korne, personal folder (trans.). Albert Smit and Wang Aitang produced a shortened version of the form, which does not ask the parents if they "accept the teaching of the Old and New Testament and the teaching of this church." Albert Selles and Qing Yage made a word-for-word translation of the form used in the CRC. Both forms are in the author's possession.

baptized the child. The child was now a member of the church, though not a communicant member until he or she made a profession of faith (i.e., accepted the promise made through his or her parents).[105]

A third key practice in the missionaries' understanding of joining the church was Communion. After a baptismal service, usually in the afternoon, a missionary served Communion to the new members and the other Christians.[106] The time and place of the service was announced several weeks in advance and included a call for converts, inquirers, and others to bring potential objections against those partaking of the sacrament. Following the Christian Reformed Church's tradition, the Sunday before the Communion service in Rugao was a "preparation" service, in which those intending to receive Communion were advised to examine themselves. Using the Apostle Paul's words, those preparing to receive the sacrament were warned that "whosoever shall eat the bread or drink the cup of the Lord in an unworthy manner, shall be guilty of the body and the blood of the Lord" (1 Cor. 11:27). They were urged to "forsake their sins and live the new life in Christ." They were also reminded that eating and drinking the body and blood of Christ was a sign of God's deep love for them and that eating together made them "one body" in Christ (*he er wei yi*).

At the afternoon service, a missionary administered the sacrament. In Rugao City, much as in the States, Communion was a solemn occasion. A liturgical form was read and the communicants were instructed to "take, eat, drink, remember, and believe." The evangelists and "elders" then took the elements and passed them on trays to the seated congregation.[107] In the countryside, Lee Huizenga wrote, "Chinese biscuits" and a bowl of wine were set on a table at front of the church. After the sermon, the missionary

---

[105] There appear to be only a few instances where baptized children made "profession of faith" in Rugao. Those who did make profession of faith appear to have been the children of the mission's evangelists, and particularly the children of those who came from a Presbyterian background. Evangelist Chen Guifan's son, for instance, was baptized in Xuzhou in 1918 at the age of two, and, after moving to Rugao in 1930, made profession of faith in 1931 at the age of fifteen. Three more professions by young women were recorded in 1948. The identity of the parents of all three are unclear. After the missionaries left in 1950, Wang Aitang recorded the profession of his daughter Wang Shuangen in 1957. Found in the Rugao church book records.

[106] Communion services were usually held three times per year, in January, April, and October.

[107] This description is based on Albert Smit's film of worship in Rugao, China Collection, Heritage Hall, Calvin College, Grand Rapid, Mich.

took the Chinese biscuits and passed it to the communicants scattered throughout the audience. Each rose at his place, offered silent prayer...and it was passed to each one standing as he took and drank of the wine. One bowl all drank from it. The roughest looking Chinamen as well as the missionaries from the homeland.[108]

Self-examination was an important part of Communion services in Rugao because it was related to a fourth important aspect of joining the church: church discipline to protect the integrity of the Christian community. Leaders at home prided themselves on the Christian Reformed Church's faithfulness in exercising discipline, calling it one of the denomination's "Three Forts."[109] Discipline was important, church leaders argued, because Christ had commanded it, because it kept the church pure, and because it served to convert "those who had gone astray."[110] The mission initiated discipline against members for a variety of reasons in Rugao. Church attendance was a common reason for starting the disciplinary process. After joining the church, some members attended worship only sporadically or not at all. Sometimes discipline was exercised in cases of financial impropriety, as happened at Dingyan in 1934 after the group's treasurer misappropriated church funds.[111] Marital abuse could also be grounds for initiating discipline. In one case, discipline was initiated when two members in Shuangdian, with the family names of Gu and Guan (Kwan), reported to evangelists Cao Zizhen that another Christian, Chen Chang, had beaten his wife two times.[112] Mina Kalsbeek initiated discipline against one of the young women that she and Liu Shuying worked with, because she had married a man who had a wife in another city.[113]

To handle these cases, the mission had formed a "discipline committee" in 1926. The committee studied individual cases and

---

[108] Huizenga, "A native church," Huizenga, CRWM folder.
[109] The other two "forts" of the CRC, R.B. Kuiper said, were doctrinal preaching and covenantal consciousness. See R.B. Kuiper, "Three Forts," *Banner* 69 (March 30, 1934): 270.
[110] Henry Kuiper, "Discipline and the Welfare of the Church," *Banner* 66 (May 29, 1931): 500-01.
[111] S. Dykstra, Annual Report 1934, S. Dykstra, CRWM folder.
[112] Chinese notes on this case are found in John De Korne's "Shuangdian folder," De Korne, personal folder.
[113] Mina Kalsbeek, "Baptized May 15, 1932: What about them since?" *Banner* 80 (Nov. 2, 1945): 1032.

made recommendations that all of the missionaries voted on.[114] Most delinquent members were indifferent to the process of discipline, but occasionally those against whom discipline was initiated became angry, and their anger made the missionaries very uncomfortable. After the Dingyan and Shuangdian groups decided in 1930 to cooperate in some activities, John De Korne encouraged them to initiate "a sort of *censura morum*" or mutual censure. Mutual censure would be "very welcome," De Korne said, "as disciplinary activities which arise among their number are taken with much better grace than those which originate with us foreign missionaries, or even than those that originate from Chinese evangelists who come to them from other places."[115] As in the Christian Reformed Church, if there was no improvement in the delinquent member's behavior, he or she was barred from taking the Lord's Supper. Repentance, which might require public admission of sin, meant that the Table was once again open to the member.[116] If negligent behavior persisted, however, the mission voted to have the names of delinquent members removed from the church list.

"Church list" was used somewhat hopefully, since for most of the 1930s there were no organized churches on the field. But belonging to a larger church body was a fifth key aspect of the missionaries' understanding of joining the church. Church members were formally "enrolled" in the Huaidong presbytery, but the mission was responsible for all matters concerning their life and faith.[117] Though enrolling members in the presbytery was mainly a formality, it revealed the missionaries' strong commitment to church associations. Soon after arriving in Rugao in 1923, they had begun participating as associate members in the local presbytery of the North Kiangsu Presbyterian Mission. After the presbytery rejected their request to organize a congregation in Rugao in 1925, the mission maintained its association with that body while following church-unifying movements taking place in other parts of China. One movement they found intriguing was the Church of Christ in China (CCC). In 1927, this union brought together Chinese Presbyterians, Reformed Baptists, Congregationalists, and independents in a body of 120,000 communicant members, a third

---

[114]   The evangelists also participated in the discussions about discipline. See minutes from church meeting (Chinese), April 1934, Rugao RAB files.

[115]   De Korne to Mission Board, June 6, 1930, De Korne, CRWM folder.

[116]   In 1933, John De Korne recorded receiving back into fellowship a member who had been under discipline for a year. De Korne Report, January 1933, De Korne, CRWM folder.

[117]   "Mission Minutes," May 7, 1934, CRWM folder.

of all Chinese Protestants.[118] Because most of the churches involved were what they termed "evangelical," the missionaries expressed some interest in joining the CCC. They were also somewhat suspicious of the union, however, since they believed a number of the leading men in the movement were "decidedly of the type that has come to be known as 'modern,'" and that the union had arisen largely out of a "rising tide of nationalism." When the Huaidong presbytery voted unanimously to reject the CCC's invitation to join, the missionaries dropped the idea of joining.[119]

The next year, in 1928, the Huaidong presbytery joined the Presbyterian Church of Christ in China (PCC), which, in uniting six presbyteries from Shandong and Jiangsu provinces, brought together 17,776 Chinese Presbyterians.[120] Because the Christian Reformed Church had no organized church in China, it could not join the denomination formally, but the mission supported the union. Despite their agreement with the doctrinal basis of the confederation, however, some of the missionaries expressed ambivalence about the body. In 1932, Harry Dykstra expressed frustration with the Huaidong presbytery, one of the important presbyteries in the denomination, since, as he said, "The mission holds the purse strings and the Chinese church is showing no tremendous strides towards independence."[121] While on furlough in 1933, John De Korne expressed concern to the Mission Board's executive committee about the "fundamentalist" elements in the Southern Presbyterian church and what he termed as "some loose tendencies in church government."[122]

Discussion about forming a Chinese Christian Reformed Church also came up in the early 1930s. The missionaries on the field were not in favor of forming "Christian Reformed churches" in Rugao. In a report studying the issues surrounding church organization, the missionaries wrote, "Aside from the racial and national factors

---

[118] Wallace Merwin, *Adventure in Unity: The Church of Christ in China* (Grand Rapids: Eerdmans, 1974): 54-55. See also Yao, *Fundamentalist Movement*, 192-93.

[119] The Huaidong presbytery declined to join the CCC because it claimed the union had too many diverse doctrinal elements, an insufficient creed, and had been imposed upon the Chinese churches. See Brown, *Earthen Vessels*, 213.

[120] Yao, *Fundamentalist Movement*, 215-16.

[121] H. Dykstra to Beets, Nov. 9, 1932, H. Dykstra, CRWM folder.

[122] From notes John De Korne made about a presentation he gave to the Mission Board's executive committee Sept. 6, 1933, De Korne, personal folder.

which would have to be considered, we can state, 1.) Historically the CRC has nothing to offer the Chinese church; and 2.) Doctrinally it is nothing sufficiently different from the existing Presbyterian Church of Christ in China."[123] They added, "Many of the reasons above would also apply to the organization of an independent church in our field closely associated with the CRC in America....It would mean little to the Chinese and would add to the Babel of confusion of the Protestant church in China.[124] After a church in Pella, Iowa, urged the synod of 1934 to force the China Mission to establish a "Christian Reformed Church in China," the missionaries were forced to take a public stand. In the *Banner*, Lee Huizenga wrote:

> None of the denominations mean anything special to the Chinese. For a salary our Chinese helpers will become Christian Reformed where formerly they were Adventists, Presbyterians, or Baptists. To them the denomination means little, Christ means more. The Christian Reformed Church has nothing sufficiently important to them to be worthwhile propagating here that is not already here. It has nothing historically to offer. It has nothing doctrinally attractive to offer. The name itself has nothing to offer.[125]

While they were opposed to creating a Chinese Christian Reformed Church, the missionaries argued that the churches the mission established would nevertheless bear the imprint of the home denomination and have a close relationship with the church in North America. The missionaries urged the home church to give them wide discretion in associating Chinese congregations, as long as they proceeded with Reformed principles of polity in mind.[126]

Red Letter Days

Though the mission saw some hopeful signs in the development of churches in Rugao County, during most of the 1930s there were few tangible results, and in their 1933 "Church Organization Report" the missionaries lamented,

[123] "Church Organization Report," December 1933, 5, CRWM folder.
[124] Ibid.
[125] Huizenga, "Letters to Philip," *Banner* 70 (March 13, 1935): 138.
[126] "Report to Synod on the Organization of Churches in China," CRWM folder.

While gratefully acknowledging God's gracious goodness in giving us a field of labor in this county...we, nevertheless, stand ashamed in the face of such small achievement. We humiliate ourselves before Almighty God asking His purging from our sins and the removing of every hindrance in the lives of us as missionaries which may obstruct the progress of God's Kingdom in this field.[127]

A survey of the field in 1937 confirms the slow progress. Of all of the field's districts, Rugao City was the most frustrating. Despite the advantages of having the hospital and the missionaries among them, the citizens of Rugao City were slow to respond to the mission's work. During the 1920s, the mission baptized seven converts, all men. Between 1929 and 1936, they baptized twenty-four, and the next year, in 1937, the mission baptized thirty-four in the city. At least four of those baptized were children of one of the Chinese evangelists. Another was a servant in the De Korne household, who, after working for the family for eight years and receiving regular Bible training, was eventually baptized. Another two converts were Rugao businessmen. The majority of the converts in Rugao during the thirties were young women who came into the church through contact with Mina Kalsbeek and Liu Shuying.

By 1937, though there were as many as two hundred worshipers in Rugao on some Sundays, the city group was still a long way from being organized as a church. Albert Smit wrote home with this assessment:

Although our mission has been working in Jukao [Rugao] for fifteen years, the results in our membership are meager....In all we now have forty-two Christians. Most of these are women, due to the splendid efforts of the Misses Kalsbeek and Liu. We have a few men Christians, but as yet [they are] not material for elders and deacons. They are not well enough grounded in the truth, and besides, some are very poor and are to a certain extent dependent upon charity. And we are not yet as ready to organize a congregation.[128]

Just north of Rugao, across the county line, Smit also worked in Haian (Hai'an), a city with a population of around eighty thousand. When the outstation was opened in 1926, the mission was enthusiastic about prospects for work in the city, since "many of the better class"

---

[127] "Church Organization Report," 7, CRWM folder.
[128] Smit, "Letter of Albert Smit," *Missionary Monthly* 41:480 (June 1937): 135.

showed interest in Christianity. In 1930, five adults and one child were baptized in the city. But the group showed resistance to the mission's effort to force it in the direction of financial independence. In 1933, Smit wrote: "We have continued the regular Sunday services, but have urged the Christians to provide their own meeting place. However, this has not met with the hoped for response, but instead has aroused some opposition. It seems hard for the Chinese Christians to appreciate our object in making these changes."[129]

In other places where Smit worked, opposition came from outside the church. In Tongchen (Tong-ch'en) just east of Rugao, members of a cult stiffly resisted the mission's efforts to establish work there. Evangelist Wang Aitang, discouraged by the opposition and lack of results, asked to be moved. The work in Shizhuang (Shih Ch'uang), a market town forty miles south of Rugao on the banks of the Yangzi, had gotten off to a promising start in the early 1930s, but the town, noted both for its cottage-industry textiles and for bandits, also proved hostile to a Christian presence.[130] After a local man named Zhang converted, some of his neighbors burned his house, nearly killing his entire family.[131] The man refused to be intimidated, and the group in the town grew, until nine adults and five children were baptized there in 1937. The group remained too weak, however, to be organized as a church.

Nor were results in other locations very promising. In 1932, Albert Selles opened a mission station in Jingjiang (Tzing Kiang) County, southwest of Rugao on the banks of the Yangzi River. In the county seat, a walled city with a population of about sixty thousand, Selles and his evangelist, An Guangrong, followed the methods used in Rugao to organize groups for study and worship. Soon after opening a work in the city, he baptized his first convert there, whom he named "Lydia of Tsingkiang," after St. Paul's first convert in the city of Philippi (Acts 16:14–15). But the work progressed slowly, and when voices at home complained about the lack of results in China, the mission board discussed closing the Jingjiang station in 1934.[132] The missionaries were

---

[129]   Smit, Annual Report, Dec. 1933, Smit, CRWM folder.

[130]   According to Barkan, the whole western edge of Rugao County along the eastern border of Taixing County was a haven for Communist activity in the late 1920s and early 1930s. See Barkan, "Nationalists, Communists, and Rural Leaders," 493.

[131]   Smit to Beets, n.d. (probably 1935), Smit, CRWM folder.

[132]   In response to the mission board's suggestion that the mission close Jingjiang, the missionaries wrote: "The China Mission in answer to the

able to keep the station open, and by 1937 there were between twenty and thirty Christians and inquirers meeting in the city.[133]

In the market town of Baibu (Pai P'u), to the southeast of Rugao along the border of Nantong County, the mission's work also progressed slowly. When Harry Dykstra tried to rent a building there in 1930, neighbors put up posters condemning the landlord: "Mr. Song you are a Chinese. Your ancestors were born in China. Why do you act as a trailing dog to these foreigners in preaching this worthless Christianity? We advise you to come to your senses quickly."[134] Once the mission had set up in Baibu, however, hostility quickly turned to indifference. In his 1934 annual report, Dykstra expressed discouragement about work in the city:

> After five years the results are indeed insignificant. Had I known this five years ago I would hardly have had the courage to start. A missionary likes to make converts and start churches. There are converts in Pai P'u but many of them are not the material from which to build churches.[135]

In 1936, Dykstra did baptize three women, but the next year the work suffered a major setback when the Chen family, prominent members of the Christian group, left after the death of their son.

In contrast to these other stations on the field, one district to the northeast of Rugao proved very receptive, and the work went quickly there. Soon after his return to China in 1929, Sam Dykstra had begun using the "broadcast method" of evangelism in the towns and villages to the northeast of Rugao. Quickly the market town of Libao became the center of the mission's effort in the area. Then in early 1930, while attending a presbytery meeting in Shandong, Dykstra had met a recent graduate of the Presbyterian seminary in Tengxian, Shandong Province, named Li Sunde, who agreed to work at Libao. After renting a courtyard house for Li's family, the mission invited several of its evangelists and

---

Board's suggestion of retreat respectfully recommends a policy of steady advance." "Mission Minutes," Sept. 24, 1934, CRWM folder.

[133] According to Sheng Songru, who attended the mission's Sunday school in Jingjiang and whose parents rented property to Selles, the only people who joined the group were widows and people of low standing. See Sheng Songru, "Xie le si zai jingjiang," ("Selles in Jingjiang") *Jingjiang wen shi ci liao* 3 (Aug. 1983): 420.

[134] H. Dykstra, "The beginning of work at Pai P'u," 3 pts., *Banner* 65 (March 21, April 4, and April 18, 1930): 276-77, 327, and 378-79.

[135] H. Dykstra, Annual Report, 1934, H. Dykstra, CRWM folder.

a group of Christians from Haian to hold a week-long set of intensive evangelistic meetings in Libao. Following morning devotions, the group would divide in two, with half remaining for Bible study and prayer and the rest going out to invite the townspeople to afternoon meetings. The afternoon meetings were well attended and resulted in several inquirers being enrolled in June 1930. By the end of the year, Dykstra reported twelve inquirers in Libao, with some already requesting baptism.

From Libao, the mission's work spread into the surrounding villages. Dykstra and evangelist Li soon discovered even greater interest in two villages about five miles to the south of Libao. In response to the interest in the village of Tanjiasuo, the mission made an exception to the Korean Plan and bought a small building there in May 1931 for Christian activities. Close by in the village of Guanba (Kuan Pah), the response was even more encouraging. By the middle of 1932, more than a dozen "earnest inquirers" were requesting baptism in Guanba. Some of these candidates were "promising," reported Dykstra, but he was slow to baptize when he realized that one of the candidates had "two wives, children with each, and [had made] false oaths in court...[and others were leading] the adulterous life."[136] Six months later, however, he baptized six adults and nine children from Tanjiasuo and Guanba. The number included a doctor's family, whom the mission had aided after the family's house burned down. This doctor, Cong Xinzhen, who, in addition to practicing traditional medicine, had a school in his home for teaching children and adults to read, soon became an important leader in the Guanba group. Not long after receiving baptism, he began helping Dykstra and evangelist Li with evangelistic activities in the area and with visiting the homes of inquirers neglecting church attendance.

Not everyone in the Guanba Christian group was a village native. Five people who were baptized there in 1933 belonged to families from Haimen, a magistracy about thirty miles southeast of Nantong. Dykstra found that these Haimen transplants in the Libao area faced some of the same issues that Dutch immigrants to North America had encountered, including financial difficulties and "haughty treatment" from the natives.[137] One man from Haimen, Qi Jiazhen (Chy Chia

---

[136] S. Dykstra to First CRC, Grand Rapids, July 1, 1932, S. Dykstra, CRWM folder.

[137] S. Dykstra, "Thanksgiving Day letter," 1934, S. Dykstra, CRWM folder. Sam Dykstra had worked with Dutch immigrants in Canada after being repatriated in 1927. It is unclear why or when these Haimen families had moved to the Libao area. Several of the families were tailors and may have moved to the area to set up tailoring businesses.

Chen), taught forty pupils in a school near Guanba. After becoming an inquirer, he began teaching his students Christian songs and Bible stories, and he allowed the mission to organize Bible classes in his school. After his conversion, Qi became the *voorlezer*, or "first reader," of the Haimen Christian group and, according to Dykstra, he "brought many of his tribe in touch with the gospel."[138]

The Haimen Christians included two of Qi Jiazhen's brothers, Qi Qingkui (Chy Chying Kuei) and Qi Qingde (Chy Chying De). These brothers were slower to be received into the church because the mission wanted them to join with their whole families. Qi Qingkui was committed enough to the faith to pay for his daughter Molan to attend a Christian high school in Shanghai, but his wife Qi Lingguang (Chy Ling Kuang) resisted accepting Christianity. When she did convert and had passed the mission's examination, she and her husband and his brother's family were all baptized in the fall of 1934, a "red letter day," as Dykstra related to his home church.[139] As the heads of large families, the Qi brothers played a key role in the leadership of the Guanba group. They also eagerly participated in the mission's evangelistic activities, using their work as tailors to introduce Christianity in the homes of Guanba's wealthier families.

By 1936, there was a thriving Christian group in the area of Guanba and Tanjiasuo. On Sundays, between forty and fifty worshipers—men, women, and children—crowded into their meeting hall, with numbers divided almost equally between the local people and the Haimen immigrants. In spite of differences in dialect, Dykstra noted, "The two elements in this group are congenial through their common faith in Christ."[140] He marveled that these Christian families prayed together in unison and about their concern for their "unsaved neighbors."[141] Some of the immigrants urged their relatives in Haimen to accept Christianity. Dr. Cong's brother, who had temporarily gone insane over his brother's conversion, became a Christian. Another young man named Xin came to faith through schoolteacher Qi. Initially

138   See S. Dykstra to First CRC, Grand Rapids, Feb. 2, 1933, S. Dykstra, CRWM folder. In CRC Dutch immigrant circles, a *voorlezer* was the most respected elder in a congregation, who read the sermon when the congregation was without a pastor and chaired the group's meetings.
139   S. Dykstra to First CRC, Grand Rapids, "Thanksgiving Day 1934," S. Dykstra, CRWM folder.
140   S. Dykstra to First CRC, Grand Rapids, March 1936, S. Dykstra, CRWM folder.
141   S. Dykstra to First CRC, Grand Rapids, Jan. 3, 1936, S. Dykstra, CRWM folder.

his parents had opposed his being baptized strenuously, threatening to disown him if he did, but eventually, they, too, as Dykstra put it, "joined him in seeking the Savior."[142]

The Guanba Christians were not interested in sharing their new-found faith with only kin and kith, however. Many volunteered to help evangelist Li with wider evangelistic campaigns. Organizing an "evangelistic band," the group began sending out several of the husbands and wives, who, carrying white canvas bags with red crosses on them, distributed tracts in the surrounding villages and countryside.[143] At local festivals, they carried a "beautifully embroidered gospel flag," advertising their church. A "common laborer" named Zhang (Chang), who had been converted by Qi Jiazhen, became the leader of the band. Band members met once a month to discuss the results of their trips and to pray for those with whom they had come into contact. Occasionally band members traveled to Taizhou to participate in evangelistic rallies and training sessions organized by the Southern Presbyterian mission. Results were not long in coming. During 1935, Dykstra baptized twenty-eight more men and women and celebrated the Lord's Supper two times. Converts continued to join, and on January 3, 1936, Dykstra baptized seven adults and thirteen "covenant children." By the end of the year, he had baptized another forty-three adults.

With so many new people joining the church, adequate worship space quickly became a problem, forcing the group to purchase a church building. In keeping with its policy of encouraging self-support, the mission only paid for the stones in the floor and wooden benches; the members paid for the rest.[144] Doctor Cong purchased the building. One of the Qi brothers donated a dozen of the "neat swinging windows." Other members gave the mottoes on the walls and the framed Bible pictures. A teacher in the group donated a bell.[145] Everyone in the group pitched in: "The men and women seated each on their own side of the aisle, made their individual donations, some of a dollar, others of a

---

[142] Ibid.

[143] Description of the group's evangelistic activities comes from S. Dykstra, Annual Report, 1935, S. Dykstra, CRWM folder.

[144] A description of this building is in S. Dykstra to First CRC, Nov. 2, 1936, S. Dykstra, CRWM folder.

[145] According to Price, Bible pictures, evangelistic pictures, public health posters, New Life Movement pictures, and charts decorated the walls of fifty-five of the sixty churches surveyed in the Yangzi delta region. Forty-six churches possessed some kind of bell for calling members to worship. Price, *Rural Church in China*, 114-15.

half dollar, and a few bringing forward ten or twenty cents from their poverty."[146] At the dedication service in November 1936, the village head spoke kind words of welcome; Dr. Cong, the earliest convert, gave a historical sketch of the group; evangelist Li recalled the dedication of the temple in the Old Testament; and missionary Dykstra preached a sermon based on the words, "The church of the living God, the pillar and ground of the truth on the church of the living God" (1 Tim. 3:15).

Though Dykstra and evangelist Li played central roles in the dedication service, the Guanba group was rapidly developing its own leadership. Because it took him almost a day to bike to the Libao area, sometimes longer when bridges were out and he had to ford canals, Dykstra only went to the church occasionally. Evangelist Li lived in the area, but in keeping with the mission's policy of not allowing an evangelist to give all of his time to one group, he had responsibilities with other groups and could only be in Guanba once or twice a month. To provide regular preaching and leadership, the group invited an elder named Wang, who had helped the mission in tent work in other locations, to serve as its evangelist. The group paid for his food and lodgings, and he divided his time between Guanba and another worship point a few miles away in Bancha (Pancha). When Wang was away, Dr. Cong led worship and preached. To develop his own skills as a lay leader, Cong began traveling at his own expense with evangelist Li to other parts of the Libao district.

The growth of the Guanba group reached a crescendo in the spring of 1937 when a delegation from the church, headed by Cong, requested organization as a church. After presenting a letter thanking the mission for its work in the Libao area and sketching the growth of the group in Guanba, the delegation requested church organization. The mission approved the request. The week before the official organization service took place, Dykstra baptized eighteen more adults and six children. Then on April 4, 1937, almost fifteen years after the missionaries' arrival in Rugao County, Sam and Harry Dykstra led a worship service organizing the fifty-three members of the Libao congregation as a church.

Describing the organizational service for the church at home, Harry Dykstra wrote the following:

> The little building was crowded when we entered. There was a subdued excitement because those gathered knew that we had

[146] S. Dykstra to First CRC, Grand Rapids, Nov. 2, 1936, S. Dykstra, CRWM folder.

First Chr. Reformed Church in China – 1937

The First Christian Reformed Church in China was established in April 1937 in the town of Libao, about twenty-five miles northeast of Rugao City: (*first row seated, center*) Cornelia Dykstra; (*first row standing, third and fourth from left*) Jean and Connie Dykstra; (*fourth row, center*) Sam Dykstra; (*second from end*) Harry Dykstra.

come as a committee delegated by the Mission to carry out their request for organization. Even though they had been told what is implied in such organizing, I suppose, many of them still felt a little uneasy in the face of a new experience.

First everybody listened to the explanation of the Sunday School lesson by the local Chinese evangelist [Li Sunde]. Mrs. S.A. Dykstra took her place at the little organ and the daughters supported the mother in leading the singing of Chinese hymns. Rev. S.A. Dykstra had been trying for some time to make the country people understand the simplified music of the new Chinese hymnbooks and his efforts are being rewarded. Considering that singing the foreign way is strange to the people, it must be admitted that they did well.

Soon after the church service began one of the newly elected elders stood up and made an acceptable speech in which he emphasized his lack of training and courage necessary for carrying out of the responsible office of elder. The second elder and the two deacons did likewise. Such procedure was of course expected of them by their fellow-Chinese. Expressions of humility and inadequacy are demanded by the standards of Chinese politeness here. There was a tone of sincerity and modesty. I could not refrain from smiling when one of the deacons suggested as a way out of the difficulty that two additional elders and two additional deacons should be added to their number. Their objections were finally overruled by the missionary who showed them that humility and sincere dependence upon God are the very requisites demanded.

After the names of the members had been read, these elders and deacons were duly installed upon the reading of a translation of the form used in our churches at home. The sermon was preached on the theme, "The Rock of the Church." In this sermon the responsibilities of the office bearers and the congregation were pointed out and it was made clear that the church can stand only when it is built on the Rock.[147]

In the spring of 1937, there were other "red letter"days for the Rugao mission, but this flowering was cut short in the summer of that year, when war broke out between China and Japan. When Chiang Kai-shek ordered his troops to open fire on Japanese troops in Shanghai in July of 1937, Japanese troops returned fire, setting off a fierce conflict that raged into the fall, with Chinese troops suffering casualties of 250,000.[148] In November, Japanese troops pursued Nationalist troops fleeing up the Yangzi River delta toward central China. The Japanese systematically bombed the cities lining the river. The American Hospital of the Christian Mission in Nantong was destroyed in the attack, and several hospital employees and patients were killed. Jingjiang was bombed, too, though not nearly as severely as Nantong or Jiangyin, just across the river. Rugao was spared the initial bombing, but seven months later, in March of 1938, it was taken by Japanese troops. The ensuing conflict all but closed mission work for the next eight years.

Though it took almost seventeen years, a church was finally established on the Rugao field in 1937. In some respects, the formation of the Libao church must have taken the missionaries by surprise. For one thing, this first church organized on the field was not in Rugao City, where the mission's forces and resources were concentrated, but in the countryside, where the mission's presence and activities were more limited. Even more surprisingly, the formation of the Libao church took place largely through Chinese efforts—both the evangelism and the efforts to organize and to lead the church—efforts that the mission merely guided rather than initiated. Finally, they did not foresee that

[147] H. Dykstra, "The church at Li Pao," *Missionary Monthly* 41:483 (Sept. 1937): 24-25.
[148] Spence, *The Search for Modern China*, 447.

Christian Reformed covenant theology could provide a new way of belonging, a way for transplants from the Haimen district to the southeast of Rugao County to create community with local residents in a worshiping body centered in Jesus Christ. While it is unclear (perhaps even unlikely) that the evangelists, converts, or inquirers fully understood the abstract theological concepts behind covenant theology, the idea of joining the faith *as family* and *as community* clearly resonated with the Chinese, particularly in the countryside, and especially in Libao. Thus, what some had originally hoped would be "many points of contact" turned out to be one important point of contact at the very heart of the Christian Reformed Dutch immigrant community, and this connection was made through discovery—on the part of both the missionaries and the Chinese converts—much more than through advanced planning.

CHAPTER 6

The Furnace of Affliction:
The War Years, 1937-1949

Wheat and Tares

The church work in Rugao was interrupted a second time by
the Japanese occupation of China, beginning in the summer of 1937.
The war with Japan that engulfed China in 1937 had been brewing
for decades. Since the Sino-Japanese war of 1894–95, Japan had been
slowly, inexorably appropriating Chinese territory and resources. In
1931, the Japanese took over the resource-rich Northeast. Despite
bloody conflicts in Shanghai the following year and a national boycott
against Japanese goods, war was avoided because Chiang Kai-shek
was preoccupied with eradicating communism.[1] When another
conflict between the two countries occurred in the summer of 1937

---

[1]   Though there were rumors that the cities along the Yangzi would be
overrun by Japanese troops in 1931, war was averted when Chiang Kai-shek
signed a peace pact with the Japanese. A 1931 boycott of Japanese goods
extended to Rugao, where bands of schoolboys checked the goods coming
into the city from Shanghai. The boycott lasted until the fall of 1932, when
it became too great a burden for local merchants. See "Anti-Japanese move
at Jukao: Students Search Shops for Goods Sent from Shanghai," *North*

A 1946 view of the Harry Dykstra house in Rugao, after it was bombed by the Japanese during WWII. The missionaries' homes were safe havens for hundreds of women and children during the first few months of the war, which began in 1937, but they were later destroyed by the Japanese to prevent Chinese resistance activity.

at the Marco Polo Bridge outside of Beijing, Chiang could no longer avoid confronting the Japanese. His troops attacked Japanese troops stationed in Shanghai in July, and fighting quickly spread throughout the Yangzi delta region.

Because there were no large cities in Rugao County close to the Yangzi River, Rugao was initially spared the violence that ravaged the cities along both banks of the Yangzi during the fall of 1937, as the Japanese pushed toward the Nationalist government's capital of Nanjing. Japanese aerial bombing leveled much of Nantong, the large city to Rugao's southeast, killing thousands. Among the casualties were Chinese staff and patients killed when the Christian Mission's hospital was destroyed. The Nantong mission's gymnasium and one missionary residence were also destroyed, though no one was killed. Japanese bombs also destroyed much of Jingjiang, to Rugao's southwest, and Jiangyin across the river from Jingjiang.[2] Not only was Rugao spared the violence of the initial assault, it prospered economically for a short time after the Chinese government laid a boom of sunken junks and other boats across the Yangzi River, forcing shipping to pass through the county's canals.[3]

China Herald (June 14, 1932): 408, and "The Boycott at Jukao" (Oct. 19, 1932): 92.

[2]   The mission's compound in Jingjiang was looted after the assault, but no one related to the mission was injured or killed.

[3]   See "The Yangzi Boom Circumvented," *North China Herald* (Nov. 17, 1937): 252. See also Harry Dykstra, "Effects of the war on our Rugao Field during October and November," unpub., art., n.d., probably late fall 1937, H. Dykstra, CRWM folder. In another article, written during the fall of 1937, Dykstra noted that Rugao's farmers continued to go about their business, and the large cotton mills at nearby Tang Jiazi (Tang Chia-tze) were still operating. See "Carrying On," unpub., art., n.d., H. Dykstra, CRWM folder.

Wilhemina ("Mina") Kalsbeek and ("Ruby") Liu Shuying with their adopted daughters Jean and Helen, 1940s.

When war had broken out in July of 1937, only the Lee Huizenga family was in Rugao. The other mission families were vacationing at Guling (Kuling). Albert Smit and Harry Dykstra made several trips from there to Rugao during the summer and fall and were surprised to find the city calm. At the urging of the American consulate, the Huizenga family moved to Shanghai. In December, the Smit and Harry Dykstra families, with Magdalena Koets, a single missionary, joined three hundred passengers of various nationalities who were evacuated from Guling on an international train to Hong Kong, which the Japanese had promised not to bomb. Mina Kalsbeek chose to remain in Guling with her Chinese Bible woman, Liu Shuying, who as a Chinese national was not allowed to take the train. From Hong Kong, the Christian Reformed refugees moved up the coast to Shanghai, where, as in 1927, they hoped once again to direct the work in Rugao from a safe distance and to wait out the storm until they could return to the city.

Quiet prevailed in Rugao until the following spring, but it was shattered Thursday, March 17, 1938, when the Japanese began to bomb the city. The day after the bombing commenced, at about 9:30 in the morning, gunfire signaled the advance of Japanese troops from Nantong to Rugao. Troops entered the city from the south and east gates and captured it with little resistance. After its capture, the city remained quiet for a brief period before the invading Japanese troops unleashed a wave of violence and terror. They plundered homes, brutally killed thousands of men, and savagely raped women and girls. At the end of a week of rape and pillage, only an estimated 10,000 of Rugao's 130,000 residents remained in the city. Most residents had fled to the countryside, but many also took refuge in Shanghai. The violence then moved to the countryside, where Japanese troops pushed north to pursue fleeing Chinese troops.

For the next ten weeks, the mission compounds were transformed into a refugee camp. One of the mission houses served as the only hospital in the Rugao area, manned by Dr. Chu, whose hospital in Nantong had been destroyed.[6] The missionaries, their Chinese colleagues, and Rugao

Albert Smit and Harry Dykstra were in Rugao several days before the Japanese took the city on March 18. Taking the bombing as advance warning of an imminent attack by ground troops, they moved all of the hospital equipment and furniture into their compounds outside the east gate, even as enemy planes roared overhead and the streets were filled with frightened people.[4] In their compounds, they cached five thousand pounds of rice, sixty gallons of kerosene, and stores of salt, matches, and other supplies. When Japanese troops entered the city the next day, close to nine hundred women and children took refuge in the mission compounds. Perched on the roofs of adjacent buildings and peering over the walls of the compound from horseback, Japanese soldiers "considered the possibilities," as the missionaries reported, but did nothing. At this early stage in the conflict between China and Japan, the Japanese respected the rights of foreigners and especially showed restraint in dealing with missionaries.[5]

---

[4]   H. Dykstra to Board of Missions, May 19, 1938, 2, H. Dykstra, CRWM folder. Dykstra's folder contains detailed reports, letters, and unpublished articles describing events from the summer of 1937 through the spring of 1941, when he returned to America on furlough.

[5]   Timothy Brook, "Christianity under the Japanese Occupation," in *Christianity in China*, ed. Daniel Bays (Stanford: Stanford Univ. Press, 1996), 324.

[6]   Just before the Japanese took Rugao, Lee Huizenga, without telling either the Rugao hospital staff or his mission colleagues, had departed for an international conference on leprosy in Cairo. The Christian Mission's Dr. Chu took charge of the hospital established in the mission house until the

Christians who stayed in the city provided sanctuary and ministry to the refugees crowded within their compounds. They opened a school, organized Bible studies, and on Sundays led worship services. "Never before," wrote Harry Dykstra, "did we experience such interest and response from these people temporarily rendered hopeless and homeless by the upheaval of this terrible catastrophe [*sic*]."[7]

But the mission's refugee work came to an abrupt halt at the beginning of June, when the occupying Japanese forces ordered the mission to transfer all of the refugees to a middle school inside the city walls that had been converted to a camp. Because they were given two days advance warning by a Japanese captain, most of the Chinese refugees had already fled into the countryside when the troops arrived to make the transfer. Furious to find that only the missionaries, the evangelists, and Rugao's Christians remained, the Japanese ordered the evangelists and Christians, nearly 170 in all, to march to the detention camp in the city walls, where they were held for three weeks before being allowed to return to the mission compound. After their release, some of the evangelists and Christians took up residence in the mission houses. When their colleagues and the Rugao Christians had been released, Albert Smit and Harry Dykstra, via a circuitous route through the countryside, returned to Shanghai and their own families.

After the situation in Rugao County had begun to stabilize, barricades were established in the northern parts of the county to demark the battle lines dividing Free China from Occupied China. Rugao City and all of the market towns and villages to the south were under Japanese control, while several of the markets and villages to the north and east remained in the hands of Chinese troops and guerrillas, though the Japanese eventually took these districts as well. Crossing from north to south in the county meant passing through territory held by the Japanese, the Nationalists, and, in a few places, Communist guerrillas. When occasional battles broke out, the lines might shift in one direction or the other, but the troop movements mostly just intensified the suffering of the rural population. Japanese troops were particularly vicious in terrorizing the local population in their pursuit of Chinese soldiers and ferreting out Chinese suspected of spying.

Japanese forced the mission to close it ten weeks later. Although Huizenga died in 1945, this incident and others related to him dogged the mission all the way to its closure in 1949. See H. Dykstra to Beets, March 11, 1938, H. Dykstra, CRWM folder.
[7]   H. Dykstra to Westside CRC, June 25, 1938, H. Dykstra, CRWM folder.

Until the end of the war in 1945, the Japanese maintained control of most of the county's districts through puppet governments but had to guard continually against attacks from Nationalist and Communist guerrillas.

Until the outbreak of war between Japan and the United States in December 1941, the missionaries continued their church work from Shanghai as best they could. Only the Selles family could occupy its home in Jingjiang, and only then, on the advice of the American consulate, by flying an American flag outside the gate.[8] The other missionaries, including the two single women, traveled back and forth between Shanghai and Rugao, carrying on what little mission work they could in a region occupied by three hostile armies. Getting passes to cross lines was difficult, and crossing lines could be a life-threatening experience. At one checkpoint, a Japanese soldier tossed Sam Dykstra's bike into a canal and threatened to shoot him. Whenever and wherever they could, with American flags attached to their bicycles, the missionaries crisscrossed Rugao County visiting workers, holding Bible studies and worship services in the homes of converts and inquirers, and passing out tracts. When some of the members of the Libao church returned to their ancestral home in Haimen, the mission instructed Sam Dykstra to explore developing church work in that locale. The missionaries also distributed rice and wheat to the destitute in the county, focusing particularly on the Christians and inquirers in Rugao and the outstations.[9]

Though their activities were severely limited by being forced to live in Shanghai and by the constraints of the war situation in Rugao, Harry Dykstra reported in1940 that "the effects of the war have by

---

[8]   Before December 7, 1941, the missionaries encountered few incidents with the Japanese in the cities, but in one incident at a Jingjiang City checkpoint, a Japanese soldier slapped Albert Selles, knocking his glasses off. When he complained to the garrison chief about the incident, the soldier was beaten in Selles's presence. See Sheng Songru, "Xie le si zai Jingjiang" ("Selles in Jingjiang"), *Jingjiang wen shi zi liao*, 3:2 (Aug. 1983): 421.

[9]   Before the Japanese advanced on Rugao, the "Red Swastika Society," a local Buddhist relief organization, was doing extensive refugee work in the county. After some of the mission's evangelists discovered that some "destitute" Christians had been forced to "take part in Buddhist worship" before they could receive aid, the mission, working through the International Red Cross, initiated relief work focusing primarily on its own converts and inquirers in the county. See H. Dykstra to Board, May 19, 1938, H. Dykstra, CRWM folder. See also Sam Dykstra to First CRC, Grand Rapids, March 31, 1940, S. Dykstra, CRWM folder.

no means been of a negative character." He went on to explain the following spiritual benefits to serving during wartime:

> ...Witnessing the furnace of affliction through which others have passed and being privileged to a small extent of becoming sharers in their sufferings, has brought about a more complete trust in the leading and love of God. Also a deeper assurance of the supreme efficacy of the Christ whom we seek to bring as the savior from sin and its terribly destructive power.[10]

Though they took "great care...in admitting new members" during these desperate times, the mission found the people of Rugao responding to the Christian message in record numbers.[11] Between 1937 and the departure of the last missionary from the Rugao field in June of 1942, the missionaries baptized 183 men, women, and children. In addition to baptisms in Rugao, Lee Huizenga, who had taken up refugee work in Shanghai and started a church among leper patients, baptized ninety patients at a tuberculosis hospital and another twenty-two Jewish refugees at the Hebrew Mission.[12]

But this phenomenal rate of conversions did not last. After the United States declared war on Japan December 8, 1941, the one missionary caught in Rugao and the family living in Jingjiang were interned by the Japanese for six months before being repatriated on the *Conte Verde* and exchanged for Japanese nationals off the coast of Lourenco Marques in Mozambique in June 1942. In early 1943, the Japanese interned Mina Kalsbeek, who had remained in Shanghai with Liu Shuying and their "adopted" Chinese daughters. The Huizenga family was also interned in Shanghai around the same time. Though Kalsbeek was repatriated by the end of 1943, the Huizengas remained in the Zhabei (Chapei) camp until the end of the war. Lee Huizenga died there of peritoneal cancer just weeks before the United States dropped atomic bombs on Hiroshima and Nagasaki in August 1945. Except for a few letters filtering out of China, contact among the missionaries, their evangelists, and the Rugao Christians was effectively cut off. The weight of the Christian movement in Rugao was now on the Chinese evangelists and the Chinese Christians themselves.

---

[10] *Acts of Synod*, 1940, 263.
[11] Mission Report for 1940, CRWM folder.
[12] Huizenga, with some other missionaries in Shanghai, helped open a gospel mission for Jewish refugees in Shanghai. L. J. Lamberts, *The Life Story of Dr. Lee S. Huizenga* (Grand Rapids: Eerdmans, 1950), 183.

The shift toward the Chinese taking responsibility for the Christian movement had already begun when war with Japan broke out in the summer of 1937. While the calm lasted in Rugao during the fall and winter of 1937–38, all of the evangelists had remained at their posts, carrying on with church work and evangelism. But when the bombs started to fall in March 1938, some of the evangelists fled. One family, that of evangelist Xia Guoye (Hsa Kuo-yih), working in Sanshili close to Baibu (Pai P'u) and Nantong, escaped south across the Yangzi River to his family's ancestral home. The Chinese Bible woman in Baibu, Sun Engui, also fled to her home. The other evangelists had fled from their stations, not home, but to the refuge of the missionary compounds outside Rugao's east gate. There they enjoyed protection and shared in the tasks of refugee work. After the Japanese released them from detention in the city in late June, some of these evangelists and their families returned to the missionary compounds or occupied other mission properties, both for refuge and for protection of the mission's property, since the Japanese initially afforded them some of the same protections given to foreign missionaries.[13]

Between 1938 and 1941, the evangelists continued the church's work. Because the missionaries were living in Shanghai and could only get to the city infrequently, most of this work was carried out without them. On Sundays, the evangelists held worship services in the mission compounds or in the homes of Christians or inquirers in the countryside. They also taught Bible classes for men and for women, though the latter activity took place only in the city, since it was dangerous for women to gather in the countryside. In other parts of China, despite (or perhaps because of) the swirling of death and destruction, churches reported packed crowds, an acknowledgment of the church's finally having earned a "respectable place" in China.[14] The record number of baptisms in Rugao shows that the response there was equally enthusiastic to the response in other parts of the country.

The evangelists also continued their church work in the countryside between 1938 and 1941, despite great risks. Though the Japanese extended some privileges and protections to the evangelists, they also treated them as a potential source of resistance, especially since they were seen as representatives of a foreign government. Some of the evangelists complained that they were afraid to work in Japanese territory, and not only because they were afraid of the Japanese. Some

---

[13]   Brook, "Christianity," 324.
[14]   Brown, *Earthen Vessels*, 278ff.

worried that some of their own compatriots might complain about them to the Japanese, since there were "plenty of people who would gladly make such complaints even when not true."[15] The evangelist at Baibu (Pai P'u), Xia Guoye, told Harry Dykstra that as soon as he went up the street he was "immediately surrounded by a crowd of Chinese more interested in politics than the gospel," and he feared complications with the Japanese, who were very plentiful at Baibu.

Conflicts with Japanese soldiers did occur. North of Rugao, Japanese soldiers killed a Southern Presbyterian evangelist and his father with bayonets.[16] Though none of the Christian Reformed mission's evangelists were killed or injured, they had several terrifying experiences. On one afternoon in the fall of 1941, Japanese soldiers held several of the mission's evangelists captive and threatened their lives. Around the same time, Li Xiupei (Li Hsioh-peh) "stood his ground" against the Japanese, and though his life was spared "he was thoroughly robbed....All his trunks were emptied, his bedding, and clothing stolen to the hat and shoes he wore."[17] When cycling through the countryside to visit outstations, Albert Smit and the Jingjiang evangelist An Guangrong (An Kuang-yung) learned that there was a Japanese checkpoint ahead, and An refused to proceed. When he also refused to return alone to Rugao, Harry Dykstra was forced to come and meet him halfway to accompany him back to the city.

From the few letters the evangelists sent to missionaries waiting out the war in the United States, it is clear that the evangelists carried on church work as best they could after the missionaries were forced to leave the country in 1942. As in other parts of Occupied China, the Japanese allowed them to carry on Christian work, as long as they steered clear of Western contact.[18] But this need for distance was not appreciated by all of the missionaries. After being repatriated, Sam Dykstra complained that his evangelists had treated him poorly at his departure, despite his financial generosity to them. When Albert Smit heard about this, he sided with the evangelists, writing to mission secretary John De Korne:

[15]   H. Dykstra to Mission Board, Sept. 7, 1938, H. Dykstra, CRWM folder. It is unclear why their compatriots would want to betray them. Perhaps this was due to jealousy, since the evangelists received some of the same protections as the foreign missionaries. See Brook, "Christianity," 324.

[16]   S. Dykstra to First CRC, Grand Rapids, Sept. 30, 1941, S. Dykstra, CRWM folder.

[17]   Ibid.

[18]   Brook, "Christianity," 332.

I don't at all sympathize with Sam when he spoke of the Chinese forsaking him. What else did he expect? He should have urged them to keep clear of him, for surely they could not do him any good and would hurt themselves. Knowing the ruthlessness of the Japanese he should have thought of their safety.[19]

Japan's larger purpose in cutting off contact with the West was to rally Chinese sentiment against Western imperialism. But the Japanese also viewed the Christian movement in China as a way to consolidate its hold on the country, and thus Japan promoted a religious policy of church unification.[20] The Church of Christ in China functioned throughout the war relatively unhindered by Japanese interference. As in some other parts of Occupied China, the evangelists in Rugao at first declined Japanese invitations to participate in efforts to enlist the support of the church.[21] Later, however, at least in some parts of the county, the mission's evangelists acquiesced. In answer to a letter he had sent from Free China in 1944, Smit received a short answer from evangelist Sun Zhifang (Suen Chih-fang) on stationery with the heading: "Jukao Church of Christ.[22]

The little contact the missionaries did have with the evangelists during the war years had to do with money. Missionary visits to Rugao after the war began in 1937 were to check on the work, to provide "spiritual supervision" to their evangelists, and above all to pay salaries. Because of astronomical inflation, the mission had begun paying in *piculs* of rice (approximately 133 pounds) before the missionaries departed. Still concerned about raising salary expectations too high (which might make it difficult for churches to pay salaries after the war), the missionaries decided in 1940 to give each worker an "emergency bonus" of rice rather than a salary increase.[23] Before leaving Rugao in 1942, Sam Dykstra had contemplated sending all of the evangelists home. But at senior evangelist Wang Aitang's suggestion and when they all agreed to take a cut in salary, Dykstra decided to keep them on after his departure. He gave them each 500 *yuan* and permission to sell the hospital's medicine and the gas and kerosene stored in the missionary compounds.

As in 1927, money created the potential for trouble. Salary disputes continued to arise even after the Japanese invasion. In the

19   Smit to De Korne, Jan. 18, 1943, Smit, CRWM folder.
20   Brook, "Christianity," 332.
21   Albert Smit, "Rugao as I found it," *Banner* 81 (Jan. 18, 1946): 80.
22   Smit to De Korne, July 15, 1944, 3, Smit, CRWM folder.
23   De Korne to Smit, April 22, 1940, Smit, CRWM folder.

fall of 1938, Sun Zhiping (Suen Chih-ping), who had served as a rural evangelist and in the hospital, along with his daughter, Sun Engui (Suen Ung-kuei), who had worked for Kalsbeek as a Bible woman, asked for salary increases.[24] The mission rejected their request, stating that these kinds of disputes should not be coming up in such turbulent times. But Sun continued to demand higher wages. Finally, in 1940, the missionaries decided to raise his salary because they valued his years of faithful work and because, as one missionary commented, "The old gentleman is bound to bring it up again and again."[25] One of Albert Smit's evangelists got into serious trouble over money. When the mission discovered that Zhou Fengwu (Chow Feng-wu), who had come from the Southern Presbyterian mission at Haizhou (Haichow), had misused money designated for relief work, Smit was forced to let him go, even though he had always found him otherwise a conscientious worker. Zhou did not take the dismissal well, accusing Smit and the mission of "everything low."[26]

Even after the last missionary was either interred or repatriated in 1942, other issues involving money continued to arise. While doing relief work with the National Christian Council in western China, Albert Smit sent a few letters to the evangelists living in Rugao: Sun Zhifang, Chen Guifan, and Wang Aitang. He also contacted An Guangrong, the evangelist in Jingjiang, and Liu Shuying, Kalsbeek's Bible woman, who was living in Shanghai with their two Chinese foster daughters. Through various people traveling between Free China, Shanghai, and Rugao, Smit sent small amounts of money. Because contact with Westerners was dangerous for the Chinese, Smit sent this money in the

[24]   About the salary dispute, Sun had stated to Harry Dykstra it was "a matter of inequality compared with that of the other preachers." He claimed that he had graduated from a Northern Presbyterian Mission literary college in Huaiyin, Jiangsu, in 1903 and studied in the theological department of Chefoo (Yantai) University for one year. He also claimed that he had labored as a preacher and conducted grade school for twenty years. During the eight years he had worked for the mission, he had worked with Lee Huizenga in the hospital and had served at the outstation of Shuangdian. Though Dykstra was unhappy about the timing of the salary dispute, he stated, "The salary issue notwithstanding, Mr. Suen is a faithful worker and justice must be done him in this matter." See H. Dykstra Report, March 7, 1940, H. Dykstra, CRWM folder. About Sun's daughter, Sun Engui, whom Kalsbeek enlisted as a Bible woman, she reported in 1940, "Efficient at Sunday school, but not mature enough for visiting in the homes of older women." Kalsbeek Report, March 13, 1940, Kalsbeek, CRWM folder.

[25]   H. Dykstra to De Korne, March 7, 1940, H. Dykstra, CRWM folder.

[26]   Smit to De Korne, April 17, 1940, Smit, CRWM folder.

name of one of the mission's former colporteurs, Song Liansen (Song Lien-sen), but he was never sure the money got through to the intended person.

Evangelist An Guangrong repeatedly pleaded with the mission to send him funds. His letter to Albert Selles in November 1944 clearly indicated he wanted financial help from the mission, though it did not explicitly request money.

> I write you a letter every month. Do you receive nearly all of them? Communications are so poor. It seems easier to add our memory (than to write). However, on August 27 I received a letter from Mrs. Price stating that she received a letter from you. This greatly comforted us. We are happy that God is so richly blessing you.
>
> At present the attendance at public worship certainly does not decrease. With the exception of those who live inside of the West Gate nearly all regularly attend worship. Mrs. Ch'ien has been to her daughter's home for a few months and therefore could not attend worship. Mr. Hwang received a gunshot wound and for a few weeks was not able to attend worship. Mr. Hwang's wound has now been healed. Mrs. Hwang has given birth to a son, who is already twenty-five days old. All are well. Mrs. Tzu had boils on her feet. She is well again now. Mr. Liu and his wife and his mother are all well. They regularly attend worship. Mr. Chen's sickness has also healed. The attendance at Sunday School is 120. This is a great pleasure.
>
> At present rice is sold for $11,000 per *tan* [about 112 pounds]. The children go out daily into the country to gather weeds for fuel, so that we can cook a little rice gruel. We daily are two-third's part hungry. Besides the difficulty of obtaining food we still have the housing problem. A small five-room house inside the city, which is not better than a mat-shed, rents for half to one *teo* of rice per month (about eleven pounds).
>
> During these few years we have all been sick and always requested the help of Dr. Ch'iao. Because we have all been reduced to poverty he does not charge us anything. This is God's grace to us.
>
> Mrs. An and the children all greet you. All the church members greet you. I myself respectfully greet you.
>
> Wishing you a blessed Christmas and a happy new year.[27]

[27] An Guangrong to Selles, Nov. 25, 1944, Selles, CRWM folder. This letter was translated by Albert Selles and sent to mission secretary De Korne. The Dr. Ch'iao whom An mentions worked at the Jiangyin Mission's hospital.

An's letters were passed along to the mission through Elsie McClure Price and Frank Price, Southern Presbyterian missionaries who worked for the Church of Christ in China in Chongqing during the war years.[28] When An "complained bitterly" to the Southern Presbyterians in 1944 about his desperate circumstances, they advanced him a hundred dollars on behalf of the mission. Despite holding a job in a Japanese-run school, An received the most aid of all of the mission's evangelists during the war years, even as Smit worried that if the Japanese ever got hold of his letters, it would endanger his life and those of the Christians in Jingjiang.[29]

The mission's other evangelists all faced economic hardship during the war years, but they supported themselves through work outside the church. A letter Albert Smit received from Wang Aitang, also written in 1944, provides a record of how some of the mission's evangelists supported their families.

> Greetings: A few days ago I received your letter. I was very very happy and wrote immediately to the other workers telling them the news. The hearts of all of us are filled with joy. I met Miss Liu [Liu Shuying] today and when she heard the news she just shouted out. We are so glad that you are safely here and we take new courage again.
>
> At present all our workers are here. On the one hand we try to provide for our families and on the other hand to preach the gospel, although I wish to tell you honestly that the work of preaching is not like formerly.
>
> Let me briefly explain the circumstances of each of the workers.
>
> a. Ch'en [Chen Guifan] still has his cotton machine (loom) and makes a living with that at present.
> b. T'ien [Tian Zhitong] has opened a little medicine shop.
> c. Hua [Hua Fuquan] has returned to his former business of making cloth.
> d. Hsia [Xia Guoye] is the only one who has no work.
> e. Ch'en [Chen Fang] is living with his two sons who are making soap.

According to Song Shengru, An Guangrong taught in a Japanese-run school during the war years. Interview with author Feb. 28, 2002.

[28] Frank Price is the author of *The Rural Churches in China*, a survey of the Yangzi delta region.

[29] Smit to De Korne, Jan. 29, 1944, Smit, CRWM folder.

    f. Suen [Sun Zhiping] has opened a little cloth shop and sells medicine on the side.

    g. Li [Li Yuantong] owns land and does business with the things given him.

    h. And I [Wang Aitang] buy things and sell them here.

No one is suffering unbearable hardship, which I am sure you will be glad to know.

When you write to your family and the church, please send my greetings.

Goodbye and may the Lord bless you and may we soon meet again.[30]

Except for these letters filtering out from the evangelists, there are few other details about what was happening in Rugao between 1943 and the beginning of 1946. A survey of news from the *Rugao Daily* (*Rugao ri bao*) during an eighteen-month period shows a city under a Japanese puppet government but functioning somewhat normally.[31] Schools were open and recruiting students. Announcements were made about the reopening of the Nantong Christian hospital and other aid organizations such as an orphans' institute and the Red Swastika Society.

One fragmentary document that survives from this period appears to show that if the church in Rugao was not actively involved in development and relief work in society, at least the subject was on the minds of some Christians in the city. During the latter part of the Sino-Japanese War, someone in the church, perhaps Liu Shuying, Mina Kalsbeek's partner, gave a talk entitled, "Christian Work on Behalf of Society and the Welfare of Children." What follows is a translation of the talk.

> The topic we want to study is the work of the church in its neighborhood on the behalf of society and for the benefit of children. It will be very helpful first to analyze our terms. What is working for society? If we refrain from technical or systematic terms, a simple definition is as follows: "Work for society is a group or a person's total work to lift higher or benefit other people in society." This includes the following activities:
>
> helping the poor;
> improving sanitary conditions;

30   Wang Aitang to Smit, 1944. The letter was translated by Albert Smit and sent to John De Korne, Smit, CRWM folder.

31   *Rugao ri bao* (*Rugao Daily*), July 23, 1943-Dec. 30, 1944.

providing literacy classes.

What is work for the welfare of children? Work for the welfare of children is one aspect of work for society. Because of its urgent and critical need it acquired independent status, so that especially since the Sino-Japanese War even more attention has been paid to it. Work for the welfare of children now includes the following:

prenatal care;

infant care;

improving the situation of children.

This kind of work [for children] includes:

outpatient care for pregnant women;

outpatient care for infants;

nursing clinics, nutrition clinics, "porridge" clinics;

orphanages;

supervision of games;

children's classes;

Sunday school classes;

boys' and girls' clubs;

short-term Bible school.

Whatever kind of works that improves the conditions [for children should be included in this list].

Why do we need to work for the benefit of society and the welfare of children? Because of its urgent need. From ancient times, we [Chinese people] have had a very deep concept of the family, but toward society our view has been one of indifference [*mo*];[32] consequently, we always have the idea of taking care of the snow in front of our own gate, [and] not considering other people's affairs, so long as we are good. As the premier has said, "Chinese society is like grains of sand in the desert unconnected to each other." [We] must know in every place the people who don't enjoy [a decent standard of living]. [We] must not only seek to do [this work] but also to safeguard the above kinds of work. If every place looked after the poor in its area, the pain after this war and the war with the Communists could be avoided, because their slogan is...[33]

---

[32] The Chinese word for "indifference" here can also mean "desert" and may be a word play connected to the subsequent quote from the premier about Chinese society being "like grains of sand."

[33] This handwritten Chinese document was found on a scrap of notebook paper in Mina Kalsbeek's personal folder. Because of its native penmanship

Unfortunately the rest of the document is missing, but it appears to show that in contrast to the missionaries—the ordained men, anyway—some of the Chinese workers were interested in preaching Christianity *and* working to alleviate a number of social problems, especially those of women and children.

It is unclear where this talk was given, but it could have been given in the context of a church meeting in Rugao, since it is clear that church activities continued during the war. After the occupation of Rugao in 1938, the evangelists living in the mission compounds opened the residences for worship services. Many more women than men attended these services, since the attendance of men tended to draw the attention of the Japanese. Occasionally, the group was forced to meet for only prayer and preaching, since singing drew unwanted attention. The messages at these meetings were very simple, so that "beginners also could learn."[34] As late as September 1941, Sam Dykstra reported visiting homes in Rugao with evangelist Sun Zhiping and that some of the "better class" were attending church services.[35]

Church records from the period also give a hint of what was happening with the Christians in Rugao during the war years.[36] Many

---

and fluency, which includes aphorisms and quotes from the premier (Chiang Kai-shek), it was almost certainly written by a Chinese person. Moreover, it was quite likely a Bible woman, since the men, both the missionaries and evangelists, were not nearly as concerned about work with women and children as were the Bible women. Finally, since the "talk" was found in Mina Kalsbeek's folder, the author and speaker was probably Liu Shuying, Kalsbeek's inseparable partner worker, though how the document got there remains a mystery. The fact that the end of the Sino-Japanese War is mentioned and the coming war with the Communists is in sight strongly suggests the talk was given sometime between 1944 and 1945, Kalsbeek, personal folder (trans. author).

[34] The simplicity of these messages was probably to accommodate the new converts that had come into the church through refugee work. H. Dykstra, March Report, 1938, H. Dykstra, CRWM folder.

[35] S. Dykstra to First CRC, Grand Rapids, Sept. 30, 1941, S. Dykstra, CRWM folder.

[36] These records come from notes the author made from the content of church books found in the Rugao Religious Affairs Bureau office June 2, 2002. They record names, age at baptism, and status in the church. By the fluency of the Chinese penmanship, the records appear to have been kept by a Chinese Christian. For many of the members baptized in the 1930s, however, there are annotations written in English with a blue pencil explaining that person's status up to 1941. These notes were probably written by Sam Dykstra, the last missionary to leave Rugao in June 1942.

of the believers and inquirers, after initially taking refuge in the mission compound, simply fled Rugao. But at least one member, Ding Shuai, returned and attended services frequently. Some of the Christians not native to Rugao returned to their ancestral homes or to other cities in the Yangzi delta region, such as Shanghai, Nantong, Nanjing, and Taizhou. Tang Wenxiu, one of Mina Kalsbeek and Liu Shuying's circle of young women, moved to Shanghai and married Liu Shuhua, Liu Shuying's brother. Several of the Christians went to other towns in Rugao County and stayed there permanently after the war. Two Christian young women from Rugao married Christians who belonged to other denominations. Liu Meizhen (Loh Mei Dzen), after moving to the village of Chahe (Ch'a-ho) where the mission had an outstation, married a Christian there.[37] Another young woman named Liu married a man living close to Jingjiang City; during the war she started a Sunday school on her own that continued even after she ran out of picture cards. Many of the Christians who left Rugao appear never to have returned.

Several of those who stayed received comments in the margins of their church record which suggest that they were regular attendees at church services and faithful to other church activities. One member, a twenty-eight-year-old woman named Zhang Chunfang, who had been a servant of the De Korne family and had come to be a Christian through the work of Kalsbeek and Liu, "was quite faithful in church attendance." Another former mission employee, Hu Yinglai, a man in his fifties who had worked as the watchman at the west gate chapel, was reported to be a "good man." Hua Yungsheng, another man in his fifties who worked in "textiles," was reported along with his family to be "faithful church members." Others in the records received comments such as "good Christian woman," "attends services," "well spoken of," and "well reported." One woman in her fifties named Huo Aizhu was recorded as a "good Christian lady," though, the record noted, she "can't attend because she's blind."

Some of the records also contain information during the war period, when the missionaries were gone from the summer of 1942 until the spring of 1946. It is unclear who kept church records during the war with Japan, but it was probably senior evangelist Wang Aitang, who took over the record keeping in 1950, after the last missionary departed.

37   In one of the twenty-fifth anniversary articles appearing in the *Banner* in 1945, Mina Kalsbeek wrote about the last she had heard about a group of women converts that had been baptized thirteen years earlier in 1932. See Wilhemina Kalsbeek, "Baptized May 15, 1932: What about Them Since?" *Banner* 80 (Nov. 2, 1945): 1032.

Some who stayed in Rugao, however, were not faithful in attending worship. About these members, their records simply note: "No longer attends services." But about Chen Ji'an, a thirty-six-year-old peasant who had been baptized in 1936, the record notes that he "seems a good boy but has neglected coming to church." The record of one woman in her thirties who had become a Christian through the work of Kalsbeek and Liu notes that she "has not attended for two and a half years, shows no interest." About Chen Youwen, a twenty-three-year-old shoemaker who was baptized in 1934, it was noted: He "has not been interested since the summer of 1938...doesn't attend services."

Some of the comments appear to indicate moral lapses. Out of a total of forty-four records, eight members received negative comments. Most of those with bad reputations were young women. Hua Baishen— a young woman in her twenties baptized in 1935 by Lee Huizenga—Liu Zhicheng, and her sister Liu Zhide—both young women in their late teens who had been baptized by Smit in 1937—all received the comment "bad reputation, doesn't attend," with no further explanation. Others received similarly negative comments such as "reputation at Rugao not good," "daughter of Christian parents, bad reputation," and "delinquent." Sun Zhifang, a young woman originally from Yangzhou who had moved to Rugao and was baptized by John De Korne in 1930 at the age of 18, was reported in the summer of 1938 to be living with a man named Luo (Loh) in Jingjiang who had a wife in another city. Sun had borne Luo a child. Zhang Fuzhen, who had also been baptized in 1930 but had not attended church since 1931, was reported in 1941 to be living with a Japanese soldier in Nantong.[38] Another woman, Chen Xiuzhen, a woman in her mid-twenties baptized by Smit in 1937, was reported to be a "concubine for a military man in Shanghai."

Of the six male church members labeled with a bad reputation, explanation is given for only one. About this Rugao businessman, who was baptized at age thirty-six by Albert Smit in 1937, it was recorded: "reputation bad, uses opium, died in an accident outside west gate 1941." Though the record is unclear about this church member's name, he may have been the husband of Yong Aitang. Baptized in 1932 at the age of twenty-five through the work of Kalsbeek and Liu, Yong had left Rugao in 1938 with her two children, following her husband into what was still Free China.[39] Yong's husband had joined the guerrilla forces and, because he was unable to feed his family as a soldier, had sold

[38]   Kalsbeek, "Baptized," 1032.
[39]   Ibid.

opium on the side. After he was killed "in action," Yong carried on his opium business to support her children "until she became a victim to the dread habit of smoking it." "When I last saw her," Kalsbeek reported, "she had sunk very low. She was not ashamed to beg and rumor said she was living with a man who was not her husband."[40]

In the same article, Kalsbeek mentions the wartime whereabouts of another 1932 convert and her husband. After her baptism at the age of sixteen, Tang Wenzhen (Tang Weng Dzen) had married William Guan (Kwan), whom the mission had hoped would develop into a Christian leader in Rugao.[41] When the Japanese had taken Rugao in the spring of 1938, they had placed a price on Guan's head because of some patriotic essays he had written that they found in the city. The couple drifted about the Jiangsu area before returning to the city and seeking help from the mission. The mission gave them a small amount of capital to start a business.

Instead of starting a business, however, the family had moved into Rugao City with their children, and, according to Kalsbeek, "Soon there were reports that he was working for the enemy."[42] Guan was first reported to be spying for the guerrilla forces, and then, after a narrow brush with death, for the Japanese, "who watched him closely." The last time Kalsbeek saw the couple, just before her internment at the end of February 1943, Guan insisted that he was loyal to the forces of Chiang Kai-shek. Because they were "heartily despised" by the people of Rugao, the family stopped attending church, "Lest they bring reproach upon the whole group."[43] Tang Wenzhen, however, confided to Kalsbeek that she continued with her daily devotions and "never ceased to love the Lord Jesus Christ."[44]

To the north, in Haian, the second largest city within the mission's scope, the Christian work came to a virtual standstill during the war years. Evangelist Tian Zhitong remained at his post and sold medicine in the front of his residence, but Christian meetings were difficult to hold because Japanese soldiers occupied part of the house. Small worship services were held in the guestroom, severely limiting the numbers that could attend. Cholera epidemics swept through Haian several times during the war, wiping out large numbers of the population, including members of the Haian church. Though the group continued to meet,

[40]   Ibid.
[41]   Ibid.
[42]   Ibid.
[43]   Ibid.
[44]   Ibid.

by the end of the war many of the Christians had left the city. In some of the smaller market towns in southern Rugao County, where there was a stronger Japanese presence, the Christians were under greater pressure, and many fled. Evangelist Xia Guoye, who had fled when war broke out, returned to Sanshili but was restricted in what he could do there because the Japanese occupied the mission's property. But just before Japan's attack on Pearl Harbor in December of 1941, he had baptized eleven people, and the group was holding crowded meetings in nearby Pingqiao village.

The Christians in the countryside fared generally better than those in the cities and larger market towns. The group at Libao, just inside Free China, continued to grow during the early years of the war. Because it was in "no man's land" between the three armies, the district had remained quiet initially, with life going on more or less as usual.[45] In 1938, the church group in Libao not only continued worship services and Bible meetings, but a group of the Haimen immigrants had traveled back to their ancestral home to organize evangelistic meetings there. During January and February of 1939, Harry Dykstra and evangelist Li Sunde examined forty inquirers and baptized five communicant members there.[46] After a Communion service celebrating the baptism, the Libao congregation donated eight hundred pounds of rice to the Christians in Rugao. During the next two years, twenty-one more people were baptized in Libao.

Though there were moments of deep disappointment, such as when the evangelist of many years had to be dismissed for a moral lapse, the signs of progress in the "infant church" were much greater.[47] The group's church building had to be enlarged to accommodate the

---

[45] Selles, Report on visit to Rugao, May 1946, Selles, CRWM folder.

[46] H. Dykstra, Report, Jan. and Feb. 1939, H. Dykstra, CRWM folder.

[47] Sam Dykstra does not mention the name or the circumstances surrounding the dismissal of this evangelist, but it was almost certainly Li Sunde, who had been instrumental in the formation of the congregation. At a mission meeting in the spring of 1940, the mission discussed a discipline case concerning evangelist Li Sunde. Upon receiving a letter from Cong vouching for the character of the evangelist and explaining "the possible origin of his disease," the mission decided to drop the case and let the consistory take further responsibility in the affair. Apparently the situation was not resolved and Dykstra dismissed Li several months later. About this dismissal, Dykstra wrote, "Severed relations with a valued worker who had been as it were my right hand during seven years. Moral confusion accompanies material havoc." See "Mission Minutes," 1194, May 1, 1940, 2, CRWM folder; S. Dykstra, Report, July 8, 1940, S. Dykstra, CRWM folder.

influx of new members, an enlargement for which members paid two hundred dollars and the mission only thirty. The church leadership had grown to three elders and five deacons. The leading member of the congregation, Dr. Cong, considered opening a Christian school for covenant children.[48] When the group decided to send their evangelist Ying Chengpeng (Yien Cheng-peng) south to the town of Liming near the city of Haimen, the ancestral home of the Haimen immigrants, the elders rotated leadership of the worship services and elder Wang gave the sermon. Just before the Japanese bombed Pearl Harbor, Dykstra traveled to the town of Liming and baptized twenty converts, among them members of three generations of the Fan family: grandparents, parents, and children.[49]

The Libao congregation maintained its momentum at the beginning of the war. By the end, however, because many of the Haimen immigrants, who were the backbone of the group, returned to their ancestral home to the south, the church was severely weakened. By the time the war was over, one elder had died and another had moved away, leaving only one elder to lead the group.

It is clear that the war years put a severe strain on the Christian movement in Rugao County. After the war, evangelist Chen Guifan (Ch'en Kuei-fan) wrote about this period:

> During the eight years of war the evangelists and Christians of Rugao church, because of the hard environment for spiritual life and morality, both alike received a shock, but wheat and tares can be distinguished and seen with the eye. God bears the unbearable and finally the church is cleansed and purified.[50]

Thanking the mission for the money he and the other evangelists had received during the war, Chen wrote: "Sirs of the mother church! Consider and excuse these feelings and make suitable arrangements for Rugao. Speedily send foreign missionaries to China to administer all things."[51] From Chen's thanks and plea, it is clear that the Christians in Rugao felt highly ambivalent about the independence from mission control they had experienced during the war years.

---

[48] It is unclear whether Cong opened the school.
[49] S. Dykstra to First CRC, Grand Rapids, Dec. 1, 1941, S. Dykstra, CRWM folder.
[50] Chen Guifan to De Korne, trans. Smit, n.d. (probably late 1945 or early 1946), Smit, CRWM folder.
[51] Ibid.

Civil War and the End of the Mission: 1946–1951

The end of World War II left China off guard, and this was nowhere more true than in Rugao. During the war, the Japanese had held the cities in the county, but the countryside was divided between Nationalist troops and Communist guerrillas. In the year following the war, however, Rugao was mostly in the hands of the troops of the Communist New Fourth Army. By dispatching thousands of troops to the area, the Nationalists had taken back the cities of Rugao County at the end of 1946. But after the Nationalists retook Rugao City, Communist troops still held pockets in the countryside, and much of the county was dotted with checkpoints, between stretches of no-man's land, where every man was a "law unto himself," making travel to many parts of the county impossible.[52]

This was a period of great suffering for the people of Rugao. When the Nationalist troops were taking Rugao back, the city was under siege for more than forty days, and the population within the walls was reduced to a "starvation diet."[53] Once the siege ended, the suffering took on new dimensions. During the next two years, inflation skyrocketed— at one point prices shot up between 400 and 1,000 percent in less than ten days.[54] In the countryside, where the Communists held sway, the population hunkered down, waiting to see who would ultimately prevail. Though the Communists held out the promise of "deliverance" from the Nationalists, to the missionaries many Communist guerrillas in the countryside appeared to be no more than "unscrupulous men who serve anyone for personal gain."[55]

Despite the uncertainty of the future, the missionaries began returning to Rugao at the beginning of 1946 with plans to expand their ranks, their territory, and their program. Only two of the families in China before the war and three of the single Bible women returned to China after the war, but four new families and two single Bible women joined the group between 1946 and 1947, making the largest group of missionaries in Rugao since the peak year of 1926.[56] With this enlarged force, the missionaries hoped to expand their program. Among the new

---

[52]   Selles, Report, May 1946, Selles, CRWM folder.
[53]   Selles, Report, Oct. 4, 1946, Selles, CRWM folder.
[54]   Selles to De Korne, Nov. 8, 1948, Selles, CRWM folder.
[55]   Selles to De Korne, April 18, 1946, Selles, CRWM folder.
[56]   The missionaries who arrived after WWII were Henry and Eunice (Smit) Bruinooge, Thelma and Peter De Jong, Rozena and Evert Van Reken, Marion De Young, and Magdelena Koets.

The first celebration of Christmas in Rugao after WWII, 1946. The shot was taken in front of the Lee Huizenga house inside the Rugao City walls. Seated in the middle of the third row (*left to right*) are Magdalena Koets, Peter De Jong, Thelma De Jong, Eunice (Smit) Bruinooge, Henry Bruinooge, William Smit, Hazel Smit, Albert Smit, and Dora Smit; in the top row (*sixth from the left*) is Wang Aitang.

group were a doctor and a nurse who planned to reopen the mission hospital, which had been closed since 1938. Albert Smit had explored expanding the mission's territory by opening a mission station in western China, but when it became obvious that the Christian Mission in Nantong was reducing its work in the territory adjacent to Rugao County, the missionaries instead obtained permission to expand their work into Tongzhou County, the rural areas surrounding Nantong City.[57]

The missionaries also intended to implement some new methods. They dropped the Korean Plan that they had adopted in 1929 in favor of a new approach allowing individual missionaries the freedom to adopt methods appropriate to their districts. Related to this decision, the missionaries decided not to rebuild two of their homes in Rugao, which were destroyed during the war.[58] Spreading their forces out into

---

[57] While doing relief work in western China during the war, Smit had negotiated with the China Inland Mission for the CRC to take over a section of the Gansu Corridor. See *Acts of Synod*, 1946, 76.

[58] The missionaries also believed that the houses they had built in 1922 were "too conspicuous" in Rugao. See Albert Smit, "Missionary Smit unburdens his heart," *Banner* 82 (March 7, 1947): 300.

the countryside, they believed, would reduce some of the problems of having too many workers in one place and would shift the focus from Rugao to the outlying areas.[59] The missionaries also decided to emphasize Christian education. Because of government restrictions on missionary education in the 1930s, the mission had not done any formal educational work since 1926. When the Nationalist government relaxed its regulations for mission-run schools at the end of the war (perhaps as a way to bolster American support for the Nationalist regime), the missionaries saw an opportunity for what they believed was a pressing need in Rugao: Christian schools. These schools would be primarily for the children of Christian parents and, to maintain this dominance, the mission proposed to offer enrollment to the children of believers, inquirers, and non-Christians, in that order. They hoped to start out with primary and middle schools and later develop a high school program.

The missionaries initiated other new work as well. Working with the Christian Reformed radio program, *The Back to God Hour*, Christian programs were broadcast from Shanghai that could be heard clearly in Rugao.[60] In cooperation with missionaries from another conservative Reformed denomination, the Orthodox Presbyterian Church, the Christian Reformed missionaries raised funds from home to translate Louis Berkhof's *Manual of Reformed Doctrine*. This translation and others were part of the missionaries' plan to train theologically "fit" church leaders. Since they did not have a force large enough to start their own theological institution, they decided to support the North China Theological Seminary in Tengxian, Shandong Province, with money and a teacher.[61]

A year after the missionaries had begun returning to the field, in the spring of 1947, Albert Smit reported in the *Banner* that the Nationalists had retaken Rugao and that things were rapidly returning to "normal." But normal turned out to be short-lived. After finishing

---

[59] Smit also believed this would reduce some of the friction among the missionaries. See Smit to De Korne, Oct. 13, 1944, Smit, CRWM folder.

[60] Selles, Report, Feb. 8, 1948, Selles, CRWM folder.

[61] The CRC favored this institution because its teaching was conservative, it was under Chinese church control, and most of its faculty was Chinese. See Brown, *Earthen Vessels*, 209-11; and Yao, *Fundamentalist Movement in China*, 139-82. Albert Smit was in favor of placing a CRC missionary at the NCTS, but he believed it would be years before any of the new arrivals would have the Chinese language facility to teach there. See Smit to De Korne, Jan. 22, 1948, Smit, CRWM folder.

如皋基督教會耶穌堂

一九四八年三月八號復活節受洗之成人及兒童六十四位興教節施顧王欉彭記念

This group of sixty-four adults and children was baptized in Rugao City on Easter Sunday, 1948, and was the largest baptismal celebration in the thirty-year history of the China Mission. Standing in the third row (*from the bottom, left to right*) are Albert Smit and Wang Aitang with Wilhemina Kalsbeek seated at the far right of the same row.

language study in Beijing, only two of the newly arrived families had moved to Rugao before clouds of war once again appeared on the horizon. When Nationalist troops evacuated Xuzhou (just several hundred miles northwest of Rugao) in early December of 1948, the people in the areas to the south along the north bank of the Yangzi River "became jittery."[62] On the advice of local officials, the missionaries in Rugao and Jingjiang left for Shanghai, hoping to return later if the situation changed.

In Shanghai, the missionaries held heated discussions about what to do next. Albert Smit was eager for all to stay, even if that meant that the families had to move to Yunnan Province in the Southwest to wait while events unfolded. Others, like Albert Selles, believed that staying on would be like pushing "money down into a rat hole," and he did not want to put Chinese Christians in jeopardy, if association with them

---

[62] Smit to Mission Board, Dec. 20, 1948, Smit, CRWM folder.

(*Left to right*) Peter De Jong, Albert Smit, Henry Bruinooge, and Wang Aitang visit the church work in Haian, 1948. The Haian members sought formal recognition as a congregation and established a Christian school in December 1948, just weeks before the missionaries were evacuated.

would cause trouble.[63] Moreover, Selles argued, "It has proved more than once to be a good thing for a group of native Christians to be left to their own resources; since it developed their initiative and feeling of independence."[64] Unlike the evacuation of 1927, when the mission had ordered families to return home, this time each family was given the freedom to decide whether to stay or to leave the country. Four of the families decided to leave, and on December 31, 1948, they left China on the *U.S.S. General Breckenbridge*. The remaining families shared a house in Shanghai's French Concession, where former mission Bible woman Liu Shuying taught Chinese to the new missionaries. In March 1949, the remaining families left, leaving three missionaries behind in China to see how the situation would develop.

[63] Selles, "Why I left our China mission field," *Banner* 84 (Dec. 30, 1949): 1543. The "rat hole" quote comes from a letter by a Mr. Scratch of the Assemblies of God mission. See Selles to De Korne, Aug. 11, 1948, Selles, CRWM folder.

[64] Selles to De Korne, Dec. 10, 1948, Selles, CRWM folder.

When his family returned in March to the United States, Albert Smit was in Rugao. He had decided to return in January to help the evangelists and Christians there as long as he could. He hoped that some church activities would be possible, but mostly he believed that by staying he would encourage the evangelists to remain at their posts. He worried that if they left, they would not be able to return, because the Communists would take their flight as sympathy for the Nationalists. If the evangelists stayed in Rugao, however, Smit believed that their presence would save the mission's property and enable the evangelists to continue their work after the Communists took the city. If the church was destroyed and the Christians scattered, he feared it would be almost impossible to start again.

When the Communists took Rugao at the end of January 1949, Smit found their arrival and the departure of the Nationalists a study in contrast. Three days before the old regime left the city, the Nationalists locked the city gates and demanded 600,000 *yuan* as a prize for keeping the local garrison from looting the city.[65] Nationalist soldiers had brutally forced their way into homes and seized young and middle-aged men, herding them like cattle into a building to serve as conscripts. Smit hid fifty men under the floor of his house. Once the local officials had fled, Nationalist troops looted the city anyway. In contrast, when the Communists troops arrived, "They showed perfect discipline."[66] After they had taken the city peacefully, one of the Rugao Christians whom the missionaries thought had died a few years earlier, and whose "widow" the mission had helped from time to time, turned up at his door, now part of the new government.[67] When other Communist officials began to arrive at his door, Smit found them remarkably restrained and tolerant in their dealings with him. In fact, he found them friendlier than the Nationalists had been when they had first arrived in the city more than twenty years earlier. The Communists already knew a lot about him, but they continued to pepper his workers, neighbors, and acquaintances for information.[68] Because he received "strong endorsements," the government left him in peace.

Other things about the Communists surprised Smit as well. Despite talk of anti-Americanism, stirred up by articles in the daily papers in the summer of 1949, Smit reported in September of 1949: "Not once have I been molested, nor has my liberty been interfered with,

---

65   Smit to De Korne, June 14, 1949, Smit, CRWM folder.
66   Ibid.
67   Ibid.
68   Ibid.

except that no pass has been given me and therefore I have not been able to visit the outstations."[69] He also believed that in some respects things in Rugao were much better than they had been under the old regime. This was not to say he endorsed the basic Communist philosophy or its avowed aim, but he found that "present affairs are run pretty much like formerly, except that the present government has cleaned up a great deal." He went on to add,

> Many improvements and reforms have been introduced that are praiseworthy. Under the KMT graft and bribery were carried on almost openly, especially towards the last. That has all been stamped out now. Land reforms which were long overdue have now been introduced. Absentee landlordism has been abolished, and the peasants have been given the land. I like the unpretentiousness of the present leaders and feel that they are giving the people an honest government. They are doing what we had always hoped the old government would do.[70]

From what he saw, Smit believed that the Chinese way of life would not change drastically, but that wealth would be more equally distributed and the poor would be given a chance to obtain a better standard of living. Several months after the Communists' arrival in the city, Smit said he could "heartily endorse" what he saw.

While government officials continued to treat him politely, by the end of 1949 he began to believe they were trying to squeeze him and all of the other missionaries out of the interior. After a year of living under the Communist regime, Smit came to the conclusion that the usefulness of foreign missionaries in China had come to an end, and by January 1950 he had decided to leave. He had suggested in 1948 that if the mission had an established medical or educational work, remaining in Rugao after the Communist takeover would be easier.[71] But since the mission had focused almost exclusively on evangelism, by the end of 1949 his place in the city was become increasingly difficult. Students no longer dared to come to his home, and it was becoming more and more difficult for him to go to the homes of the Christians and inquirers in the city. Being associated with an American was becoming a liability for the Chinese. His relationship with the Chinese evangelists was affected, too. They had all but stopped evangelistic work, but there was little he

---

[69] Smit to Mission Board, Sept. 14, 1949, Smit, CRWM folder.
[70] Smit to Mission Board, Feb. 28, 1950, Smit, CRWM folder.
[71] Smit to Mission Board, Dec. 20, 1948, Smit, CRWM folder.

could do about it, Smit admitted, "For to go with them would make it that much harder."[72] He concluded that to stay on in Rugao "could serve no good purpose and in a way the workers and the Christians are now better off without me."[73] As a reason for applying for a permit to Shanghai, Smit cited some difficulty he was having with his eyes and traveled there for treatment at the end of January 1950. Two months after arriving in Shanghai, he departed for the United States. Evangelist Wang Aitang and his family saw Smit off at the dock where his ship departed. After almost thirty years in Rugao, the Christian Reformed Church's China work had come to an end.

While the work in Rugao had made great strides during the Nanjing Decade, including the formation of the Libao church, the first church established by the mission, much of what was accomplished in the 1930s was destroyed by the Japanese invasion in the summer of 1937. Following the invasion, mission work in Rugao was limited because of a reduced number of missionaries and because of the difficulties of working during the subsequent Japanese occupation. Although the missionaries thought the important relief efforts at the beginning of the war might result in a better situation for the church, ultimately these efforts did not bring an influx of new members. Following the bombing of Pearl Harbor in 1941, all of the missionaries were eventually evacuated, and the Rugao church was on its own. By making adjustments (i.e., joining the Japanese-sanctioned Church of Christ in China) some of the churches and meeting points near Rugao remained open and, though certainly constrained in the scope of their work, continued to minister in the county. Following World War II, the missionaries returned and resumed work, with a new strategy and plan for expanding their work into Nantong County to the east. But the chaos of the civil war that almost immediately engulfed the country made mission work nearly impossible, and on the eve of the Communist victory in 1949, all but a few missionaries returned home. When Albert Smit left in March 1950, after almost thirty years in the country, the Christian Reformed Church's work in China had come to an end. The questioned remained, however, would the church established by the mission in Rugao remain open? And if it did continue, would it be a Reformed church?

---

[72] Smit to Mission Board, Feb. 28, 1950, Smit, CRWM folder.
[73] Ibid.

CHAPTER 7

A Real Chinese Christian Church:
The Church in Rugao, 1950-1966

Once back in the United States, some of the repatriated missionaries expressed the opinion that the Communist period would be only an interlude and that eventually missionaries would be allowed to return. "The present picture is a very dark one," reported Albert Selles to the Mission Board shortly after his repatriation, but he believed that "the 'red' of China will gradually fade into 'pink' and that ultimately the doors will be opened again."[1] Others in the mission were not so sure, believing rather that the days of the foreign missionary were over for good. One missionary suggested hopefully that the hostile Communist movement might mean the end of the liberal church union movement. Though the Communist takeover put the Chinese church in "the position of the often persecuted Christian groups of which we read in scripture," he wrote, "let us hope and pray...[that this experience makes] it a real Chinese Christian church."[2] All agreed, however, that the closing of the mission—whether for a season or forever—had the

---

[1] Selles at Mission Board Meeting, April 4, 1949, Selles, CRWM folder.
[2] Peter De Jong, "The China Mission Field as I See It," *Banner* 85 (July 7, 1950): 843.

potential to benefit the Christian movement both in Rugao and across China. Even before he left China, Albert Smit had suggested that although the Christians in Rugao had not made great progress toward self-support, these new circumstances would "make it necessary for the Chinese church to take over and carry on independently. It will be hard for a time," Smit said, "but it may be a blessing in disguise."[3]

Though the details are sketchy, there are some hints about what happened to the Christians in the Rugao countryside when land reform was implemented shortly after the Communist victory.[4] Although church activities and worship services were initially disrupted all over the county, eventually Christians began holding regular worship services again.[5] In some places, Christians were required to apply for permits to meet for activities and to furnish the authorities with the names of all those who attended. If the government had seized their mission-rented property for its own use, Christians could continue meeting only if they furnished their own meeting place, usually in the house of one of the members.[6] But in three districts where the mission had lost contact with the Christians because of the civil war, the situation after the Communist takeover appears to have been somewhat better. Because these Christians had been in the Communist-controlled countryside and had had a chance to become acquainted with the new

[3]   Smit to Mission Board, Feb. 28, 1950, Smit, CRWM folder.

[4]   After they assumed control in 1949, the Communists began to implement land reform in Jiangsu Province as they did all over the country. Because the pattern of tenancy along the coast and in the counties just north of the river was complex, this was a very complicated process that involved training eleven thousand cadres for the reforms in northern Jiangsu. Reports from the area indicate that there was resistance to the reforms. Some of the wealthier peasants resisted seizure of their land, animals, and tools. This resistance resulted in some violent clashes among the party, rich peasants, and poor peasants, and almost certainly made Christian activities difficult. Robert Ash, "Economic Aspects of Land Reform in Kiangsu, 1949-1952," *China Quarterly* 66 (June 1976): 277.

[5]   This information comes via Albert Smit in a Mission Report appearing in *Acts of Synod*, 1950, 438.

[6]   In some locations, the Christians had the only available space the cadres could use for their meetings, and consequently the party "borrowed" these facilities for its own meetings. According to Oi Ki Ling, before Liberation the Manchurian branch of the Church of Christ in China had 290 churches, but by the end of 1949 the number of churches had been reduced to 47, with almost none of the churches in the countryside functioning. Oi Ki Ling, *The Changing Role of the British Protestant Missionaries in China, 1945-1952* (Madison, N.J.: Associated University Presses, 1999), 113.

government, after the takeover they were allowed to hold worship services unhindered. Some of the Christians in these areas had even taken minor positions in the new government.[7]

Little is known about what took place in the Rugao countryside after 1949. At the time, there were six evangelists working in the city and in the outstations. They had all intended to flee, but they stayed because Smit stayed. Some of the Christians at the outstations in the countryside, such as Shizhuang in the south, moved to Rugao. But Smit had persuaded some of the evangelists to return to their stations. Evangelist Hua Fuquan (Hua Fu-ch'uen) agreed to return to Baibu (Pai P'u), where in the fall of 1948 only two Christians had remained, and evangelist Li Yuantong (Li Yuen-tong) agreed to take up work again at Libao. Li had followed several families from Libao to Haimen and had served there during the war. In 1949 he agreed to restart the work at Libao, which had suffered greatly during the civil war period. From a thriving church in 1937, the congregation had been reduced to a few families meeting irregularly for worship. Their building had been destroyed, some of the members had died, and many more had moved away. Until the situation stabilized, Li would live in Rugao and travel back and forth to Libao, something the evangelists were still free to do, though Smit was not.

The Christian group in Haimen, from which evangelist Li was returning, was doing surprisingly well. Some of the Haimen immigrants living in Libao, who had been instrumental in starting the church in 1937, had returned to their ancestral home during the war and had started church work there among their families. Smit visited them after the war and found a small but thriving group. They had grown from six Christians to forty families by 1949. Evangelist Li reported in 1949 that many in this group were requesting baptism. Because the group did not have a building or even a fixed meeting place, it met in various homes under the leadership of some of the Christians who had returned from Libao during the war. In the fall of 1949, these Christians requested that the mission supply them with an evangelist to give them further instruction and, presumably, to help them organize a Haimen congregation.[8] Nothing else is known about the fate of this group.

More details are recorded about the situation of the Christian groups in Jingjiang City and Haian City (Hai'an). The small Christian

[7]   Smit to Mission Board, *Acts of Synod*, 1950, 438.
[8]   Edward Van Baak and Henry Bruinooge to the Executive Committee of the Mission Board, Nov. 10, 1949, CRWM folder.

group in Jingjiang, about twenty miles southwest of Rugao, did not survive long after the city was liberated. Having heard, he said later, "about persecutions of Christians, even crucifixions and other forms of executions," evangelist An Guangrong fled with his family, two other Christian workers with their servants and families, and several of the Christian families in the city, crossing the river to Jiangyin before the Communists arrived in Jingjiang.[9] When they returned after the Communists had taken control of the city, all of the Christians were under suspicion of being "pro-Nationalist" (i.e., anti-Communist), and evangelist An was kept under house arrest for a time.

After releasing him, the government did not allow evangelist An to preach or the Jingjiang Christians to hold worship services, since their mission-rented facilities were being used for political meetings. The remaining small group of Christians was afraid to have contact with An. In September of 1949, An reported to Smit, who passed the information along to the Mission Board, that one of the families, the Liu family, "the most important Christian family" in the city, "has now renounced Christianity and refuses to have him visit them or lead them in Bible study."[10] Evangelist An reported that another Christian had turned against him and threatened to turn him in to the local authorities for carrying on religious activities, a charge that An believed could mean a lengthy prison term. After some pleading, evangelist An received Smit's permission to move to Rugao with his family. The Christian group in Jingjiang appears to have stopped completely after An's departure from the city.[11]

Although going strong before Liberation, the Christians in Haian, a city about twelve miles north of Rugao, did not fare much better than those in Jingjiang after the arrival of the Communists. The missionaries had started working in Haian just before they had been evacuated from Rugao in 1927. As one of the mission's oldest stations, it had experienced both peaks of hope and valleys of disappointment. The period following the war with Japan had been particularly difficult, because many of the members had died when several cholera epidemics hit the city.[12] But after the war the Christian work had begun to grow

---

[9]   Selles, "Why I left our China mission field," *Banner*, 1543. There is no record of Communist executions or "crucifixions" either before or after their taking over the county.

[10]   Smit to Mission Board, Sept. 14, 1949, Smit, CRWM folder.

[11]   Sheng Songru in interview with author Feb. 28, 2002.

[12]   Smit to De Korne, May 30, 1948, Smit, CRWM folder.

again, and in the late spring of 1948, Albert Smit baptized ten adults and fourteen children in the Haian church. Then in the fall of the same year, just before the missionaries were evacuated to Shanghai, the Haian Christians sent two letters to the mission: one asking for help organizing and operating a Christian school specifically for the children of the church, and the other asking to be organized as a congregation. Representing the Haian congregation, Zhang Saoxian (Chang Sao-hsien), Zhu Shian (Ch'u Shih-An), and Zhu Baoxian (Chu Pao-Hsien) attended a mission meeting to present the church's requests in person.

They addressed the mission with the following letter:

When Rev. Smit reported to us last year that you were planning to open a school in Hai'an we were indeed very happy. Later, because of disturbed conditions in China, it was decided to postpone the opening of the school till later.

However, we find that the children of our Christians and Inquirers greatly lack Christian training. It is essential that they be trained in the Christian religion from an early age. And although there are public schools in Hai'an, the children do not receive Christian training there. Also the tuition is very high so that many are not able to send their children to school.

In view of this, we feel it is imperative that some sort of Christian school be started in Hai'an. Therefore, although financially we really are not strong enough to do so, we have now opened a Christian school and are going forward in faith. We now have 93 pupils. The children of Christians and inquirers are over half of the pupils. In all we have four teachers and one servant.

We have purchased necessary equipment, but for salaries, rent and misc. expenses we need about 15 *piculs* (about 2,000 pounds of rice). We are hoping to add two more classes next spring and expect to have about two hundred pupils then, with resultant increased expenses. At present we have the first four years of the primary school.

Our strength is still very limited. We have exerted our utmost to begin this school, buying the necessary equipment, etc., but by ourselves we will not be able to carry on. Will your mission therefore please consider the possibility of helping us with this project by taking a share in the work? Then this school can become a great blessing for the church at Hai'an and the people of this city.

Will you please give this your kind consideration?

Respectfully submitted,
(Signed)
        Chang Sao-Hsien
        Ch'u Shih-An
        Chu Pao-Hsien
Representing the Hai'an Christian group
Hai'an, Oct. 1, 1948[13]

At a meeting a few weeks later, the mission, believing this might "prove to be a valuable mission agency," decided to help with the school "started by the Haian believers on their own initiative." On the condition that the mission would be given a say in choosing teachers, in the number and quality of students admitted, in setting the tuition rates, in registering with the government, and in plans for expansion, the mission provided the new school with a forty-dollar (seven and a half *piculs*, or almost a thousand pounds of rice) monthly grant for the rest of the year.

At the same meeting in which the members from Haian requested help with their Christian school, they also wrote asking that the mission formally organize the Christians in their city into a congregation:

> At present Hai'an is an important city on the canal between Nantung (Nantong) and Yangchow (Yangzhou) and also an important sectional point on the auto road between Nantung and Haichow (Haizhou). The city is a gateway for east-west and north-south traffic. It is, therefore, a prosperous business center and thickly populated. Therefore, it is one of the important cities in the district. Although it has suffered from communist troubles, so that many rich people have moved away, and business has declined a little, yet the population is well over 40,000.
>
> Looking back over the past twenty years we see that due to the grace of our God and your untiring efforts and care, the Gospel has been brought to this district. Through your persistent efforts in spite of hardships, the truth of the gospel and the love of Christ have been made known to many in this city and surrounding district. So that now, by the grace of God, there are in Hai'an 52 Christians and 25 inquirers. And there are 9

[13]   Haian Christian School Committee to Mission, "Mission Minutes" (trans.), Oct. 20-23, 1948, 7, CRWM folder.

Christians and 4 inquirers in the adjoining district. Also there are 5 Christians who were baptized elsewhere living in Hai'an. Therefore in all we have 66 Christians and 29 inquirers. We praise the Lord for this. But of course, there are still thousands living here who do not know Christ. The harvest is truly great but the laborers are few.

Now we Christians of Hai'an are doing our best to help the evangelist with making the gospel known through our testimony and that gives us much satisfaction. But we are living in unusual and uncertain times. If suddenly there should be a complete change in the political situation and we, against our will, were cut off from the Mission, the work would suffer greatly. Of course, we who have accepted the Lord would not become disloyal to the gospel, but we would be loosely united, and many of the Inquirers who are still weak might fall away. As the Bible says: "the devil goes about as a roaring lion seeking whom he may devour." If the devil used such an opportunity it would be very sad. We therefore feel if the above should happen and we were then organized as a congregation we would stand much stronger. We have a large loyal group of Christians, and although financially we are not as yet strong, yet we would like to be formed into a church. Then we are closer joined together and with the help and advice of the Mission will carry on the work at Hai'an, and spread the gospel in this district.

Therefore we are especially writing this letter, petitioning the Mission to consider whether it is possible to grant our request to be organized into a congregation so that we can elect elders and deacons and also call a pastor, if possible. We realize that we are not strong enough to take full responsibility for the salary of the pastor. We therefore ask the Mission to help us with this. If our request is granted, will the Mission please decide what portion of the salary we would be responsible for? We hope that we will be able to take increasingly greater responsibility for this.

We, also, petition the Mission to be permitted to use the mission building at Hai'an after we have been organized, until we are strong enough to provide a place of our own.

We are sending three representatives who will gladly answer any questions you may have and explain the condition of our Hai'an Christian group.

With Christian greetings,

> Respectfully submitted,
> (Signed)
>   Chang Sao-Hsien
>   Ch'u Shih-An
>   Chu Pao-Hsien
> Representing the Hai'an Christian group[14]
> Hai'an, Oct. 1, 1948

In response, the mission expressed gratitude for the growth in Haian and, "after a lengthy conference with the delegation from the church," agreed to allow the church to continue meeting in the mission building until it could provide its own facility, and to provide half the salary for a pastor.[15]

On December 22, 1948, Smit participated in the formal organization of the Haian church and the election of two elders and two deacons to govern the congregation. Smit was the lone missionary present because all the others had evacuated to Shanghai. Less than a month later, when the Nationalists had left the city, the Communists claimed it as "liberated." After the takeover, evangelist Tian, who had been living in a mission-rented house, immediately fled to Rugao and the safety of the mission compounds, but Smit persuaded him and his two sons to return to Haian. In the summer of 1949, however, after a short illness, evangelist Tian died, leaving a widow and six children. After Tian's death, the new Haian government refused to grant permission for another evangelist to replace him, and a labor union seized the church's mission-rented building.[16] For a while the elders continued to hold worship services in the "little Christian school building." In other cities, Communist governments applied pressure to Christian schools, especially primary and middle schools, socking them with high taxes in an effort to force them to close.[17] It is highly doubtful the school lasted very long after the arrival of the new regime in the city. Nor did the Haian congregation survive very long in "new" China.[18]

The picture from Rugao City emerges the most clearly. Before leaving Rugao, Albert Smit had tried to prepare the evangelists and

---

14   Haian Church Delegation, Mission Meeting Minutes (trans.), Oct. 20-23, 1948, 7, CRWM folder. The Bible reference is a paraphrase of 1 Pet. 5:8.
15   Ibid.
16   China Mission Report, *Acts of Synod*, 1950, 438.
17   Ling, *Changing Role*, 133.
18   According to the Haian gazetteer, the church closed soon after the city was liberated in 1949. *Haian Xian zhi (Haian Gazetteer)*: 1056.

Christians for being cut off from the missionaries. As with the two previous evacuations (1927 and 1937), money was a key issue. In December 1949, several of the missionaries had hired coolies to help them cart from Shanghai several billion *yuan* back to Rugao. Smit used this money to pay in advance several years of property taxes and the "salary of a caretaker," with whom, he told De Korne, the "stuff is stored."[19] Because Smit believed that the evangelists would have to work outside of the church, as they had done during the Sino-Japanese war, he also wanted, if possible, to provide for the "needs of the churches and evangelists...since many of the Christian groups are supplied by the evangelists and are small and weak financially."[20] Before his departure in January 1950, Smit paid several months' advance salary to the evangelists in the city who agreed to stay on after he left. After he returned to the United States, he suggested that the Christian Reformed Church continue to remit a hundred dollars a month to Rugao for the use of the evangelists and Christians there. This money, he believed, would express the home church's feelings toward the Christians in Rugao and maintain contact with the group there until missionaries could return.[21] Some money appears to have gotten through to Rugao, but political complications arising from the Korean War in the fall of 1950 brought this help to an end.[22]

Before leaving Rugao, Smit also worried about the future leadership of the church. Because there were no Christians in Rugao when they arrived, the missionaries had been forced to hire evangelists from other parts of the country. They preferred workers trained by the Presbyterians—Northern or Southern—but they had been forced by

---

[19] The "stuff" referred to was equipment from the mission hospital. De Korne suggested that Smit sell the equipment to the Christians in Rugao, so that Wang Aitang's brother-in-law, who was a surgeon, could open a hospital in the city. Since the Christians in Rugao could not buy the equipment, Smit had to store it. From notes John De Korne made of a phone conversation with Albert Smit from Shanghai Jan. 30, 1950, Smit, CRWM folder.

[20] *Acts of Synod*, 1950, 76.

[21] Albert Smit's appearance before the Mission Board, Nov. 1950, Smit, CRWM folder.

[22] After the outbreak of the Korean War and in response to the U.S. Government's freezing of Chinese assets in the United States, China demanded in December 1950 that all Christian churches, hospitals, and schools completely sever their relationships with American mission boards. The Christian Church of China sent a statement to overseas mission boards citing the demands of the Chinese state council and asking that the remittance of funds be discontinued.

necessity to hire others from missions as diverse as the Baptists and the Adventists. Though these Chinese associates were the backbone of the Christian movement in Rugao, not one had been formally ordained to lead a congregation as pastor when the missionaries decided to leave in 1949. Over the years, the mission had provided seminary training for a number of promising converts, hoping that someday one of these young people would return to work in Rugao; none had returned, though a few of the evangelists' children were working for other missions.

One major concern about leaving the Christians in Rugao without leadership was related to the administration of the sacraments. In the fall of 1949, Smit and mission secretary John De Korne had discussed this problem. With no ordained minister in Rugao, they wondered, who would perform the sacraments for the 350 adults and 150 children in the county's church groups? De Korne had acknowledged that the Christians in Rugao could, if they had to, live without the sacraments, but they were important since, he said, "The Lord has given the sacraments to his church...for the purpose of strengthening the faith of believers."[23] Putting aside the issue of who would pay salaries, De Korne suggested that Smit work out an arrangement with the Huaidong Presbytery to ordain a pastor for Rugao. "Just how it would be worked out would be left to local circumstances," wrote De Korne, adding, "but I would emphasize the need of the sacraments, as our Lord told us to remember his death until he comes and He has also commanded us to baptize those who believe and their children."[24]

After receiving De Korne's letter, Smit contacted the Huaidong presbytery and requested that the body ordain two of the mission's Presbyterian evangelists.[25] For Smit the choice of whom to ordain was obvious: Chen Guifan (Ch'en Kuei-fen) and Wang Ai T'ang (Wang Ai-tang) were both trained by Presbyterians, and they had worked for the mission for more than twenty years. Both of the evangelists agreed to join the Huaidong Presbytery, because, as Smit explained to De Korne, "It connects them with a larger body."[26]

A native of Xuzhou (Hsuchow) in northern Jiangsu Province, Chen Guifan was born in 1905 and baptized at the age of sixteen by

---

23   De Korne to Smit, Nov. 23, 1949, Smit CRWM folder.
24   Ibid.
25   There is no record of Smit's correspondence with the Huaidong Presbytery about ordaining pastors in Rugao. The name of the presbytery was changed to "Kiangpei (Jiangbei) Presbytery" sometime during the 1930s. See Brown, *Earthen Vessels*, 185-86.
26   Smit cablegram to De Korne, via U.S. State Department, n.d., Smit, CRWM folder.

the Southern Presbyterian missionary, the Reverend Mark Grier. He was a middle school graduate who had three and a half years of college training and also studied at the North China Theological Seminary in Tengxian, Shandong Province. Before moving to Rugao, Chen worked at the Presbyterian mission in Yancheng under the fiery conservative Hugh White. In 1929, Chen and his family moved to Rugao, where he took up work with the Christian Reformed mission for the next twenty years. The Chen family lived in the north gate chapel, and evangelist Chen worked with John De Korne in Rugao City. Together they prepared sermons, did evangelistic work, visited homes, prepared copy for newspaper advertisements, translated liturgical forms, and attended church and presbytery meetings. Not long after arriving in Rugao, Chen also requested that the mission give his wife, Chen Xiuying, a salary for her work with the mission. The mission turned down the request on the grounds that the "wives of evangelists are expected to volunteer as their time and talents allow."[27] Even without the salary, in 1933 Chen Xiuying was doing church work four afternoons a week in Baibu (Pai P'u) with Lillian Bode, one of the mission's foreign Bible women.

Sometime after John De Korne returned to the United States in 1934, Chen and his family moved to the rural outstation of Dongchen (Tong-ch'en). The work there was slow and difficult, yet evangelist Chen turned down a request for him to return to the city in 1939.[28] There were only two Christians in Dongchen, but Chen also ran a daily Bible school for young men, with an enrollment of thirty students.[29] During the war with Japan, Chen continued his church work while supporting his family by operating a cotton machine (loom). After the war, Chen continued his duties as evangelist and served the mission, upon occasion, as courier or "handy cargo man," transporting millions of *yuan* between Shanghai and Rugao.[30] Because Chen had impeccable Presbyterian credentials and had been loyal to the mission and faithful in his work, Smit arranged for the Huaidong Presbytery to ordain him

[27] The mission turned down the request for salary but offered to pay for the family to hire a servant to facilitate Chen Xuying's work outside their home. "Mission Minutes," Jan. 6, 1930, CRWM folder.

[28] Smit to De Korne, Nov. 14, 1939, Smit, CRWM folder. One of the difficulties of Dongchen was the presence of a secret society there that was strongly opposed to Christianity. See Smit to Beets, March 1933, Smit, CRWM folder.

[29] Smit in church book, Feb. 29, 1940. Copy of notes from church records in the Rugao RAB office.

[30] Selles to Mission Board, Jan. 27, 1948, Selles, CRWM folder.

in April 1949. But just before the presbytery met, Chen fell ill and was not able to attend the meeting.[31]

Thus, when Smit left Rugao in January of 1950, he left behind only one ordained man, senior evangelist Wang Aitang, who had worked in Rugao for almost twenty-five years. Sam Dykstra first met Wang Aitang in Nanjing in 1926. Immediately impressed by the recent Nanking Seminary graduate, "who kept his appointment" in meeting him on a boat on the Yangzi River, Dykstra had "come to terms" with the young evangelist for work in Rugao.[32] Wang, whose father was a Presbyterian evangelist in Xuzhou, northern Jiangsu Province, moved with his family to Rugao shortly after the meeting and began working as Dykstra's language teacher and evangelist.[33] This arrangement helped Dykstra increase his preaching proficiency in Chinese and allowed Wang to ease gradually into the task of preaching almost every day in the north gate chapel, which Dykstra believed was "by no means an easy task to remain fresh and interesting."[34]

Wang easily filled the role of preaching evangelist; he was reputed to be a man of "impressive bearing" and one of the best preachers in the mission, with not only sound theology but also excellent communication skills. One of the missionaries called him "a natural leader of his countrymen."[35] Though he had been implicated initially by his colleagues in the evangelists' strike of 1927, when three other evangelists threatened to quit unless their salaries were increased, Wang proved a faithful worker and loyal to the mission, rising to the position of senior evangelist. He had started out working at the north gate chapel, and then moved to Haian to begin Christian work there. Later, he moved back to Rugao so that his daughter who was suffering

---

[31] Though the records are inconclusive, it does not appear that Chen ever received ordination.

[32] S. Dykstra to First CRC, Grand Rapids, June 6, 1926, S. Dykstra, CRWM folder.

[33] Wang Aitang was born and raised in Xuzhou, Jiangsu Province. According to Wang Shuangen, Wang's youngest daughter, her father's father had been an educated man who when he first came into contact with Christianity rejected the faith, but later through reading became a Christian. Wang Aitang's father later became an evangelist in the Southern Presbyterian mission in Xuzhou. Interview with Wang Shuangen in Nanjing March 19, 2007.

[34] Ibid.

[35] Albert Selles, "Our Native Evangelists," *Banner* 80 (Nov. 2, 1945): 1032. Edward Van Baak, who met Wang in the late 1940s, confirms the impression of Wang's bearing and preaching skills, Edward Van Baak in interview with author, April 15, 2003.

from tuberculosis could receive better care. Wang also helped at various times with the Christian groups in Libao, Dongchen, and Motou.

In 1940, Wang contemplated moving his family to "Free China," but he and his family stayed on in Rugao to oversee the Christian groups there. His family moved into one of the mission's vacant houses, protecting the property and taking over the piano the De Korne family had left in 1934, an instrument both Wang and his daughter enjoyed playing.[36] Like the other evangelists, Wang found work outside the church to support his family during the war years, buying and selling goods between Rugao and Shanghai.[37] Despite this outside work, he served the Christians in Rugao faithfully after the missionaries left and was given the highest bonus allowed by the mission after the war.[38] At the end of the war Wang, in broken English, wrote to the mission secretary, John De Korne, saying,

> [We] have walked through valley of the shadow of death. But have no hurt from the day of the war in Pacific. We work in Jukao just like the disciples after Jesus hang on the cross. Inside is fear, outside have truly dangers. That is called the Great War. Please our mother church have missionaries come to help us.[39]

After the war, Wang worked with the returning missionaries to strengthen the Christian groups in Rugao. But he did more than strictly "Christian work." Like Chen Guifan, he was an intrepid bearer of money and messages through barbed-wired checkpoints between Rugao and Shanghai.

On the eve of the Communists' arrival, perhaps because he sensed things would go easier for the church, for Wang Aitang, and for himself once the Communists took the city, Albert Smit "officially" transferred the leadership of the Rugao church group to Wang. At a meeting led by evangelist Wang Friday, January 21, 1949, Smit reported that all of the other missionaries had returned to America.[40] The discussion then

---

[36]   S. Dykstra to De Korne, Spring 1941, S. Dykstra, CRWM folder.
[37]   Wang Aitang to Smit, 1944 (trans.), Smit, CRWM folder.
[38]   The highest amount of the bonuses was $125 and the lowest was $50. These amounts were given on the basis of how much church work each evangelist had done during the war years. Wang received the highest amount, while Chen Guifan, who supported himself with his cotton machine, received the lowest. "Mission Minutes," Jan. 26, 1946, CRWM folder.
[39]   Wang Aitang to De Korne, 1945, Smit, CRWM folder.
[40]   Minutes, church meeting, Jan. 21, 1949. These minutes were found in the Rugao church book in the Rugao Religious Affairs Bureau office (trans. author).

turned to preparing for the future, which included setting the dates for evangelistic meetings for the upcoming Chinese New Year and plans for organizing a "relief committee." After some discussion, seven church members were selected to serve on the relief committee, a decision that was to be ratified by the whole church at a later meeting.[41]

That later meeting took place after the worship service two days later on Sunday, January 23, 1949. At this meeting, it was announced (presumably by Albert Smit) that "Wang is now the pastor of the church."[42] Two elders were then selected to work with Pastor Wang to govern the church, Wu Tongshen as "lead elder" (*zheng hui zhang*) and Chen Yuying as "second lead elder" (*fu hui zhang*). Next, the congregation approved a motion outlining the responsibilities of the new elders. They were elected for an indefinite period of service but could request to be released from service. The elders could be released from office if three members of the congregation rejected them.[43] Their responsibilities included overseeing the work of the church, representing the congregation at the presbytery, and reporting to the congregation.

Smit left a year later in January 1950. Nothing is known about the spring of 1950 in Rugao, but on Saturday, May 13, the leaders of the Rugao church, and perhaps some of the members as well, held an afternoon meeting.[44] "Lead" elder Wu Tongsheng opened the meeting with prayer, and pastor Wang Aitang, referred to in the minutes as "teacher" (*jiao shi*), reported on new "administrative rules" (*jiao wu zhao lie*) for the church. As of today, he announced, "The Rugao church is part of the Three-Self Reform" (*san zi ge*).[45] Toward the new situation and the leadership of the movement, he said, "Everyone should work

---

[41] The next day Smit wrote to John De Korne stating his decision to remain in Rugao after the Communists' arrival to see "what their attitude will be" and to encourage the evangelists and workers. Though he did not mention the meeting of the previous day, Smit informed De Korne that he had asked Wang Aitang and his family to stay in Rugao, "since he is well acquainted here and he told me he would gladly stay if I stayed, of which I assured him." Smit to De Korne, Jan. 22, 1949, Smit, CRWM folder.

[42] Minutes, Rugao congregational meeting, Jan. 23, 1949. These minutes were found in the Rugao church book in the Rugao Religious Affairs Bureau office (trans. author).

[43] Though verses are not cited, they follow Christ's teaching in Matthew 18: 15-16 concerning the confrontation of a Christian about sin.

[44] Church meeting minutes, May 13, 1950. From minutes found in the Rugao church book in RAB office, June 2, 2002 (trans. author).

[45] Ibid.

to be positive." In the same meeting, he reported that the Rugao Public Security Bureau (*gong an ju*) had requested a list of the names of all of the "believers," a request, he added, "that could not be refused."[46] Before the meeting closed, the group spent time in "free discussion" (*zi you tan hua*).[47]

While there were unofficial stages in the development of the Three-Self Patriotic Movement, it was not officially organized until the fall of 1951, after the beginning of the Korean War.[48] Why then does the movement seem to have begun more than a year earlier in Rugao? There is no clear answer to this question. Perhaps there were greater pressures to conform in smaller cities such as Rugao, which is suggested by the Public Security Bureau's demand for membership lists and Wang's encouraging of those present at the meeting to "work to be positive." What it also suggests is that Wang Aitang, and possibly other members of the Rugao church, were early signers of a "Manifesto" promulgated by the Communist Party and prominent Protestant leaders.[49] Rugao's

---

[46]   Ibid.

[47]   Ibid.

[48]   The beginning of the Three-Self Movement can largely be traced to one person, Y.T. Wu (Wu Yaocong), who dominated the Protestant church scene during the 1950s. His radical writings in the late 1940s criticizing the church as a "tool of reactionary forces opposed to social change" had set him up to be the chief Protestant contact with the new Communist government after 1949. Out of his early meetings with the government in the spring of 1950 emerged a "Manifesto" about the state of the church under communism (c.f., note 136 below). Later, in the fall of the same year at the biannual meeting of the Chinese National Christian Council, Wu and other Protestant leaders adopted this manifesto and discussed ways to implement "Three-Self Reform" (self-government, self-support, and self-propagation). The next April the government's newly organized Religious Affairs Bureau invited 151 Protestant leaders to Beijing to deal with the problem of Christian institutions formerly receiving mission aid. One outcome of this meeting was the formal establishment of the Protestant Three-Self Reform Movement in the fall of 1951 with W.T. Wu as its chairman. G. Thompson Brown, *Christianity in the People's Republic of China* (Atlanta: John Knox, 1986), 81-84.

[49]   In April 1950, Premier Zhou Enlai met with Y. T. Wu and several other leading Protestants in Beijing to discuss how the Protestant church might "best express its loyalty to New China." Out of these and subsequent discussions, Protestant church leaders drafted a document that came to be known as the "Manifesto," which spoke strongly of Chinese patriotism and supporting the new government while at the same time soundly denounced imperialistic influences. Early drafts of the Manifesto encountered opposition from a wider circle of Protestant leaders around

relatively close proximity to Shanghai and Nanjing, both major centers of Protestant Christianity, supports this possibility. Because he had many contacts in Shanghai, it is almost certain that some of his contacts included church leaders there. There is no documentary evidence that Wang had strong church connections in Nanjing. But since Wang had graduated from Nanjing Seminary, he very likely had church contacts there, too.

After his departure from China, Smit continued to write Wang Aitang but did not receive an answer from him until sometime in either late 1950 or in 1951. Wang's handwritten letter of November 8, 1950, reads as follows:

> In reply to your kindly letter which you have written to me at the date 11/8/50 in U.S.A. and $30 and another $20 for Miss Swen [Sun Engui]. I also received that letter you sent from Japan in May. So I knew the all of what you have happened after you leave Shanghai.
>
> Thank you very much for you give me the letters and the money. You are so kind to me.
>
> Very sorry indeed. For I have not give you any letter before. Please excuse me. That is also very hard to give you a letter for me, as you know. But how ever I can give you this letter now.
>
> We all good in our preach place. Have no trouble. At the twenty-sixth of June the policemen call me to their office and told me. You take care Mr. Smit's and all the U.S.A. people's goods. When they come back you give them again. One day in July they call me to their office again. And they told me just as the first time. But this time they order me to write down all what you have in your place. So I do that. Since now we have no trouble. Even the house no body come to use.
>
> The tribute of our house change 4% to 7% they said that is because you are not here, can't say use by self.
>
> Our church just as before. At forenoon we have 80-90. At afternoon we have 40 or more. And now some new inquirers come in. Now my boy Chien En [Wang Qianen] study at Kasin

---

the country, but by the fifth draft more Protestant leaders were signing on and a campaign was launched to get all Chinese Protestants to sign. By late September 1950, more than 1,500 Chinese Protestants had signed the document; two months later more than 180,000 had signed; and within two years, more than 400,000 had signed the Manifesto. Richard C. Bush, Jr. *Religion in Communist China* (Nashville: Abingdon, 1970), 179; and Bob Whyte, *Unfinished Encounter: China and Christianity* (London: Fount Paperbacks, 1988), 210-11, 218.

Tsien's place and Lin En [Wang Linen] study at Nantung Chow the Christian church's school. Only Shwan En [Wang Shuangen] at home with us.

Hsa [Xia Guoye]. Still live at the west gate. The house which Mr. Ten [Tian Zhitong] still haven't taken back. Now can take back. But the Christians did not want to do so. They think that may make much trouble with them. So Mr. Hsa only can visit the Christians at their home one by one. Go there morning and come back at night same day.

Lee [Li Sunde]. The work just as before. They have Sunday meeting in a Christian's home freely. But the new place at the far east now cannot have meeting [probably Liming village, near Haimen, where Li had previously served the country group].

Hwa [Hua Fuquan]. The Sunday as before. But sometimes have trouble at the house, for some one want to use. But not on Sunday. So they have the Sunday meeting.

Chen [Chen Guifan]. Every Sunday have meeting at a Christian's home in the country the old place as you know, now do not prepare to move the home to the country. So now will find a new place at the same street. After a few days.

An [An Guangrong]. Live at the south by the river as you know. But at Sunday morning go the north side of that river. And have meeting at the Christian Chows. Sometimes go back the same day and sometimes go back on Monday. Last Monday he came to see me and go back afternoon.

Miss swen [Sun Engui]. Just as before. Have the women's Bible class at Thursday, except that to visit some Christians and inquirer's home.

The two old men Mr. Tsou and Mr. Chen also in their place. Mrs. Tien also.

All of our workers no one have find any works to get money in outside. Just like Noah's dove. At the first time nothing can find outside of the ark.

Every morning at 6 o'clock I and Mrs. Wang pray for you, your family, and all of our friends at your place. Please give my greetings to all of them.

This is the all of this time.

Truly your's

A.T. Wang[50]

---

50   Wang to Smit, answer to Nov. 8, 1950, letter. According to the letter, it was written and sent from 169 Yuan Ming Yuan Road in Shanghai, a residence owned by the mission.

From the letter, it is clear that the church work, though with adjustments, was being carried on throughout 1950 and into 1951. As at other times, property issues plagued the Christians, both because the authorities linked the Christians with Americans and because of tax or tribute obligations. Church services continued to be held twice on Sunday, once in the morning and once in the afternoon, though, no doubt, with reduced numbers.[51] New inquirers were coming into the church, though Wang does not state how many. Even the women's Bible classes were still being held on Thursday afternoons, and the lone Bible woman remaining in the city, Sun Engui, was visiting the homes of Christians and inquirers.[52] Five of the other evangelists, though they could not find work outside the church, appear to have been living in the city in mission property and carrying on work in the outstations as best they could.

After the receipt of this letter, no more information came directly out of Rugao to the United States, which is not surprising, since just a month before it was written China had crossed the Yalu River into North Korea and entered the conflict against American troops. In a national climate where patriotism reached fever pitch with the "Resist America—Aid Korea, Three-Self Movement," which was aimed at demonstrating the patriotism of Chinese Christians, it would have been foolish, even dangerous, for Wang Aitang or anyone else in Rugao to contact foreign Christians in the United States.[53]

---

[51] The situation for Christians in other places during these early years after Liberation appears to have been much worse. Westerners visiting China in 1952 noted that some church property was "borrowed" (i.e., seized), some pastors were forbidden to preach, and some Christians were frightened away from attending church. In some places, the leaders of indigenous Protestant churches were imprisoned and their churches were broken up. Ralph and Nancy Lapwood, *Through the Chinese Revolution* (London: People's Books Cooperative Society, 1954), 197. Quoted in Bush, *Religion in Communist China*, 206. In other places, Christians stopped coming to church activities not so much because of fear but because they simply had no time. In addition to their jobs, they had to attend political meetings, making attendance at church difficult. Thomas A. Harvey, *Acquainted with Grief* (Grand Rapids: Brazos, 2002), 68.

[52] Ten years earlier, in 1940, when Sun Engui and her father, Sun Zhiping, had requested a salary increase during the war with Japan, Mina Kalsbeek had noted that she was "Efficient at Sunday school, but not mature enough for visiting in the homes of older women." Kalsbeek Report, March 13, 1940, Kalsbeek, CRWM folder.

[53] Bush, *Religion in Communist China*, 194.

Though no direct word came out of Rugao following Wang Aitang's last letter to Albert Smit, fragments of church records Wang kept, and information from Wang's youngest daughter, Wang Shuangen, provide a glimpse of his continued work and the life of Christians in the city. The records note that in 1951 the church "received permission to continue," confirming that Wang, the other evangelists, and the church members had held "successful" denunciation meetings necessary for permission to continue and for their "tribute" to be abated.[54] Wang did not have regular work outside of the church, as he did during the Japanese occupation. He supported himself after 1950, according to his daughter, through small gifts by the Christians in Rugao and through money his eldest son, working in Shanghai, sent home.[55] After she married, Wang Shuangen and her husband lived with her parents, and she helped support them through her work as a teacher in a local elementary school. Sometime after 1950, Wang Aitang's father, a Presbyterian evangelist from Xuzhou in northern Jiangsu Province, came to live with his son and also helped with the church work in Rugao.

Records Wang kept himself also show that he continued his church work, not only holding regular church services but also holding weekly Bible studies and carrying on with evangelism. Church records show that between 1953 and 1958, Wang baptized twenty-six adults and three children.[56] Just before Christmas, on December 20, 1953,

[54]   In the spring of 1951, the government implemented a "Denunciation Movement" directed at churches and their links with imperialism as a part of a larger ideological remolding. Whyte, *Unfinished Encounter*, 223. Flyers were distributed to Christian organizations and churches around the country providing instructions for holding successful "denunciation meetings." Harvey, *Acquainted with Grief*, 64. Denunciation meetings were held all over the country for the next fifteen months. Major Protestant institutions, such as the YMCA, YWCA, and NCC, all came under attack. Individual churches also held denunciation meetings. In fact, before a church could register to have taxes abated and qualify as a branch of the Three-Self Patriotic Movement, it was required to hold "successful" accusation meetings. The meetings were usually followed by political study, and those accused had to undergo extensive thought reform. Typically, the meetings concluded with a statement from the local church supporting the Three-Self Movement and a patriotic pledge to root out all counter-revolutionary elements in the church. Ling, *Changing Role*, 171.

[55]   Interview with Wang Shuangen in Nanjing March 19, 2007.

[56]   Ibid. This reception of new members in Rugao squares with what was happening in other parts of the country in the early 1950s. Observers found "the quality of life of the churches, judged by the earnestness of

Wang baptized eighteen adults and three children. At the service, a man named Li was baptized and his twelve-year-old son received "infant" baptism. Another five-year-old boy and his two-year-old sister also received "infant" baptism. A seventeen-year-old young woman, who had been baptized by Smit in 1948 at the age of eleven, made a profession of faith. It is likely that at least half (and probably more) of the people who were baptized came with one family member or more. In addition to the Wu and Zhu families, at least three other families were represented at the December 1953 baptism ceremony. The records show that at least eleven males and six females were baptized. The ages of the group ranged between two and seventy-four. Four of those baptized, three men and one woman, were over the age of seventy.[57] Three of the men were between the ages of fifty-nine and sixty-four, and the two women were in their late fifties. Of the other three men, one was forty-one and the other two were both thirty-two. The thirty-one-year-old wife of one of these thirty-two-year-old men was also baptized, along with another woman, aged twenty-four. After the morning baptism service, Communion was served in the afternoon.

The next year, again just before Christmas, on December 19, 1954, Wang baptized six more people, four men and two women. One of the four men was sixty, two were in their forties (forty-five and forty-three, perhaps brothers), and the other man was thirty-four. One woman was sixty-three, and the other was forty-nine. At least two families appear to have been represented at the service.

The one person baptized December 22, 1957, was a seventy-year-old woman who had moved to Rugao from Wudong, Hebei Province. Wang also notes in 1957 that his daughter Wang Shuangen ("Double Grace"), who was born in Anhui Province and had been baptized at the

---

Bible study, prayer, and mutual care, are greatly improved." Many people were also baptized. In Shandong Province, one observer reported that in some places requests to be examined for baptism ranged from a handful up to two hundred, even a thousand in one instance. These figures are based on figures reported by Lewis Lancaster in the *Presbyterian Journal* and quoted by John De Korne in a 1951 *Banner* article. See John De Korne, "The Church in Red China," pt. 2, *Banner* 86 (March 9, 1951): 299. Evangelistic rallies continued to be held in Shanghai at Chinese New Year, with one church reporting over three hundred conversions and another five hundred baptisms. Bush, *Religion in Communist China*, 209.

57 Record "37" in Book Two of the church records does not give the age of a woman with the family name of Wu baptized in 1953, but since her husband was aged seventy at the time and she entered an old people's home in 1956, it is more than likely she was also close to seventy.

age of three, made "profession of faith" and "took Communion" for the first time. Other than recording that another person was baptized in 1958, Wang gives no information about that person.[58]

People joined the Rugao church during the 1950s, but they also left at a steady rate. Between 1949 and 1960, five members, all of whom had been baptized by Albert Smit in 1948, "withdrew" from membership in the church. The first to leave was a "self-employed" man of sixty-eight, who left the church in 1949, most likely some time soon after the Communists took the city. In 1950, two more members withdrew, a "businessman," aged twenty-three, and another man, aged sixty-four. Four other members baptized by Smit in 1948 simply "stopped coming" in 1950: a man, aged thirty-four, listed as a "businessman"; a young man of twenty-four listed as a "peasant"; and a young woman, aged twenty-five.[59] The last recorded member who "stopped coming" in 1950 was Hua Banqing, the fourteen-year-old son of Hua Yang (who remained a church member), a boy whom Wang Aitang had noted earlier in the records as a "Good boy and truthful." In 1952, a young woman named Weng, who had been baptized at the age of eighteen, withdrew, though her parents remained in the church. Another woman aged sixty-eight withdrew from the church in 1960.

Death also slowly reduced the number of church members during the 1950s and into the 1960s. If he was allowed, Wang Aitang may have performed at least fourteen funerals by 1962. The deaths Wang recorded give a glimpse of the church members during this period. In 1954, Hua Yongsheng, a Rugao native who worked in textiles and had been baptized by Lee Huizenga in 1934 and about whom Wang Aitang recorded "faithful church member" of twenty years, died at age sixty-nine. In 1955, a man that Wang had baptized in 1953 died at the age of seventy-two, forcing his widow to move into an "old people's home," where the church lost contact with her. Another young man that Wang had baptized in 1953 died at the age of thirty-five, and his wife, who had been baptized at the same time, moved to Shanghai. In 1956, two

58 According to Gao Wangzhi, after 1958 the Three-Self Patriotic Movement became more of a church authority, and as the whole country was being "communized" so was the church, which in the same year was forced to abandon all Protestant denominational distinctives. Many activities were also curtailed. This may account for the cessation of baptisms after 1958. See Gao, "Y. T. Wu: A Christian Leader Under Communism," in Bays, *Christianity in China*, 347.

59 Though the record is unclear, it is likely these last two members were either husband and wife or brother and sister.

members died: a businessman named Weng, who had been baptized by Albert Smit in 1948 at the same time as his wife and daughter, died at the age of seventy, and a woman, who had been baptized by Smit, died at the age of 81. In 1958, the woman who had moved to Rugao from Wudong, Hebei Province, and whom Wang had baptized in 1957, also died. Huo Aizhu, a blind woman who had not been able to attend church for years, died in 1959.

Six more members died between 1960 and 1962.[60] Four church members died in 1960 alone. Two were members baptized by Smit in 1948: a carpenter, aged fifty-eight, and a woman, aged fifty. Two other members who died that year had been baptized by Wang Aitang in 1953: a man, aged seventy-three, and a woman named Zhu, aged sixty. In 1961, two more church members died: one was a man Wang had baptized in 1954 who died at the age of forty, and the other was a man who had moved to Dongchen from Huaiyin in Subei and been baptized by Smit in 1937. The last death recorded in the church record was that of Hu Yinglai, who died in 1962. Hu, the "watchman" at the mission's west gate hospital, had been baptized in 1936 and had received the note of "good man" by Sam Dykstra during the war with Japan in 1941.

Perhaps the biggest loss to the church occurred December 7, 1956, when evangelist Chen Guifan died. In 1929, he had moved with his wife, her mother, and their four children from Xuzhou to Rugao to work with the mission. Three of their four children had been baptized in Rugao, and all had made profession of faith there, including their youngest child in 1950. Their oldest son, Yuehan ("John"), had worked for Lee Huizenga doing refugee work in Shanghai from 1941 to 1943, before moving to Taizhou to work in the Southern Presbyterian hospital there. After the death of her husband, Chen Xiuying, who had been born in Shandong and baptized at the age of fourteen, moved to Nanjing in 1958, having lived and worked in Rugao for almost thirty years.

That Wang Aitang made the last record in the church books in 1962 suggests that the church records were taken from him in that year. Perhaps the Public Security Bureau wanted church records as well as a list of the names of the members. Little is known about the Christians in Rugao between 1962 and 1966. But some information about Wang and the church in Rugao comes from Wang Shuangen,

---

[60]   It is quite likely that the high number of deaths occurring in this two-year period was the result of the man-made famine following the disastrous "Great Leap Forward."

Wang Aitang's youngest daughter. Until 1963, the family lived in the back of the main church building in Rugao, directly across from the main government building on the main street of the city. In 1963, the government moved the family into a house located close to where the Lee Huizenga family had lived, where Wang was allowed to continue his work with the Christians in the city. Ironically, given the missionaries' opposition to movies, sometime after the Wang family was moved, the church building was converted to a cinema, no doubt to screen propaganda movies supporting the Communist revolution. After 1963, Wang continued his church work in the new house, which had a large courtyard and a sitting room for church meetings. During this time, according to Wang's daughter, about twenty people continued to meet for worship services. According to Wang Shuangen, her father lost touch with the other evangelists during these years, and she believes the church work was carried on in Rugao longest because the city had been the center of the mission's work in the county. Wang was also required to meet with the other religious leaders in the city, Daoist and Buddhist priests, and according to his daughter he became friends with these other religious leaders.

At the beginning of the Cultural Revolution in 1966, when all religious practice across the country ended, Rugao City officials told Wang to stop holding church meetings.[61] Less than a year later, Wang Aitang was put in the Rugao jail, his hands tied as he was led away. After being held in jail for six months, Wang was released, and he and his wife were sent to work on a farm to the west of Rugao. They worked on the farm for almost ten years. During these years they did not have a Bible, but, according to Wang Shuangen, they were able to recite scripture from memory, especially the psalms, perhaps through the Christian Reformed Church's emphasis on the use of psalms in worship. Wang Shuangen has said that neither of her parents was bitter, continuing to believe to the end of their lives that God would provide for their needs and for the needs of the church. At the end of the Cultural Revolution in 1976, the Wangs moved to a small apartment in Shanghai, where they lived until he died in 1984 and she died in 1997. At his memorial service, the family placed his Bible next to his body.

[61]   Yan Lingsu, "Tian zhu jiao ji du jiao zai Rugao," (Roman Catholics and Protestants in Rugao). *Rugao wen shi zhi ci liao* (*Information on the history of Rugao*), vol. 8 (Rugao: Guo ying yin shua chang yin shua, 1985): 56. According to the Yan Shiji, the party secretary in Rugao, other church records and documents were all destroyed during the Cultural Revolution. Yan Shiji interview with author June 2, 2002.

From the beginning, the goal of the Christian Reformed mission was to establish a Reformed church in China, ideally one that was "self-supporting, self-governing, and self-propagating."[62] Like most Protestants, however, the mission was not able to achieve the goal of establishing an independent Chinese church before its departure from China; Chinese workers and the Chinese Christians remained dependent on the mission, especially for finances, until the very end.[63] Nevertheless, what the missionaries could not bring about, larger historical events beyond their control did, creating, as one Christian Reformed missionary called it, a "real Chinese Christian church."[64]

Not long after their departure, the missionaries lost touch with Rugao. Information pieced together from a variety of sources, however, shows that while the other churches in the county and surrounding area appear to have closed soon after 1949, the church in Rugao City stayed open another sixteen years, until the beginning of the Cultural Revolution in 1966. The continuation of the Rugao church was largely due to the commitment and faithfulness of one man, evangelist Wang Aitang. Wang made the necessary adjustments to stay open (i.e., completing "successful" denunciation meetings and joining the Three-Self Patriotic Movement organization), but he almost certainly maintained church and theology as he had received them as much as he was able. Moreover, the records Wang kept give indications that he maintained an emphasis on families coming into the church and that he continued to perform infant baptism, all marks of covenant theology. In the end, in the encounter between the missionaries and the Chinese, it appears that the strong Christian Reformed emphasis on covenant theology, which focused on belonging, communicated the Christian faith to the people of Rugao most clearly.

---

[62]   Gao, "Y. T. Wu," 346.

[63]   It is beyond the scope of this discussion to tackle the knotty issues and questions surrounding the failure of Protestant missions to realize their longstanding ideal of fostering an independent church. Indeed, that subject would require a book-length treatment. For a treatment of some of the history and issues related to the transition from mission dependence, especially after WWII, see Timothy Brook, "Christianity under the Japanese Occupation," in Bays, *Christianity in China*, 317-37.

[64]   De Jong, "China Mission Field," 843.

EPILOGUE

In the century and a half leading up to 1950, China was buffeted by a relentless wave of foreigners intent on carving up the country. With the Communist victory in October 1949, when Chairman Mao Zedong stood on the rostrum in Tiananmen Square and declared that China had stood up, an old world came to an end and a new world was born. Change swept across the country touching the lives of Chinese citizens in countless ways, both wanted and unwanted. The church was one aspect of Chinese society that bore the brunt of much of the enforced change. Ironically, under the new régime, the Chinese church was finally freed from foreign control and financial propping, only to come under the control of the Communist Party without money.

During the first decade of Communist rule, Chinese churches continued to carry on their ministries, although with some constraints. But the series of mass movements unleashed during the 1950s, all playing on virulent antiforeign sentiments, severely shrank personal freedoms, especially the practice of religion. With its connections to foreigners, the Chinese church was a particularly vulnerable target, and with the onset of the Cultural Revolution in 1966, the open practice

Through donations from members of the Christian Reformed Church, Chinese Christians in Rugao County constructed this church building in 2003.

of Christianity in China came to an end. Churches were boarded up or converted to garages and warehouses. Christians stopped meeting publicly and began meeting in secret, when they could meet at all. Bibles were stashed away to prevent confiscation or more serious repercussions. Many Christians, both inside and outside the country, feared that Christianity had once again been ripped from Chinese soil.

But what the Communist Party meant for harm turned out to benefit Chinese Christianity. During more than a decade of harsh repression, Christianity became a Chinese religion. Developing flexible structures for training leaders, Chinese Christians learned to organize themselves for ministry in secret. Pared to essentials, Chinese Christians lived and served with little, if anything at all. The attempt to pluck the seedling of Christianity from Chinese soil only caused the movement to develop a deeper root system, something that became obvious after the death of Mao in 1976 when churches began to reopen and stories of a growing house church movement began to filter out of the country. What missionaries had tried to do for 150 years, the Communist Party had inadvertently achieved in a decade: it had made the Chinese church Chinese.

Since the late 1970s, the Chinese church has continued to grow rapidly, both in house churches and in the "registered" (TSPM) churches. This explosive growth took place first in the countryside where the bulk of Chinese Christians lived, and then in the cities where it flourishes today among all walks of life. In another of God's ironies, the number of Christians in China today exceeds the number of Communist Party members, and while the number of Christians continues to grow, the number of Communist Party members continues to decline. At this writing, the trends look promising for continued growth and increasing potential for Chinese Christians to have an impact on their own government and on the development of world Christianity.

While in most places churches planted by missionaries emerged after the Cultural Revolution stronger and more Chinese, not all

American Christian Reformed Church members and Chinese Christians following the dedication ceremony of the Rugao County Protestant Church in April 2004. The U.S. delegation included the children, grandchildren, and great-grandchildren of the China missionaries.

missionary-planted churches survived the decade of chaos. Rugao is one place where the church appears to have died out. After the closure of the church in 1966 and the departure of evangelist Wang Aitang from Rugao City in 1969, the church there did not reopen. Today more than one church exists in Rugao County (including a Seventh Day Adventist church), but none of these churches appears to have a historical connection with the work of the Christian Reformed Church's China mission in the county from 1921 to 1950.

Why did the church in Rugao fail? A number of possible factors may have played a role in its demise. Because the mission came late to Rugao County (where a Christian presence had never been established) and was there for a relatively short time (three decades interrupted by war three times), the church failed to reach a sustainable level of membership that could nurture a second generation of Christians. Moreover, because the Christian Reformed mission's work focused almost exclusively on evangelism and church planting, especially in the late 1930s and 1940s, the Christian presence in Rugao was institutionally weak and thus particularly vulnerable to the pressures exerted on it by the Communist Revolution. In other words, if the Christian Reformed China mission had done more institutional work in medicine and education during the periods of turmoil, there might have been more visible and stable signs of Christianity's presence, which might have been reclaimed following the Cultural Revolution. Finally, the conservative nature of the Rugao County Government no doubt played some role in preventing the church in Rugao from reopening in the late 1970s. Whatever the reason, the church did not survive in Rugao.[1]

---

[1] Interestingly, according to the Rugao Government's website, there are more than one hundred Christians in the city, and the government would like to build a church facility in the city. One of the reasons cited by the government for building a church is the possibility of attracting foreign investment. See www.rugao.gov.cn/rgzx/print2.asp?id=1593 3K 2008-8-27 (in Chinese).

Does the absence of a Christian Reformed-related church in Rugao mean that the denomination's mission failed, despite the almost forty Christian Reformed Church members who spent time in Rugao over a thirty-year period and the hundreds of thousands of dollars spent there on Chinese personnel and buildings? Certainly the missionaries made mistakes, perhaps the biggest and most obvious being the failure to develop Chinese leadership. But most missions made *this* mistake, and *all* missions and missionaries made other mistakes. Thus, the failure of the church to take root in Rugao may ultimately be more closely related to the facts listed above than to any one mistake made by the missionaries. After all, it should be noted that the denomination was successful in other places, such as Nigeria, where in the 1930s the denomination established a mission work that today outnumbers the North American denomination.

Even if the attempt to plant a church in Rugao ultimately failed, planting a church was only one part of the larger story. For the Christian Reformed Church, the decision to go to China in the 1920s was a part of the larger process of Americanization taking place in this small Dutch immigrant group. In addition to drawing the church into the orbit of the American Protestant world, the effort in China captured the attention of many church members at an important moment in denominational history. Countless people in the denomination learned about another place. In doing so, a vision for global outreach became an important feature of the Christian Reformed Church.

APPENDIX

China Mission Personnel

Name	Hometown	Field Service	Home church
Lillian Bode	Woden, Iowa	1926-1927, 1929-37, 1946-1949	father Rev. H.C. Bode
Eunice (Smit) Bruinooge	Rugao, Jiangsu, China	1947-1949	
Henry Bruinooge	Sheboygan, Wisconsin	1947-1949	Sherman St., Grand Rapids, MI
Peter De Jong	Grand Rapids, Michigan	1947-1949	First, Ripon, CA
Thelma De Jong	Ellsworth, MI	1947-1948	
John De Korne	Grand Rapids, Michigan	1920-1934	Beckwith Hills, Grand Rapids, MI
Nettie De Korne	Grand Rapids, Michigan	1920-1934	
Nicholas De Vries	Baflo, Groningen, Netherlands	1926-1927	First, Ripon, CA
Caroline De Vries	Grand Rapids, Michigan	1926-1927	

Name	Hometown	Field Service	Home church
Marion De Young	Chicago, Illinois	1947-1948	
Harry Dykstra	Ferwerd, Friesland, Netherlands	1920-1926, 1927-1941	Alpine Ave, Grand Rapids, MI
Florence Dykstra	Grand Rapids, Michigan	1920-1926, 1927-1941	
Simon Dykstra	Ferwerd, Friesland, Netherlands	1924-1927, 1929-1943	Alpine Ave, Grand Rapids, MI
Gertrude Dykstra	Holland, MI	1924-1927, 1929-1943	
Angie Haan	Grand Rapids, Michigan	1924-1926	
Ann Huizenga	Engelwood, NJ		LaGrave, Grand Rapids, MI
Elizabeth Herema	Orange City, Iowa	1948-1949	Sherman St, Grand Rapids, MI
Eunice Huizenga	Engelwood, NJ		LaGrave, Grand Rapids, MI

Name	Hometown	Field Service	Home church
Lee Huizenga	Lioessens, Friesland, Netherlands	1920-1927, 1929-1945	LaGrave, Grand Rapids, MI
Myrtle Huizenga	Tohatchi, NM	1920-1927, 1929-1945	LaGrave, Grand Rapids, MI
Matillda Huizenga	Grand Haven, MI	1920-1927, 1929-1945	LaGrave, Grand Rapids, MI
Wilhelmina Kalsbeek	Grand Rapids, Michigan	1923-1949	Drenthe, MI
Jacob Kamps	Drenthe, Michigan	1926-1927	Drenthe, MI
Isabel Kamps	Ottawa County, MI	1926-1927	Beckwith Hills, Grand Rapids, MI
Magdalena Koets	Grand Rapids, Michigan	1937-1947	Mayfair, Grand Rapids, MI
Grace Pels	Sheridan Twp, Sioux County, IA	1936-1937	
Richard Pousma	Paterson, New Jersey	1926-1927	Prospect Park, NJ

Name	Hometown	Field Service	Home church
Ollie Pousma	Harrison, SD	1926-1927	
Albert Selles	Kampen, Utrecht, Netherlands	1926-1927, 1929-1937, 1938-1943, 1946-1949	Central Ave, Holland, MI
Trena Selles	Lansing, Illinois	1926-1927, 1929-1937, 1938-1943, 1946-1948	Central Ave, Holland, MI
Albert Smit	Nijeveen, Drenthe, Netherlands	1924-1943, 1944-45, 1946-1950	
Dora Smit	Grand Rapids, Michigan	1924-1943, 1946-1950	
Edward Van Baak	Detroit, Michigan	1948-1950	First, Detroit, MI
Fran Van Baak	Sheboygan, Wisconsin	1948-1949	
Evert Van Reken	Chicago, Illinois	1947-1948	LaGrave, Grand Rapids, MI
Rozena Van Reken	Jamestown, MI	1947-1948	

Index